ABOUT THIS PUBLICATION

FOR SERVICE ASSISTANCE

Customer Service
1.704.898.0770

North Carolina General Statues is published by The Muliti-Media Group of Greater Charlotte in Charlotte, North Carolina. Copyright 2015 by the Multi-Media Group of Greater Charlotte. This book or parts thereof may not be reproduced in any form, stored in a retrieval system, or transmitted in any form by any means—electronic, mechanical, photocopy, recording or otherwise—without prior written permission of the publisher, except as provided by United States of America copyright law.

The records required by U.S. Code 2257(a) through (c) and the pertinent regulations 28 C.F.R. Cli. 1, Part 75 with respect to this publication and all materials associated with such records are maintained by The Multi-Media Group of Greater Charlotte, Publisher and available for review by Attorney General.

www.visionbooks.org

Copyright © 2015 by MMGGC
All rights reserved!

TID: 5108012
ISBN (10) digit: 1503245373
ISBN (13) digit: 978-1503245372

123-4-56789-01239-Paperback
123-4-56789-01239-Hardback

First Edition

090520140547

Printed in the United States of America

2015 EDITION

North Carolina Criminal Law And Procedure-Pamphlet # 85

Printed In conjunction with the Administration of the Courts

North Carolina Criminal Law and Procedure
Pamphlet Reference Guide

Chapters	Pamphlet
Chapter 1 Civil Procedure	1
Chapter 1 Civil Procedure (Continue)	2
Chapter 1A Rules of Civil Procedure	2
Chapter 1B Contribution.	2
Chapter 1C Enforcement of Judgments.	2
Chapter 1D Punitive Damages.	2
Chapter 1E Eastern Band of Cherokee Indians.	2
Chapter 1F North Carolina Uniform Interstate Depositions and Discovery Act.	2
Chapter 2 - Clerk of Superior Court [Repealed and Transferred.]	3
Chapter 3 - Commissioners of Affidavits and Deeds [Repealed.]	3
Chapter 4 - Common Law	3
Chapter 5 - Contempt [Repealed.]	3
Chapter 5A - Contempt	3
Chapter 6 - Liability for Court Costs	3
Chapter 7 - Courts [Repealed and Transferred.]	3
Chapter 7A – Judicial Department	3
Chapter 7A – Continuation (Judicial Department)	4
Chapter 7A – Continuation (Judicial Department)	5
Chapter 7B - Juvenile Code	5
Chapter 8 - Evidence	6
Chapter 8A - Interpreters for Deaf Persons [Recodified.]	6
Chapter 8B - Interpreters for Deaf Persons	6
Chapter 8C - Evidence Code	6
Chapter 9 - Jurors	6
Chapter 10 - Notaries [Repealed.]	6
Chapter 10A - Notaries [Recodified.]	6
Chapter 10B - Notaries	6
Chapter 11 - Oaths	6
Chapter 12 - Statutory Construction	6
Chapter 13 - Citizenship Restored	6
Chapter 14 - Criminal Law	7
Chapter 14 –Criminal Law (Continuation)	8
Chapter 15 - Criminal Procedure	9
Chapter 15A - Criminal Procedure Act (Continuation)	10
Chapter 15A - Criminal Procedure Act (Continuation)	11
Chapter 15B - Victims Compensation	11
Chapter 15C - Address Confidentiality Program	11
Chapter 16 - Gaming Contracts and Futures	11
Chapter 17 - Habeas Corpus	11

Chapter 17A - Law-Enforcement Officers [Recodified.]	11
Chapter 17B - North Carolina Criminal Justice Education and Training System [Recodified.]	11
Chapter 17C - North Carolina Criminal Justice Education and Training Standards Commission	11
Chapter 17D - North Carolina Justice Academy	11
Chapter 17E - North Carolina Sheriffs' Education and Training Standards Commission	11
Chapter 18 - Regulation of Intoxicating Liquors [Repealed.]	12
Chapter 18A - Regulation of Intoxicating Liquors [Repealed.]	12
Chapter 18B - Regulation of Alcoholic Beverages	12
Chapter 18C - North Carolina State Lottery	12
Chapter 19 - Offenses against Public Morals	12
Chapter 19A - Protection of Animals	12
Chapter 20 - Motor Vehicles	13
Chapter 20 - Motor Vehicles (Continuation)	14
Chapter 20 - Motor Vehicles (Continuation)	15
Chapter 20 - Motor Vehicles (Continuation)	16
Chapter 21 - Bills of Lading	17
Chapter 22 - Contracts Requiring Writing	17
Chapter 22A - Signatures	17
Chapter 22B - Contracts Against Public Policy	17
Chapter 22C - Payments to Subcontractors	17
Chapter 23 - Debtor and Creditor	17
Chapter 24 – Interest	17
Chapter 25 – Uniform Commercial Code	18
Chapter 25 – Uniform Commercial Code (Continuation)	19
Chapter 25A – Retail Installment Sales Act	20
Chapter 25B - Credit	20
Chapter 25C - Sales of Artwork	20
Chapter 26 - Suretyship	20
Chapter 27 - Warehouse Receipts [Repealed.]	20
Chapter 28 - Administration [Repealed.]	20
Chapter 28A - Administration of Decedents' Estates	20
Chapter 28B - Estates of Absentees in Military Service	20
Chapter 28C - Estates of Missing Persons	20
Chapter 29 - Intestate Succession	21
Chapter 30 - Surviving Spouses	21
Chapter 31 - Wills	21
Chapter 31A - Acts Barring Property Rights	21
Chapter 31B - Renunciation of Property and Renunciation of Fiduciary Powers Act	21
Chapter 31C - Uniform Disposition of Community Property Rights at Death Act	21
Chapter 32 - Fiduciaries	21
Chapter 32A - Powers of Attorney	21
Chapter 33 - Guardian and Ward [Repealed and Recodified.]	21

Chapter 33A - North Carolina Uniform Transfers to Minors Act	21
Chapter 33B - North Carolina Uniform Custodial Trust Act	21
Chapter 34 - Veterans' Guardianship Act	22
Chapter 35 - Sterilization Procedures	22
Chapter 35A - Incompetency and Guardianship	22
Chapter 36 - Trusts and Trustees [Repealed.]	22
Chapter 36A - Trusts and Trustees	22
Chapter 36B - Uniform Management of Institutional Funds Act [Repealed.]	22
Chapter 36C - North Carolina Uniform Trust Code	22
Chapter 36D - North Carolina Community Third Party Trusts, Pooled Trusts	23
Chapter 36E - Uniform Prudent Management of Institutional Funds Act	23
Chapter 37 - Allocation of Principal and Income [Repealed.]	23
Chapter 37A - Uniform Principal and Income Act	23
Chapter 38 - Boundaries	23
Chapter 38A - Landowner Liability	23
Chapter 39 - Conveyances	23
Chapter 39A - Transfer Fee Covenants Prohibited	23
Chapter 40 - Eminent Domain [Repealed.]	23
Chapter 40A - Eminent Domain	23
Chapter 41 - Estates	23
Chapter 41A - State Fair Housing Act	23
Chapter 42 - Landlord and Tenant	23
Chapter 42A - Vacation Rental Act	23
Chapter 43 - Land Registration	23
Chapter 44 - Liens	24
Chapter 44A - Statutory Liens and Charges	24
Chapter 45 - Mortgages and Deeds of Trust	24
Chapter 45A - Good Funds Settlement Act	24
Chapter 46 - Partition	24
Chapter 47 - Probate and Registration	25
Chapter 47A - Unit Ownership	25
Chapter 47B - Real Property Marketable Title Act	25
Chapter 47C - North Carolina Condominium Act	25
Chapter 47D - Notice of Settlement Act [Expired.]	25
Chapter 47E - Residential Property Disclosure Act	25
Chapter 47F - North Carolina Planned Community Act	25
Chapter 47G - Option to Purchase Contracts	25
Chapter 47H - Contracts for Deed	25
Chapter 48 – Adoptions	26
Chapter 48A - Minors	26
Chapter 49 - Bastardy	26
Chapter 49A - Rights of Children	26
Chapter 50 - Divorce and Alimony	26
Chapter 50A - Uniform Child-Custody Jurisdiction and	

Enforcement Act	26
Chapter 50B - Domestic Violence	26
Chapter 50C - Civil No-Contact Orders	26
Chapter 51 - Marriage	26
Chapter 52 - Powers and Liabilities of Married Persons	27
Chapter 52A - Uniform Reciprocal Enforcement of Support Act [Repealed.]	27
Chapter 52B - Uniform Premarital Agreement Act	27
Chapter 52C - Uniform Interstate Family Support Act	27
Chapter 53 - Banks	27
Chapter 53A - Business Development Corporations and North Carolina Capital Resource Corporations	28
Chapter 53B - Financial Privacy Act	28
Chapter 54 - Cooperative Organizations	28
Chapter 54A - Capital Stock Savings and Loan Associations [Repealed.]	28
Chapter 54B - Savings and Loan Associations	29
Chapter 54C - Savings Banks	29
Chapter 55 - North Carolina Business Corporation Act	30
Chapter 55A - North Carolina Nonprofit Corporation Act	31
Chapter 55B - Professional Corporation Act	31
Chapter 55C - Foreign Trade Zones	31
Chapter 55D - Filings, Names, and Registered Agents for Corporations, Nonprofit Corporations, and Partnerships	31
Chapter 56 - Electric, Telegraph and Power Companies [Repealed.]	31
Chapter 57 - Hospital, Medical and Dental Service Corporations [Recodified.]	31
Chapter 57A - Health Maintenance Organization Act [Recodified.]	31
Chapter 57B - Health Maintenance Organization Act [Recodified.]	31
Chapter 57C - North Carolina Limited Liability Company Act.	31
Chapter 58 - Insurance.	32
Chapter 58 - Insurance (Continuation)	33
Chapter 58 - Insurance (Continuation)	34
Chapter 58 - Insurance (Continuation)	35
Chapter 58 - Insurance (Continuation)	36
Chapter 58 - Insurance (Continuation)	37
Chapter 58 - Insurance (Continuation)	38
Chapter 58A - North Carolina Health Insurance Trust Commission [Recodified.]	38
Chapter 59 - Partnership.	39
Chapter 59B - Uniform Unincorporated Nonprofit Association Act.	39
Chapter 60 - Railroads and Other Carriers [Repealed and Transferred.]	39
Chapter 61 - Religious Societies	39
Chapter 62 - Public Utilities	39

Chapter 62 - Public Utilities (Continuation)	40
Chapter 62A - Public Safety Telephone Service And Wireless Telephone Service	40
Chapter 63 - Aeronautics	40
Chapter 63A - North Carolina Global TransPark Authority	40
Chapter 64 - Aliens	40
Chapter 65 – Cemeteries	40
Chapter 66 - Commerce and Business	41
Chapter 67 - Dogs	41
Chapter 68 - Fences and Stock Law	41
Chapter 69 - Fire Protection	41
Chapter 70 - Indian Antiquities, Archaeological Resources and Unmarked Human Skeletal Remains Protection	42
Chapter 71 - Indians [Repealed.]	42
Chapter 71A - Indians	42
Chapter 72 - Inns, Hotels and Restaurants	42
Chapter 73 - Mills	42
Chapter 74 - Mines and Quarries	42
Chapter 74A - Company Police [Repealed.]	42
Chapter 74B - Private Protective Services Act [Repealed.]	42
Chapter 74C - Private Protective Services	42
Chapter 74D - Alarm Systems	42
Chapter 74E - Company Police Act	42
Chapter 74F - Locksmith Licensing Act	42
Chapter 74G - Campus Police Act	42
Chapter 75 - Monopolies, Trusts and Consumer Protection	42
Chapter 75A - Boating and Water Safety	43
Chapter 75B - Discrimination in Business	43
Chapter 75C - Motion Picture Fair Competition Act	43
Chapter 75D - Racketeer Influenced and Corrupt Organizations	43
Chapter 75E - Unlawful Activities in Connection With Certain Corporate Transactions	43
Chapter 76 - Navigation	43
Chapter 76A - Navigation and Pilotage Commissions	43
Chapter 77 - Rivers, Creeks, and Coastal Waters	43
Chapter 78 - Securities Law [Repealed.]	43
Chapter 78A - North Carolina Securities Act	43
Chapter 78B - Tender Offer Disclosure Act [Repealed.]	43
Chapter 78C - Investment Advisers	43
Chapter 78D - Commodities Act	43
Chapter 79 - Strays [Repealed.]	43
Chapter 80 - Trademarks, Brands, etc.	44
Chapter 81 - Weights and Measures [Recodified.]	44
Chapter 81A - Weights and Measures Act of 1975.	44
Chapter 82 - Wrecks [Repealed.]	44
Chapter 83 - Architects [Recodified.]	44

Chapter 83A - Architects	44
Chapter 84 - Attorneys-at-Law	44
Chapter 84A - Foreign Legal Consultants	44
Chapter 85 - Auctions and Auctioneers [Repealed.]	44
Chapter 85A - Bail Bondsmen and Runners [Recodified.]	44
Chapter 85B - Auctions and Auctioneers	44
Chapter 85C - Bail Bondsmen and Runners [Recodified.]	44
Chapter 86 - Barbers [Recodified.]	44
Chapter 86A - Barbers	44
Chapter 87 - Contractors	44
Chapter 88 - Cosmetic Art [Repealed.]	44
Chapter 88A - Electrolysis Practice Act	44
Chapter 88B - Cosmetic Art	45
Chapter 89 - Engineering and Land Surveying [Recodified.]	45
Chapter 89A - Landscape Architects	45
Chapter 89B - Foresters	45
Chapter 89C - Engineering and Land Surveying	45
Chapter 89D - Landscape Contractors	45
Chapter 89E - Geologists Licensing Act	45
Chapter 89F - North Carolina Soil Scientist Licensing Act	45
Chapter 89G - Irrigation Contractors	45
Chapter 90 - Medicine and Allied Occupations	45
Chapter 90 - Medicine and Allied Occupations (Continuation)	46
Chapter 90 - Medicine and Allied Occupations (Continuation)	47
Chapter 90 - Medicine and Allied Occupations (Continuation)	48
Chapter 90A - Sanitarians and Water and Wastewater Treatment Facility Operators	48
Chapter 90B - Social Worker Certification and Licensure Act	48
Chapter 90C - North Carolina Recreational Therapy Licensure Act	48
Chapter 90D - Interpreters and Transliterators	48
Chapter 91 - Pawnbrokers [Repealed.]	48
Chapter 91A - Pawnbrokers Modernization Act of 1989	48
Chapter 92 - Photographers [Deleted.]	48
Chapter 93 - Certified Public Accountants	48
Chapter 93A - Real Estate License Law	49
Chapter 93B - Occupational Licensing Boards	49
Chapter 93C - Watchmakers [Repealed.]	49
Chapter 93D - North Carolina State Hearing Aid Dealers and Fitters Board.	49
Chapter 93E - North Carolina Appraisers Act	49
Chapter 94 - Apprenticeship	49
Chapter 95 - Department of Labor and Labor Regulations	49
Chapter 95 - Department of Labor and Labor Regulations (Continuation)	50
Chapter 96 - Employment Security	50
Chapter 97 - Workers' Compensation Act	50
Chapter 97 - Workers' Compensation Act (Continuation)	51

Chapter 98 - Burnt and Lost Records	51
Chapter 99 - Libel and Slander	51
Chapter 99A - Civil Remedies for Criminal Actions	51
Chapter 99B - Products Liability	51
Chapter 99C - Actions Relating to Winter Sports Safety and Accidents	51
Chapter 99D - Civil Rights	51
Chapter 99E - Special Liability Provisions	51
Chapter 100 - Monuments, Memorials and Parks	51
Chapter 101 - Names of Persons	51
Chapter 102 - Official Survey Base	51
Chapter 103 - Sundays, Holidays and Special Days	51
Chapter 104 - United States Lands	51
Chapter 104A - Degrees of Kinship	51
Chapter 104B - Hurricanes or Other Acts of Nature	51
Chapter 104C - Atomic Energy, Radioactivity and Ionizing Radiation [Repealed and Recodified.]	51
Chapter 104D - Southern States Energy Compact	51
Chapter 104E - North Carolina Radiation Protection Act	51
Chapter 104F - Southeast Interstate Low-Level Radioactive Waste Management Compact [Repealed]	51
Chapter 104G - North Carolina Low-Level Radioactive Waste Management Authority Act of 1987 [Repealed]	51
Chapter 105 - Taxation	51
Chapter 105 - Taxation (Continuation)	52
Chapter 105 - Taxation (Continuation)	53
Chapter 105 - Taxation (Continuation)	54
Chapter 105A - Setoff Debt Collection Act	55
Chapter 105B - Defaulted Student Loan Recovery Act	55
Chapter 106 - Agriculture	55
Chapter 106 - Agriculture (Continue)	56
Chapter 106 - Agriculture (Continue)	57
Chapter 107 - Agricultural Development Districts [Repealed.]	57
Chapter 108 - Social Services [Repealed and Recodified.]	57
Chapter 108A - Social Services	57
Chapter 108B - Community Action Programs	58
Chapter 108C Medicaid and Health Choice Provider Requirements.	58
Chapter 108D Medicaid Managed Care for Behavioral Health Services.	58
Chapter 109 - Bonds [Recodified.]	58
Chapter 110 - Child Welfare	58
Chapter 111 - Aid to the Blind	58
Chapter 112 - Confederate Homes and Pensions [Repealed.]	58
Chapter 113 - Conservation and Development	58
Chapter 113 - Conservation and Development (Continuation)	59

Chapter 113A - Pollution Control and Environment	59
Chapter 113A - Pollution Control and Environment (Continuation)	60
Chapter 113B - North Carolina Energy Policy Act of 1975	60
Chapter 114 - Department of Justice	60
Chapter 115 - Elementary and Secondary Education [Repealed.]	60
Chapter 115A - Community Colleges, Technical Institutes, and Industrial Education Centers [Repealed.]	60
Chapter 115B - Tuition and Fee Waivers	60
Chapter 115C - Elementary and Secondary Education	60
Chapter 115C - Elementary and Secondary Education (Continuation)	61
Chapter 115C - Elementary and Secondary Education (Continuation)	62
Chapter 115C - Elementary and Secondary Education (Continuation)	63
Chapter 115D - Community Colleges	63
Chapter 115E - Private Educational Facilities Finance Act [Recodified]	63
Chapter 116 - Higher Education	63
Chapter 116 - Higher Education (Continuation)	63
Chapter 116A - Escheats and Abandoned Property [Repealed.]	64
Chapter 116B - Escheats and Abandoned Property	64
Chapter 116C - Continuum of Education Programs	64
Chapter 116D - Higher Education Bonds	64
Chapter 116E -Education Longitudinal Data System	64
Chapter 117 - Electrification	64
Chapter 118 - Firemen's and Rescue Squad Workers' Relief and Pension Funds [Recodified.]	64
Chapter 118A - Firemen's Death Benefit Act [Repealed.]	64
Chapter 118B - Members of a Rescue Squad Death Benefit Act [Repealed.]	64
Chapter 119 - Gasoline and Oil Inspection and Regulation	64
Chapter 120 - General Assembly	65
Chapter 120 - General Assembly (Continuation)	66
Chapter 120 - General Assembly (Continuation)	67
Chapter 120C - Lobbying	67
Chapter 121 - Archives and History	67
Chapter 122 - Hospitals for the Mentally Disordered [Repealed.]	67
Chapter 122A - North Carolina Housing Finance Agency	67
Chapter 122B - North Carolina Agricultural Facilities Finance Act [Repealed.]	67
Chapter 122C - Mental Health, Developmental Disabilities, and Substance Abuse Act of 1985	67
Chapter 122C - Mental Health, Developmental Disabilities, and Substance Abuse Act of 1985 (Continuation)	68

Chapter 122D - North Carolina Agricultural Finance Act	68
Chapter 122E - North Carolina Housing Trust and Oil Overcharge Act	68
Chapter 123 - Impeachment	69
Chapter 123A - Industrial Development [Repealed.]	69
Chapter 124 - Internal Improvements	69
Chapter 125 - Libraries	69
Chapter 126 - State Personnel System	69
Chapter 127 - Militia [Repealed.]	69
Chapter 127A - Militia	69
Chapter 127B - Military Affairs	69
Chapter 127C - Advisory Commission on Military Affairs	69
Chapter 128 - Offices and Public Officers	69
Chapter 128 - Offices and Public Officers (Continuation)	70
Chapter 129 - Public Buildings and Grounds	70
Chapter 130 - Public Health [Repealed.]	70
Chapter 130A - Public Health	70
Chapter 130A - Public Health (Continuation)	71
Chapter 130A - Public Health (Continuation)	72
Chapter 130B - Hazardous Waste Management Commission [Repealed.]	72
Chapter 131 - Public Hospitals [Repealed.]	72
Chapter 131A - Health Care Facilities Finance Act	72
Chapter 131B - Licensing of Ambulatory Surgical Facilities [Repealed.]	72
Chapter 131C - Charitable Solicitation Licensure Act [Repealed.]	72
Chapter 131D - Inspection and Licensing of Facilities	72
Chapter 131E - Health Care Facilities and Services	72
Chapter 131E - Health Care Facilities and Services (Continuation)	73
Chapter 131F - Solicitation of Contributions	73
Chapter 132 - Public Records	73
Chapter 133 - Public Works	74
Chapter 134 - Youth Development [Recodified.]	74
Chapter 134A - Youth Services [Repealed.]	74
Chapter 135 - Retirement System for Teachers and State Employees; Social Security; Health Insurance Program for Children	74
Chapter 135 - Retirement System for Teachers and State Employees; Social Security; Health Insurance Program for Children	75
Chapter 136 - Transportation	75
Chapter 136 - Transportation (Continuation)	76
Chapter 137 - Rural Rehabilitation [Repealed.]	76
Chapter 138 - Salaries, Fees and Allowances	76
Chapter 138A - State Government Ethics Act	76

Chapter 139 - Soil and Water Conservation Districts	76
Chapter 140 - State Art Museum; Symphony and Art Societies	76
Chapter 140A - State Awards System	76
Chapter 141 - State Boundaries	76
Chapter 142 - State Debt	76
Chapter 143 - State Departments, Institutions, and Commissions	77
Chapter 143 - State Departments, Institutions, and Commissions (Continuation)	78
Chapter 143 - State Departments, Institutions, and Commissions (Continuation)	79
Chapter 143 - State Departments, Institutions, and Commissions (Continuation)	80
Chapter 143A - State Government Reorganization	80
Chapter 143B - Executive Organization Act of 1973	80
Chapter 143B - Executive Organization Act of 1973 (Continuation)	81
Chapter 143B - Executive Organization Act of 1973 (Continuation)	82
Chapter 143C - State Budget Act	83
Chapter 143D - The State Governmental Accountability and Internal Control Act	83
Chapter 144 - State Flag, Official Governmental Flags, Motto, and Colors	83
Chapter 145 - State Symbols and Other Official Adoptions.	83
Chapter 146 - State Lands	83
Chapter 147 - State Officers	83
Chapter 148 - State Prison System	84
Chapter 149 - State Song and Toast	84
Chapter 150 - Uniform Revocation of Licenses [Repealed.]	84
Chapter 150A - Administrative Procedure Act [Recodified.]	84
Chapter 150B - Administrative Procedure Act	84
Chapter 151 - Constables [Repealed.]	84
Chapter 152 - Coroners	84
Chapter 152A - County Medical Examiner [Repealed.]	84
Chapter 153 - Counties and County Commissioners [Repealed.]	84
Chapter 153A - Counties	84
Chapter 153A - Counties (Continuation)	85
Chapter 153B - Mountain Resources Planning Act	85
Chapter 153C - Uwharrie Regional Resources Act	85
Chapter 154 - County Surveyor [Repealed.]	85
Chapter 155 - County Treasurer [Repealed.]	85
Chapter 156 - Drainage	85

Chapter 156 – Drainage (Continuation)	86
Chapter 157 - Housing Authorities and Projects	86
Chapter 157A - Historic Properties Commissions [Transferred.]	86
Chapter 158 - Local Development	86
Chapter 159 - Local Government Finance	86
Chapter 159 - Local Government Finance (Continuation)	87
Chapter 159A - Pollution Abatement and Industrial Facilities Financing Act [Unconstitutional.]	87
Chapter 159B - Joint Municipal Electric Power and Energy Act	87
Chapter 159C - Industrial and Pollution Control Facilities Financing Act	87
Chapter 159D - The North Carolina Capital Facilities Financing Act	87
Chapter 159E - Registered Public Obligations Act	87
Chapter 159F - North Carolina Energy Development Authority [Repealed.]	87
Chapter 159G - Water Infrastructure	87
Chapter 159H - [Reserved.]	87
Chapter 159I - Solid Waste Management Loan Program and Local Government Special Obligation Bonds	87
Chapter 160 - Municipal Corporations [Repealed And Transferred.]	87
Chapter 160A - Cities and Towns	88
Chapter 160A - Cities and Towns (Continuation)	89
Chapter 160B - Consolidated City-County Act	89
Chapter 160C - Baseball Park Districts [Repealed.]	90
Chapter 161 - Register of Deeds	90
Chapter 162 - Sheriff	90
Chapter 162A - Water and Sewer Systems	90
Chapter 162B Continuity of Local Government in Emergency.	90
Chapter 163 Elections and Election Laws.	90
Chapter 163 Elections and Election Laws. (Continuation)	91
Chapter 164 Concerning the General Statutes of North Carolina.	92
Chapter 165 Veterans.	92
Chapter 166 Civil Preparedness Agencies [Repealed.]	92
Chapter 166A North Carolina Emergency Management Act.	92
Chapter 167 State Civil Air Patrol [Repealed.]	92
Chapter 168 Persons with Disabilities.	92
Chapter 168A Persons With Disabilities Protection Act.	92

§ 153A-150. Reserve for reappraisal.

Before the beginning of the fiscal year immediately following the effective date of a reappraisal of real property conducted as required by G.S. 105-286, the county budget officer shall present to the board of commissioners a budget for financing the cost of the next reappraisal. The budget shall estimate the cost of the reappraisal and shall propose a plan for raising the necessary funds in annual installments during the intervening years between reappraisals, with all installments as nearly uniform as practicable. The board shall consider this budget, making any amendments to the budget it deems advisable, and shall adopt a resolution establishing a special reserve fund for the next reappraisal. In the budget ordinance of the first fiscal year of the plan, the board of commissioners shall appropriate to the special reappraisal reserve fund the amount set out in the plan for the first year's installment. When the county budget for each succeeding fiscal year is in preparation, the board shall review the reappraisal budget with the budget officer and shall amend it, if necessary, so that it will reflect the probable cost at that time of the reappraisal and will produce the necessary funds at the end of the intervening period. In the budget ordinance for each succeeding fiscal year, the board shall appropriate to the special reappraisal reserve fund the amount set out in the plan as due in that year.

Moneys appropriated to the special reappraisal reserve fund shall not be available or expended for any purpose other than the reappraisal of real property required by G.S. 105-286, except that the funds may be deposited at interest or invested as permitted by G.S. 159-30. If there is a fund balance in the reserve fund following payment for the required reappraisal, it shall be retained in the fund for use in financing the next required reappraisal.

Within 10 days after the adoption of each annual budget ordinance, the county finance officer shall report to the Department of Revenue, on forms to be supplied by the Department, the terms of the county's reappraisal budget, the current condition of the special reappraisal reserve fund, and the amount appropriated to the reserve fund in the current fiscal year. (1959, c. 704, s. 6; 1971, c. 806, s. 4; c. 931, s. 2; 1973, c. 476, s. 193; c. 822, s. 1; 2008-146, s. 1.3.)

§ 153A-151. Sales tax.

A county may levy a local sales and use tax under the rules and according to the procedures prescribed by the Local Government Sales and Use Tax Act (Chapter 105, Subchapter VIII). (1973, c. 822, s. 1.)

§ 153A-152. Privilege license taxes.

(a)   Authority. - A county may levy privilege license taxes on trades, occupations, professions, businesses, and franchises to the extent authorized by Article 2 of Chapter 105 of the General Statutes and any other acts of the General Assembly. A county may levy privilege license taxes to the extent formerly authorized by the following sections of Article 2 of Chapter 105 of the General Statutes before they were repealed:

G.S. 105-50	Pawnbrokers.
G.S. 105-53	Peddlers, itinerant merchants, and specialty market operators.
G.S. 105-55	Installing elevators and automatic sprinkler systems.
G.S. 105-58	Fortune tellers, palmists, etc.
G.S. 105-65	Music machines.
G.S. 105-66.1	Electronic video games.
G.S. 105-80	Firearms dealers and dealers in other weapons.
G.S. 105-89	Automobiles, wholesale supply dealers and service stations.
G.S. 105-89.1	Motorcycle dealers.
G.S. 105-90	Emigrant and employment agents.
G.S. 105-102.5	General business license.

(b)   Telecommunications Restriction. - A county may not impose a license, franchise, or privilege tax on a company taxed under G.S. 105-164.4(a) (4c).

(1973, c. 822, s. 1; 1996, 2nd Ex. Sess., c. 14, s. 22; 2001-430, s. 16.)

§ 153A-152.1. Privilege license tax on low-level radioactive and hazardous waste facilities.

(a)   Counties in which hazardous waste facilities as defined in G.S. 130A-290 or low-level radioactive waste facilities as defined in G.S. 104E-5(9b) are located may levy an annual privilege license tax on persons or firms operating such facilities only in accordance with this section.

(b)   The rate or rates of a tax levied under authority of this section shall be in an amount calculated to compensate the county for the additional costs incurred by it from having a hazardous waste facility or a low-level radioactive waste facility located in its jurisdiction to the extent to which compensation for such costs is not otherwise provided, which costs may include the loss of ad valorem property tax revenues from the property on which a facility is located, the cost of providing any additional emergency services, the cost of monitoring air, surface water, groundwater, and other environmental media to the extent other monitoring data is not available, and other costs the county establishes as being associated with the facilities and for which it is not otherwise compensated.

(c)   Any person or firm taxed pursuant to this section may appeal the tax rate to the Board, but shall pay the tax when due, subject to a refund when the appeal is resolved by the Board or in the courts. (1981, c. 704, s. 16; 1985, c. 462, s. 11; 1987, c. 850, s. 21; 1989, c. 168, s. 34.)

§ 153A-153. Animal tax.

A county may levy an annual license tax on the privilege of keeping dogs and other pets within the county. (1973, c. 822, s. 1.)

§ 153A-154: Repealed by Session Laws 2006-151, s. 11, effective January 1, 2007.

§ 153A-154.1. Uniform penalties for local meals taxes.

(a)   Penalties. - Notwithstanding any other provision of law, the civil and criminal penalties that apply to State sales and use taxes under Chapter 105 of the General Statutes apply to local meals taxes. The governing board of a taxing county has the same authority to waive the penalties for a local meals tax that the Secretary of Revenue has to waive the penalties for State sales and use taxes.

(b)   Scope. - This section applies to every county authorized by the General Assembly to levy a meals tax. As used in this section, the term "meals tax" means a tax on prepared food and drink. (2001-264, s. 1.)

§ 153A-155. Uniform provisions for room occupancy taxes.

(a)   Scope. - This section applies only to counties the General Assembly has authorized to levy room occupancy taxes.

(b)   Levy. - A room occupancy tax may be levied only by resolution, after not less than 10 days' public notice and after a public hearing held pursuant thereto. A room occupancy tax shall become effective on the date specified in the resolution levying the tax. That date must be the first day of a calendar month, however, and may not be earlier than the first day of the second month after the date the resolution is adopted.

(c)   Collection. - A retailer who is required to remit to the Department of Revenue the State sales tax imposed by G.S. 105-164.4(a)(3) on accommodations is required to remit a room occupancy tax to the taxing county on and after the effective date of the levy of the room occupancy tax. The room occupancy tax applies to the same gross receipts as the State sales tax on accommodations and is calculated in the same manner as that tax. A rental agent or a facilitator, as defined in G.S. 105-164.4(a)(3), has the same responsibility and liability under the room occupancy tax as the rental agent or facilitator has under the State sales tax on accommodations.

If a taxable accommodation is furnished as part of a package, the bundled transaction provisions in G.S. 105-164.4D apply in determining the sales price of the taxable accommodation. If those provisions do not address the type of package offered, the person offering the package may determine an allocated price for each item in the package based on a reasonable allocation of revenue that is supported by the person's business records kept in the ordinary course of business and calculate tax on the allocated price of the taxable accommodation.

A retailer must separately state the room occupancy tax. Room occupancy taxes paid to a retailer are held in trust for and on account of the taxing county.

The taxing county shall design and furnish to all appropriate businesses and persons in the county the necessary forms for filing returns and instructions to ensure the full collection of the tax. A retailer who collects a room occupancy tax may deduct from the amount remitted to the taxing county a discount equal to the discount the State allows the retailer for State sales and use tax.

(d) Administration. - The taxing county shall administer a room occupancy tax it levies. A room occupancy tax is due and payable to the county finance officer in monthly installments on or before the 20th day of the month following the month in which the tax accrues. Every person, firm, corporation, or association liable for the tax shall, on or before the 20th day of each month, prepare and render a return on a form prescribed by the taxing county. The return shall state the total gross receipts derived in the preceding month from rentals upon which the tax is levied. A room occupancy tax return filed with the county finance officer is not a public record and may not be disclosed except in accordance with G.S. 153A-148.1 or G.S. 160A-208.1.

(e) Penalties. - A person, firm, corporation, or association who fails or refuses to file a room occupancy tax return or pay a room occupancy tax as required by law is subject to the civil and criminal penalties set by G.S. 105-236 for failure to pay or file a return for State sales and use taxes. The governing board of the taxing county has the same authority to waive the penalties for a room occupancy tax that the Secretary of Revenue has to waive the penalties for State sales and use taxes.

(f) Repeal or Reduction. - A room occupancy tax levied by a county may be repealed or reduced by a resolution adopted by the governing body of the county. Repeal or reduction of a room occupancy tax shall become effective on the first day of a month and may not become effective until the end of the fiscal year in which the resolution was adopted. Repeal or reduction of a room occupancy tax does not affect a liability for a tax that was attached before the effective date of the repeal or reduction, nor does it affect a right to a refund of a tax that accrued before the effective date of the repeal or reduction.

(f1) Use. - The proceeds of a room occupancy tax shall not be used for development or construction of a hotel or another transient lodging facility.

(g) Applicability. - Subsection (c) of this section applies to all counties and county districts that levy an occupancy tax. To the extent subsection (c) conflicts with any provision of a local act, subsection (c) supersedes that provision. The remainder of this section applies only to Alleghany, Anson, Brunswick, Buncombe, Burke, Cabarrus, Camden, Carteret, Caswell, Chatham, Cherokee, Chowan, Clay, Craven, Cumberland, Currituck, Dare, Davie, Duplin, Durham, Edgecombe, Forsyth, Franklin, Granville, Halifax, Haywood, Henderson, Jackson, Madison, Martin, McDowell, Montgomery, Moore, Nash, New Hanover, Northampton, Pasquotank, Pender, Perquimans, Person, Randolph, Richmond, Rockingham, Rowan, Rutherford, Sampson, Scotland, Stanly, Swain, Transylvania, Tyrrell, Vance, Washington, and Wilson Counties, to New Hanover County District U, to Surry County District S, to Watauga County District U, to Wilkes County District K, to Yadkin County District Y, and to the Township of Averasboro in Harnett County and the Ocracoke Township Taxing District. (1997-102, s. 3; 1997-255, s. 2; 1997-342, s. 2; 1997-364, s. 3; 1997-410, s. 6; 1998-14, s. 2; 1999-155, s. 2; 1999-205, s. 2; 1999-286, s. 2; 2000-103, s. 5; 2001-162, s. 2; 2001-305, s. 2; 2001-321, s. 3; 2001-381, s. 10; 2001-434, s. 1; 2001-439, s. 18.2; 2001-468, s. 3; 2001-480, s. 14; 2001-484, s. 2; 2002-138, s. 5; 2004-106, s. 2; 2004-120, s. 3; 2004-170, ss. 36(a), 42(a); 2004-199, s. 60(a); 2005-16, s. 2; 2005-46, s. 1.2; 2005-53, s. 2; 2005-197, s. 6; 2005-233, s. 6.1; 2006-120, s. 8.1; 2006-127, s. 2; 2006-128, s. 6; 2006-129, s. 2; 2006-162, s. 20(a); 2006-167, s. 7(e); 2006-264, s. 81(a); 2007-19, s. 3; 2007-63, s. 3; 2007-223, s. 3; 2007-224, s. 5; 2007-265, s. 2; 2007-315, s. 2; 2007-318, s. 2; 2007-337, s. 3; 2007-340, s. 9; 2007-527, ss. 23, 43; 2008-33, s. 2; 2008-134, s. 12(b); 2008-187, s. 31; 2009-112, s. 4; 2009-157, s. 2; 2009-297, s. 3; 2010-31, ss. 31.6(c), (d); 2010-78, s. 10; 2010-123, s. 10.2; 2011-113, s. 4; 2011-115, s. 4; 2011-170, s. 5; 2012-100, s. 1; 2012-144, s. 4; 2012-194, s. 35; 2013-255, s. 3.)

§ 153A-156. Gross receipts tax on short-term leases or rentals.

(a) As a substitute for and in replacement of the ad valorem tax, which is excluded by G.S. 105-275(42), a county may levy a gross receipts tax on the gross receipts from the short-term lease or rental of vehicles at retail to the general public. The tax rate shall not exceed one and one-half percent (1.5%) of the gross receipts from such short-term leases or rentals.

(b) If a county enacts the substitute and replacement gross receipts tax pursuant to this section, any entity required to collect the tax shall include a provision in each retail short-term lease or rental agreement noting that the percentage amount enacted by the county of the total lease or rental price, excluding highway use tax, is being charged as a tax on gross receipts. For purposes of this section, the transaction giving rise to the tax shall be deemed to have occurred at the location of the entity from which the customer takes delivery of the vehicle. The tax shall be collected at the time of lease or rental and placed in a segregated account until remitted to the county.

(c) The collection and use of taxes under this section are not subject to highway use tax and are not included in the gross receipts of the entity. The proceeds collected under this section belong to the county and are not subject to creditor liens against the entity.

(d) A tax levied under this section shall be collected by the county but otherwise administered in the same manner as the tax levied under G.S. 105-164.4(a)(2).

(e) The following definitions apply in this section:

(1) Short-term lease or rental. - Defined in G.S. 105-187.1(4).

(2) Vehicle. - Any of the following:

a. A motor vehicle of the passenger type, including a passenger van, minivan, or sport utility vehicle.

b. A motor vehicle of the cargo type, including cargo van, pickup truck, or truck with a gross vehicle weight of 26,000 pounds or less used predominantly in the transportation of property for other than commercial freight and that does not require the operator to possess a commercial drivers license.

c. A trailer or semitrailer with a gross vehicle weight of 6,000 pounds or less.

(f) The penalties and remedies that apply to local sales and use taxes levied under Subchapter VIII of Chapter 105 of the General Statutes apply to a tax levied under this section. The county board of commissioners may exercise any power the Secretary of Revenue may exercise in collecting local sales and use taxes. (2000-2, s. 2; 2000-140, s. 75(b).)

§ 153A-156.1. Heavy equipment gross receipts tax in lieu of property tax.

(a) Definitions. - The following definitions apply in this section:

(1) Heavy equipment. - Earthmoving, construction, or industrial equipment that is mobile, weighs at least 1,500 pounds, and meets any of the descriptions listed in this subdivision. The term includes an attachment for heavy equipment, regardless of the weight of the attachment.

a. It is a self-propelled vehicle that is not designed to be driven on a highway.

b. It is industrial lift equipment, industrial material handling equipment, industrial electrical generation equipment, or a similar piece of industrial equipment.

(2) Short-term lease or rental. - Defined in G.S. 105-187.1.

(b) Tax Authorized. - A county may, by resolution, impose a tax at the rate of one and two-tenths percent (1.2%) on the gross receipts from the short-term lease or rental of heavy equipment by a person whose principal business is the short-term lease or rental of heavy equipment at retail. The heavy equipment subject to this tax is exempt from property tax under G.S. 105-275, and this tax provides an alternative to a property tax on the equipment. A person is not considered to be in the short-term lease or rental business if the majority of the person's lease and rental gross receipts are derived from leases and rentals to a person who is a related person under G.S. 105-163.010.

The tax authorized by this section applies to gross receipts that are subject to tax under G.S. 105-164.4(a)(2). Gross receipts from the short-term lease or rental of heavy equipment are subject to a tax imposed by a county under this section if the place of business from which the heavy equipment is delivered is located in the county.

(c) Payment. - A person whose principal business is the short-term lease or rental of heavy equipment is required to remit a tax imposed by this section to the county finance officer. The tax is payable quarterly and is due by the last day of the month following the end of the quarter. The tax is intended to be added to the amount charged for the short-term lease or rental of heavy equipment and paid to the heavy equipment business by the person to whom the heavy equipment is leased or rented.

(d) Enforcement. - The penalties and collection remedies that apply to the payment of sales and use taxes under Article 5 of Chapter 105 of the General Statutes apply to a tax imposed under this section. The county finance officer has the same authority as the Secretary of Revenue in imposing these penalties and remedies.

(e) Effective Date. - A tax imposed under this section becomes effective on the date set in the resolution imposing the tax. The date must be the first day of a calendar quarter and may not be sooner than the first day of the calendar quarter that begins at least two months after the date the resolution is adopted.

(f) Repeal. - A county may, by resolution, repeal a tax imposed under this section. The repeal is effective on the date set in the resolution. The date must be the first day of a calendar quarter and may not be sooner than the first day of the calendar quarter that begins at least two months after the date the resolution is adopted. (2008-144, s. 2.)

Article 8.

County Property.

Part 1. Acquisition of Property.

§ 153A-157: Recodified as § 153A-158.1(a) by Session Laws 1995, c. 17, s. 15(a).

§ 153A-158. Power to acquire property.

A county may acquire, by gift, grant, devise, exchange, purchase, lease, or any other lawful method, the fee or any lesser interest in real or personal property for use by the county or any department, board, commission, or agency of the county. In exercising the power of eminent domain a county shall use the procedures of Chapter 40A. (1868, c. 20, ss. 3, 8; 1879, c. 144, s. 1; Code, ss. 704, 707; Rev., ss. 1310, 1318; C.S., ss. 1291, 1297; 1973, c. 822, s. 1; 1981, c. 919, s. 21; 1995, c. 17, s. 14; 2011-284, s. 106.)

§ 153A-158.1. Acquisition and improvement of school property.

(a) Acquisition by County. - A county may acquire, by any lawful method, any interest in real or personal property for use by a school administrative unit within the county. In exercising the power of eminent domain a county shall use the procedures of Chapter 40A. The county shall use its authority under this subsection to acquire property for use by a school administrative unit within the county only upon the request of the board of education of that school administrative unit and after a public hearing.

(b) Construction or Improvement by County. - A county may construct, equip, expand, improve, renovate, or otherwise make available property for use by a school administrative unit within the county. The local board of education shall be involved in the design, construction, equipping, expansion, improvement, or renovation of the property to the same extent as if the local board owned the property.

(c) Lease or Sale by Board of Education. - Notwithstanding the provisions of G.S. 115C-518 and G.S. 160A-274, a local board of education may, in connection with additions, improvements, renovations, or repairs to all or part of any of its property, lease or sell the property to the board of commissioners of the county in which the property is located for any price negotiated between the two boards.

(d) Board of Education May Contract for Construction. - Notwithstanding the provisions of G.S. 115C-40 and G.S. 115C-521, a local board of education may enter into contracts for the erection of school buildings upon sites owned in fee simple by one or more counties in which the local school administrative unit is located.

(e) Scope. - This section applies in every county. (1868, c. 20, ss. 3, 8; 1879, c. 144, s. 1; Code, ss. 704, 707; Rev., ss. 1310, 1318; C.S., ss. 1291, 1297; 1973, c. 822, s. 1; 1981, c. 919, s. 21; 1991, cc. 120, 533; 1991, c. 1001, s. 2; 1991 (Reg. Sess., 1992), c. 832, s. 1; c. 848, s. 1; c. 865, s. 1; c. 1001, s. 1; 1993 (Reg. Sess., 1994), c. 611, ss. 1.1, 2; c. 612, ss. 1-3; c. 614, ss. 1-4; c. 622, ss. 1-3; c. 623, ss. 1-3; c. 642, s. 3(a), (c), (d); c. 655, ss. 1-3; 1995, c. 17, ss. 15(a), (b), 16; c. 251, ss. 1, 2; 1995 (Reg. Sess., 1996), c. 651, s. 1; c. 702, s. 1; c. 703, s. 1; c. 705, s. 1; c. 737, s. 1; 1996, 2nd Ex. Sess., c. 11, s. 1; 1997-24, s. 1; 1997-162, s. 1; 1997-190, s. 1; 1997-236, s. 3; 1997-409, s. 1; 1998-33, s. 1; 1998-48, s. 1; 1998-201, s. 1; 1999-65, s. 1; 2001-76, s. 1; 2001-427, s. 7(a); 2003-89, s. 1; 2003-355, s. 1.)

§ 153A-158.2. Acquisition and improvement of community college property.

(a) Acquisition. - A county may acquire, by any lawful method, any interest in real or personal property for use by a community college within the county. In exercising the power of eminent domain for real property, a county shall use the procedures of Chapter 40A of the General Statutes.

(b) Construction; Disposition. - A county may construct, equip, expand, improve, renovate, repair, or otherwise make available property for use by a community college within the county and may lease, sell, or otherwise dispose of property for use by a community college within the county for any price and on any terms negotiated by the board of county commissioners and the board of trustees of the community college.

(c) Public Hearing. - A county may use its authority under this section to acquire an interest in real or personal property for use by a community college within the county only upon request of the board of trustees of the community college for which property is to be made available. The board of county commissioners shall hold a public hearing prior to final action. A notice of the public hearing shall be published at least once at least 10 days before the date fixed for the hearing. (1999-115, s. 1.)

§§ 153A-159 through 153A-162. Repealed by Session Laws 1981, c. 919, s. 20.

§ 153A-163. Acquisition of property at a judicial sale, execution sale, or sale pursuant to a power of sale; disposition of such property.

A county, city, or other unit of local government may purchase real property at a judicial sale, an execution sale, or a sale made pursuant to a power of sale, to secure a debt due the county, city, or other unit. The purchasing government may sell any property so acquired by private sale for not less than the amount of its bid or may sell or exchange the property for any amount according to the procedures prescribed by Chapter 160A, Article 12. (1868, c. 20, s. 8; 1879, c. 144, s. 1; Code, s. 707; Rev., s. 1318; C.S., s. 1297; 1973, c. 822, s. 1.)

§ 153A-164. Joint buildings.

Two or more counties, cities, other units of local government (including local boards of education), or any combination of such governments may jointly acquire or construct public buildings to house offices, departments, bureaus, agencies, or facilities of each government. The governments may acquire any land necessary for a joint building or may use land already held by one of the governments.

In exercising the powers granted by this section, the governments shall proceed according to the procedures and provisions of Chapter 160A, Article 20, Part 1. (1965, c. 682, s. 1; 1973, c. 822, s. 1.)

§ 153A-165. Leases.

A county may lease as lessee, with or without option to purchase, any real or personal property for any authorized public purpose. A lease of personal property with an option to purchase is subject to Chapter 143, Article 8. (1973, c. 822, s. 1.)

§§ 153A-166 through 153A-168. Reserved for future codification purposes.

Part 2. Use of County Property.

§ 153A-169. Care and use of county property; sites of county buildings.

The board of commissioners shall supervise the maintenance, repair, and use of all county property. The board may issue orders and adopt by ordinance or resolution regulations concerning the use of county property, may designate and redesignate the location of any county department, office, or agency, and may designate and redesignate the site for any county building, including the courthouse. Before it may redesignate the site of the courthouse, the board of commissioners shall cause notice of its intention to do so to be published once at least four weeks before the meeting at which the redesignation is made. (1868, c. 20, ss. 3, 8; Code, ss. 704, 707; Rev., ss. 1310, 1318; C.S., ss. 1291, 1297; 1925, c. 229; 1927, c. 91, ss. 11, 13; 1957, c. 909, s. 1; 1961, c. 811; 1967, c. 581, s. 1; 1973, c. 822, s. 1.)

§ 153A-170. Regulation of parking on county property.

A county may by ordinance regulate parking of motor vehicles on county-owned property. Such an ordinance may be enforced pursuant to G.S. 153A-123. In addition, the ordinance may provide that vehicles parked in violation thereof may be removed from the property by the county or an agent of the county to a storage area or garage. If a vehicle is so removed, the owner, as a condition of regaining possession of the vehicle, shall be required to pay to the county all reasonable costs incidental to the removal and storage of the vehicle and any fine or penalty due for the violation. (1961, c. 191; 1971, c. 109; 1973, c. 822, s. 1.)

§§ 153A-171 through 153A-175. Reserved for future codification purposes.

Part 3. Disposition of County Property.

§ 153A-176. Disposition of property.

A county may dispose of any real or personal property belonging to it according to the procedures prescribed in Chapter 160A, Article 12. For purposes of this section references in Chapter 160A, Article 12, to the "city," the "council," or a specific city official are deemed to refer, respectively, to the county, the board of commissioners, and the county official who most nearly performs the same duties performed by the specified city official. For purposes of this section, references in G.S. 160A-266(c) to "one or more city officials" are deemed to refer to one or more county officials designated by the board of county commissioners. (1868, c. 20, ss. 3, 8; Code, ss. 704, 707; Rev., ss. 1310, 1318; C.S., ss. 1291, 1297; 1973, c. 822, s. 1; 1983, c. 130, s. 2.)

§ 153A-177. Reconveyance of property donated to a local government.

If real or personal property is conveyed without consideration to a county, city, or other unit of local government to be used for a specific purpose set out in the instrument of conveyance and the governing body of the county, city, or other unit of local government determines that the property will not be used for that purpose, the county, city, or other unit of local government may reconvey the property without consideration to the grantor or his heirs, assigns, or nominees. Before it may make a reconveyance, the county, city, or other unit of local government shall publish once a week for two weeks notice of its intention to do so. (1937, c. 441; 1973, c. 822, s. 1.)

§ 153A-178. Disposition of county property for a State psychiatric hospital.

When the Secretary of Health and Human Services selects a county for the location of a new State psychiatric hospital as authorized by law, the county selected for the location of the new State psychiatric hospital is authorized under the general law to acquire real and personal property and convey it to the State under G.S. 160A-274 or other applicable law for use as a psychiatric hospital. The county may acquire the property by eminent domain, and the power under this section is supplementary to any other power the county may have to take property by eminent domain. (2003-314, s. 3.2.)

§§ 153A-179 through 153A-184. Reserved for future codification purposes.

Article 9.

Special Assessments.

§ 153A-185. Authority to make special assessments.

A county may make special assessments against benefited property within the county for all or part of the costs of:

(1)   Constructing, reconstructing, extending, or otherwise building or improving water systems;

(2)   Constructing, reconstructing, extending, or otherwise building or improving sewage collection and disposal systems of all types, including septic tank systems or other on-site collection or disposal facilities or systems;

(3)   Acquiring, constructing, reconstructing, extending, renovating, enlarging, maintaining, operating, or otherwise building or improving

a.   Beach erosion control or flood and hurricane protection works; and

b.   Watershed improvement projects, drainage projects and water resources development projects (as those projects are defined in G.S. 153A-301).

(4)   Constructing, reconstructing, paving, widening, installing curbs and gutters, and otherwise building and improving streets, as provided in G.S. 153A-205.

(5)   Providing street lights and street lighting in a residential subdivision, as provided in G.S. 153A-206.

A county may not assess property within a city pursuant to subdivision (1) or (2) of this section unless the governing board of the city has by resolution approved the project. (1963, c. 985, s. 1; 1965, c. 714; 1969, c. 474, s. 1; 1973, c. 822, s. 1; 1975, c. 487, s. 1; 1979, c. 619, s. 11; 1983, c. 321, s. 1; 1989 (Reg. Sess., 1990), c. 923, s. 1.)

§ 153A-186. Bases for making assessments.

(a) For water or sewer projects, assessments may be made on the basis of:

(1) The frontage abutting on the project, at an equal rate per foot of frontage; or

(2) The street frontage of the lots served, or subject to being served, by the project, at an equal rate per foot of frontage; or

(3) The area of land served, or subject to being served, by the project, at an equal rate per unit of area; or

(4) The valuation of land served, or subject to being served, by the project, being the value of the land without improvements as shown on the tax records of the county, at an equal rate per dollar of valuation; or

(5) The number of lots served, or subject to being served, by the project when the project involves extension of an existing system to a residential or commercial subdivision, at an equal rate per lot; or

(6) A combination of two or more of these bases.

(b) For beach erosion control or flood and hurricane protection works, watershed improvement projects, drainage projects and water resources development projects, assessments may be made on the basis of:

(1) The frontage abutting on the project, at an equal rate per foot of frontage; or

(2) The frontage abutting on a beach or shoreline or watercourse protected or benefited by the project, at an equal rate per foot of frontage; or

(3) The area of land benefited by the project, at an equal rate per unit of area; or

(4) The valuation of land benefited by the project, being the value of the land without improvements as shown on the tax records of the county, at an equal rate per dollar of valuation; or

(5) A combination of two or more of these bases.

(c) Whenever the basis selected for assessment is either area or valuation, the board of commissioners shall provide for the laying out of one or more benefit zones according (i), in water or sewer projects, to the distance of benefited property from the project being undertaken and (ii), in beach erosion control or flood and hurricane protection works, watershed improvement projects, drainage projects and water resources development projects, to the distance from the shoreline or watercourse, the distance from the project, the elevation of the land, or other relevant factors. If more than one benefit zone is established, the board shall establish differing rates of assessment to apply uniformly throughout each benefit zone.

(d) For each project, the board of commissioners shall endeavor to establish an assessment method from among the bases set out in this section that will most accurately assess each lot or parcel of land according to the benefit conferred upon it by the project. The board's decision as to the method of assessment is final and not subject to further review or challenge. (1963, c. 985, s. 1; 1965, c. 714; 1973, c. 822, s. 1; 1983, c. 321, ss. 2, 3.)

§ 153A-187. Corner lot exemptions.

The board of commissioners may establish schedules of exemptions from assessments for water or sewer projects for corner lots when water or sewer lines are installed along both sides of the lots. A schedule of exemptions shall be based on categories of land use (residential, commercial, industrial, and agricultural) and shall be uniform for each category. A schedule may not allow exemption of more than seventy-five percent (75%) of the frontage of any side of a corner lot, or 150 feet, whichever is greater. (1963, c. 985, s. 1; 1973, c. 822, s. 1.)

§ 153A-188. Lands exempt from assessment.

Except as provided in this Article, no land within a county is exempt from special assessments except land belonging to the United States that is exempt under the provisions of federal statutes and, in the case of water or sewer projects, land within any floodway delineated by a local government pursuant to Chapter 143, Article 21, Part 6. In addition, in the case of water or sewer projects, land owned, leased, or controlled by a railroad company is exempt from assessments by a county to the same extent that it would be exempt from assessments by a city under G.S. 160A-222. (1963, c. 958, s. 1; 1973, c. 822, s. 1.)

§ 153A-189. State participation in improvement projects.

If a county proposes to undertake a project that would benefit land owned by the State of North Carolina or a board, agency, commission, or institution of the State and to finance all or a part of the project by special assessments, the board of commissioners may request the Council of State to authorize the State to pay its ratable part of the cost of the project, and the Council of State may authorize these payments. The Council of State may authorize the Secretary of Administration to approve or disapprove requests from counties for payment pursuant to this section, but a county may appeal to the Council of State if the Secretary disapproves a request. The Council of State may direct that any payment authorized pursuant to this section be made from the Contingency and Emergency Fund of the State of North Carolina or from any other available funds. Except as State payments are authorized pursuant to this section, state-owned property is exempt from assessment under this Article. (1973, c. 822, s. 1; 1975, c. 879, s. 46.)

§ 153A-190. Preliminary resolution; contents.

Whenever the board of commissioners decides to finance all or part of a proposed project by special assessments, it shall first adopt a preliminary assessment resolution containing the following:

(1) A statement of intent to undertake the project;

(2) A general description of the nature and location of the project;

(3) A statement as to the proposed basis for making assessments, which shall include a general description of the boundaries of the area benefited if the basis of assessment is either area or valuation;

(4) A statement as to the percentage of the cost of the work that is to be specially assessed;

(5) A statement as to which, if any, assessments shall be held in abeyance and for how long;

(6) A statement as to the proposed terms of payment of the assessment; and

(7) An order setting a time and place for a public hearing on all matters covered by the preliminary assessment resolution. The hearing shall be not earlier than three weeks and not later than 10 weeks from the day on which the preliminary resolution is adopted. (1963, c. 985, s. 1; 1965, c. 714; 1973, c. 822, s. 1.)

§ 153A-191. Notice of preliminary resolution.

At least 10 days before the date set for the public hearing, the board of commissioners shall publish a notice that a preliminary assessment resolution has been adopted and that a public hearing on it will be held at a specified time and place. The notice shall describe generally the nature and location of the improvement. In addition, at least 10 days before the date set for the hearing, the board shall cause a copy of the preliminary assessment resolution to be mailed by first-class mail to each owner, as shown on the county tax records, of property subject to assessment if the project is undertaken. The person designated to mail these resolutions shall file with the board a certificate stating that they were mailed by first-class mail and on what date. In the absence of fraud, the certificate is conclusive as to compliance with the mailing requirements of this section. (1963, c. 985, s. 1; 1965, c. 714; 1973, c. 822, s. 1.)

§ 153A-192. Hearing on preliminary resolution; assessment resolution.

At the public hearing, the board of commissioners shall hear all interested persons who appear with respect to any matter covered by the preliminary assessment resolution. At or after the hearing, the board may adopt a final assessment resolution directing that the project or portions thereof be undertaken. The final assessment resolution shall describe the project in general terms (which may be by reference to projects described in the preliminary resolution) and shall set forth the following:

(1) The basis on which the special assessments will be made, together with a general description of the boundaries of the areas benefited if the basis of assessment is either area or valuation;

(2) The percentage of the cost of the work that is to be specially assessed; and

(3) The terms of payment, including the conditions, if any, under which assessments are to be held in abeyance.

The percentage of cost to be assessed may not be different from the percentage proposed in the preliminary assessment resolution, nor may the project authorized be greater in scope than the project described in that resolution. If the board decides that a different percentage of the cost should be assessed than that proposed in the preliminary assessment resolution, or that the project should be greater in scope than that described in that resolution, it shall adopt and advertise a new preliminary assessment resolution as provided in this Article. (1963, c. 985, s. 1; 1965, c. 714; 1973, c. 822, s. 1.)

§ 153A-193. Determination of costs.

When a project is complete, the board of commissioners shall determine the project's total cost. In determining total cost, the board may include construction costs, the cost of necessary legal services, the amount of interest paid during construction, the cost of rights-of-way, and the cost of publishing and mailing notices and resolutions. The board's determination of the total cost of a project is conclusive. (1963, c. 985, s. 1; 1965, c. 714; 1973, c. 822, s. 1.)

§ 153A-193.1. Discounts authorized.

The board of commissioners is authorized to establish a schedule of discounts to be applied to assessments paid before the expiration of 30 days from the date that notice is published of confirmation of the assessment roll pursuant to G.S. 153A-196. Such a schedule of discounts may be established even though it was not included among the terms of payment as specified in the preliminary assessment resolution or final assessment resolution. The amount of any discount may not exceed thirty percent (30%). (1983, c. 381, s. 1.)

§ 153A-194. Preliminary assessment roll; publication.

When the total cost of a project has been determined, the board of commissioners shall cause a preliminary assessment roll to be prepared. The roll shall contain a brief description of each lot, parcel, or tract of land assessed, the basis for the assessment, the amount assessed against each, the terms of payment, including the schedule of discounts, if such a schedule is to be established and the name of the owner of each lot, parcel, or tract as far as this can be ascertained from the county tax records. A map of the project on which is shown each lot, parcel, or tract assessed, the basis of its assessment, the amount assessed against it, and the name of its owner as far as this can be ascertained from the county tax records is a sufficient assessment roll.

After the preliminary assessment roll has been completed, the board shall cause the roll to be filed in the clerk's office, where it shall be available for public inspection, and shall set the time and place for a public hearing on the roll. At least 10 days before the date set for the hearing, the board shall publish a notice that the preliminary assessment roll has been completed. The notice shall describe the project in general terms, note that the roll in the clerk's office is available for inspection, and state the time and place for the hearing on the roll. In addition, at least 10 days before the date set for the hearing, the board shall cause a notice of the hearing to be mailed by first-class mail to each owner of property listed on the roll. The mailed notice shall state the time and place of the hearing, note that the roll in the clerk's office is available for inspection, and state the amount as shown on the roll of the assessment against the property of the owner. The person designated to mail these notices shall file with the board a certificate stating that they were mailed by first-class mail and on what date. In the absence of fraud, the certificate is conclusive as to compliance with the mailing requirements of this section. (1963, c. 985, s. 1; 1965, c. 714; 1973, c. 822, s. 1; 1983, c. 381, s. 2.)

§ 153A-195. Hearing on preliminary assessment roll; revision; confirmation; lien.

At the public hearing the board of commissioners shall hear all interested persons who appear with respect to the preliminary assessment roll. At or after the hearing, the board shall annul, modify, or confirm the assessments, in whole or in part, either by confirming the preliminary assessments against any lot, parcel, or tract described in the preliminary assessment roll or by cancelling, increasing, or reducing the assessments as may be proper in compliance with the basis of assessment. If any property is found to be omitted from the preliminary assessment roll, the board may place it on the roll and make the proper assessment. When the board confirms assessments for a project, the clerk shall enter in the minutes of the board the date, hour, and minute of confirmation. From the time of confirmation, each assessment is a lien on the property assessed of the same nature and to the same extent as the lien for county or city property taxes, under the priorities set out in G.S. 153A-200. After the assessment roll is confirmed, the board shall cause a copy of it to be delivered to the county tax collector for collection in the same manner (except as provided in this Article) as property taxes. (1963, c. 985, s. 1; 1965, c. 714; 1973, c. 822, s. 1.)

§ 153A-196. Publication of notice of confirmation of assessment roll.

No earlier than 20 days from the date the assessment roll is confirmed, the county tax collector shall publish once a notice that the roll has been confirmed. The notice shall also state that assessments may be paid without interest at any time before the expiration of 30 days from the date that the notice is published and that if they are not paid within this time, all installments thereof shall bear interest as determined by the board of commissioners. The notice shall also state the schedule of discounts, if one has been established, to be applied to assessments paid before the expiration date for payment of assessments without interest. (1963, c. 985, s. 1; 1965, c. 714; 1973, c. 822, s. 1; 1983, c. 381, s. 3.)

§ 153A-197. Appeal to the General Court of Justice.

If the owner of, or any person having an interest in, a lot, parcel, or tract of land against which an assessment is made is dissatisfied with the amount of the assessment, he may, within 10 days after the day the assessment roll is confirmed, file a notice of appeal to the appropriate division of the General Court of Justice. He shall then have 20 days after the day the roll is confirmed to serve on the board of commissioners or the clerk a statement of facts upon which the appeal is based. The appeal shall be tried like other actions at law. (1963, c. 985, s. 1; 1965, c. 714; 1973, c. 822, s. 1.)

§ 153A-198. Reassessment.

When in its judgment an irregularity, omission, error, or lack of jurisdiction has occurred in any proceeding related to a special assessment made by it, the board of commissioners may set aside the assessment and make a reassessment. In that case, the board may include in the total project cost all additional interest paid, or to be paid, as a result of the delay in confirming the assessment. A reassessment proceeding shall, as far as practicable, follow the comparable procedures of an original assessment proceeding. A reassessment has the same force as if it originally had been made properly. (1963, c. 985, s. 1; 1965, c. 714; 1973, c. 822, s. 1.)

§ 153A-199. Payment of assessments in full or by installments.

Within 30 days after the day that notice of confirmation of the assessment roll is published, each owner of assessed property shall pay his assessment in full, unless the board of commissioners has provided that assessments may be paid in annual installments. If payment by installments is permitted, any portion of an assessment not paid within the 30-day period shall be paid in annual installments. The board shall in the assessment resolution determine whether payment may be made by annual installments and set the number of installments, which may not be more than 10. With respect to payment by installment, the board may provide

(1) That the first installment with interest is due on the date when property taxes are due, and one installment with interest is due on the same date in each successive year until the assessment is paid in full, or

(2) That the first installment with interest is due 60 days after the date that the assessment roll is confirmed, and one installment with interest is due on that same day in each successive year until the assessment is paid in full. (1963, c. 985, s. 1; 1965, c. 714; 1973, c. 822, s. 1.)

§ 153A-200. Enforcement of assessments; interest; foreclosure; limitations.

(a) Any portion of an assessment that is not paid within 30 days after the day that notice of confirmation of the assessment roll is published shall, until paid, bear interest at a rate to be fixed in the assessment resolution. The maximum rate at which interest may be set is eight percent (8%) per annum.

(b) If an installment of an assessment is not paid on or before the due date, all of the installments remaining unpaid immediately become due, unless the board of commissioners waives acceleration. The board may waive acceleration and permit the property owner to pay all installments in arrears together with interest due thereon and the cost to the county of attempting to obtain payment. If this is done, any remaining installments shall be reinstated so that they fall due as if there had been no default. The board may waive acceleration and reinstate further installments at any time before foreclosure proceedings have been instituted.

(c) A county may foreclose assessment liens under any procedure provided by law for the foreclosure of property tax liens, except that (i) lien sales and lien sale certificates are not required and (ii) foreclosure may be begun at any time after 30 days after the due date. The county is not entitled to a deficiency judgment in an action to foreclose an assessment lien. The lien of special assessments is inferior to all prior and subsequent liens for State, local, and federal taxes, and superior to all other liens.

(d) No county may maintain an action or proceeding to foreclose any special assessment lien unless the action or proceeding is begun within 10 years from the date that the assessment or the earliest installment thereof included in the action or proceeding became due. Acceleration of installments under subsection (b) of this section does not have the effect of shortening the time within which foreclosure may be begun; in that event the statute of limitations continues to run as to each installment as if acceleration had not occurred. (1963, c. 985, s. 1; 1965, c. 714; 1973, c. 822, s. 1.)

§ 153A-201. Authority to hold assessments in abeyance.

The assessment resolution may provide that assessments made pursuant to this Article shall be held in abeyance without interest for any benefited property assessed. Water or sewer assessments may be held in abeyance until improvements on the assessed property are connected to the water or sewer system for which the assessment was made, or until a date certain not more than 10 years from the date of confirmation of the assessment roll, whichever event occurs first. Beach erosion control or flood and hurricane protection assessments may be held in abeyance for not more than 10 years from the date of confirmation of the assessment roll. When the period of abeyance ends, the assessment is payable in accordance with the terms set out in the assessment resolution.

If assessments are to be held in abeyance, the assessment resolution shall classify the property assessed according to general land use, location with respect to the water or sewer system (for water or sewer assessments), or other relevant factors. The resolution shall also provide that the period of abeyance shall be the same for all assessed property in the same class.

Statutes of limitations are suspended during the time that any assessment is held in abeyance without interest. (1963, c. 985, s. 1; 1965, c. 714; 1973, c. 822, s. 1.)

§ 153A-202. Assessments on property held by tenancy for life or years; contribution.

(a)   Assessments upon real property in the possession or enjoyment of a tenant for life or a tenant for a term of years shall be paid pro rata by the tenant and the remaindermen after the life estate or by the tenant and the owner in fee after the expiration of the tenancy for years according to their respective interests in the land as calculated pursuant to G.S. 37-13.

(b)   If a person having an interest in land held by tenancy for life or years pays more than his pro rata share of an assessment against the property, he may maintain an action in the nature of a suit for contribution against any delinquent party to recover from that party his pro rata share of the assessment, with interest thereon from the date of the payment; and in addition, he is subrogated to the right of the county to a lien on the property for the delinquent party's share of the assessment. (1963, c. 985, c. 1; 1965, c. 714; 1973, c. 822, s. 1.)

§ 153A-203. Lien in favor of a cotenant or joint owner paying special assessments.

Any one of several tenants in common or joint tenants (other than copartners) may pay the whole or any part of a special assessment made against property held in common or jointly. Any amount so paid that exceeds his share of the assessment and that was not paid through agreement with or on behalf of the other joint owners is a lien in his favor upon the shares of the other joint owners. This lien may be enforced in a proceeding for actual partition, a proceeding for partition and sale, or by any other appropriate judicial proceeding. This lien is not effective against an innocent purchaser for value until notice of the lien is filed in the office of the clerk of superior court in the county in which the land lies and indexed and docketed in the same manner as other liens required by law to be filed in that clerk's office. (1963, c. 985, s. 1; 1965, c. 714; 1973, c. 822, s. 1.)

§ 153A-204. Apportionment of assessments.

If a special assessment has been made against property that has been or is about to be subdivided, the board of commissioners may, with the consent of the owner of the property, (i) apportion the assessment among the lots or tracts within the subdivision, or (ii) release certain lots or tracts from the assessment if, in the board's opinion, the released lots or tracts are not benefited by the project, or (iii) both. Upon an apportionment each of the lots or tracts in the subdivision is released from the lien of the original assessment, and the portion of the original assessment assessed against each lot or tract has, as to that lot or tract, the same force as the original assessment. At the time the board makes an apportionment under this section, the clerk shall enter on the minutes of the board the date, hour, and minute of apportionment and a statement to the effect that the apportionment is made with the consent of the owners of the property affected, which entry is conclusive in the absence of fraud. The apportionment is effective at the time shown in the minute book. Apportionments may include past due installments with interest, as well as installments not then due; and any installment not then due shall fall due at the same date as it would have under the original assessment. (1963, c. 985, s. 1; 1965, c. 714; 1973, c. 822, s. 1.)

§ 153A-204.1. Maintenance assessments.

(a) In order to pay for the costs of maintaining and operating a project, the board of commissioners may annually or at less frequent intervals levy maintenance and operating assessments for any project purpose set forth in G.S. 153A-185(3) on the same basis as the original assessment. The amount of these assessments shall be determined by the board of commissioners on the basis of the board's estimate of the cost of maintaining and operating a project during the ensuing budget period, and the board's decision as to the amount of the assessment is conclusive. In determining the total cost to be included in the assessment the board may include estimated costs of maintaining and operating the project, of necessary legal services, of interest payments, of rights-of-way, and of publishing and mailing notices and resolutions. References to "total costs" in provisions of this Article that apply to maintenance and operating assessments shall be construed to mean "total estimated costs." Within the meaning of this section a "budget period" may be one year or such other budget period as the board determines.

(b) All of the provisions of this Article shall apply to maintenance and operating assessments, except for G.S. 153A-190 through G.S. 153A-193. (1983, c. 321, s. 4.)

§ 153A-205. Improvements to subdivision and residential streets.

(a) A county may finance the local share of the cost of improvements made under the supervision of the Department of Transportation to subdivision and residential streets that are a part of the State maintained system located in the county and outside of a city and shall levy and collect pursuant to the procedures of Article 9 of Chapter 153A of the General Statutes special assessments against benefited property to recoup that portion of the costs financed by the county. The local share is that share required by policies of the Secondary Roads Council, and may be paid by the county from funds not otherwise limited as to use by law. Land owned, leased, or controlled by a railroad company is exempt from such assessments to the same extent that it would be exempt from street assessments of a city under G.S. 160A-222. No project may be commenced under this section unless it has been approved by the Department of Transportation.

(b) A county may finance the local share of the cost of improvements made under the supervision of the Department of Transportation to subdivision and residential streets located in the county and outside of a city in order to bring those streets up to the standards of the Secondary Roads Council so that they may become a part of the State-maintained system and shall levy and collect pursuant to the procedures of Article 9 of Chapter 153A of the General Statutes special assessments against benefited property to recoup that portion of the costs financed by the county. The local share is that share required by policies of the Secondary Roads Council, and may be paid by the county from funds not otherwise limited as to use by law. Land owned, leased, or controlled by a railroad company is exempt from such assessments to the same extent that it would be exempt from street assessments of a city under G.S. 160A-222. No project may be commenced under this section unless it has been approved by the Department of Transportation.

(c)   Before a county may finance all or a portion of the cost of improvements to a subdivision or residential street, it must receive a petition for the improvements signed by at least seventy-five percent (75%) of the owners of property to be assessed, who must represent at least seventy-five percent (75%) of all the lineal feet of frontage of the lands abutting on the street or portion thereof to be improved. The petition shall state that portion of the cost of the improvement to be assessed, which shall be the local share required by policies of the Secondary Roads Council. A county may treat as a unit and consider as one street two or more connecting State-maintained subdivision or residential streets in a petition filed under this subsection calling for the improvement of subdivision or residential streets subject to property owner sharing in the cost of improvement under policies of the Department of Transportation.

Property owned by the United States shall not be included in determining the lineal feet of frontage on the improvement, nor shall the United States be included in determining the number of owners of property abutting the improvement. Property owned by the State of North Carolina shall be included in determining frontage and the number of owners only if the State has consented to assessment as provided in G.S. 153A-189. Property owned, leased, or controlled by railroad companies shall be included in determining frontage and the number of owners to the extent the property is subject to assessment under G.S. 160A-222. Property owned, leased, or controlled by railroad companies that is not subject to assessment shall not be included in determining frontage or the number of owners.

No right of action or defense asserting the invalidity of street assessments on grounds that the county did not comply with this subsection in securing a valid petition may be asserted except in an action or proceeding begun within 90 days after the day of publication of the notice of adoption of the preliminary assessment resolution.

(d)   This section is intended to provide a means of assisting in financing improvements to subdivision and residential streets that are on the State highway system or that will, as a result of the improvements, become a part of the system. By financing improvements under this section, a county does not thereby acquire or assume any responsibility for the street or streets involved, and a county has no liability arising from the construction of such an improvement or the maintenance of such a street. Nothing in this section shall be construed to alter the conditions and procedures under which State system streets or other public streets are transferred to municipal street systems pursuant to G.S. 136-66.1 and 136-66.2 upon annexation by, or incorporation of, a municipality. (1975, c. 487, s. 2; c. 716, s. 7; 1981, c. 768.)

§ 153A-206. Street light assessments.

(a)   Authorization. A county may annually levy special assessments against benefited property in a residential subdivision within the county and not within a city for the costs of providing street lights and street lighting pursuant to the procedures provided in this Article. The provisions of this Article, other than G.S. 153A-186, G.S. 153A-187 and G.S. 153A-190 through G.S. 153A-193, apply to street light assessments under this section.

(b)   Basis of Assessment. The estimated costs of providing street lights and street lighting shall be apportioned among all benefited property on the basis of the number of lots served, or subject to being served, by the street lights, at an equal rate per lot.

(c)   Amount of Assessment. The county shall determine the amount of the assessments on the basis of an estimate of the cost of constructing or operating the street lights during the ensuing year, and the board of commissioners' determination of the amount of the assessment is conclusive. In determining the total cost to be included in the assessment, the board may also include estimated costs of necessary legal services, projected utility rate increases, and the costs to the county of administering and collecting the assessment.

(d)   Procedure. The county may approve the levy of street light assessments under this section upon petition of at least two-thirds of the owners of the lots within the subdivision. The request or petition shall include an estimate from the appropriate utility of the charge for providing street lights and street lighting within the subdivision for one year. Upon approval of the petition, the petitioning owner or owners shall pay to the tax collector the total estimated assessment amount for the ensuing year as determined by the county. This payment shall be set aside by the county tax office in escrow as security for payment of the assessments.

(e) Collection and Administration. The county shall levy the street light assessments on an annual basis and shall pay the costs of providing street lights and street lighting to the appropriate utility on a periodic basis. The assessment amount shall be adjusted on an annual basis in order to maintain in the escrow account an amount equal to the estimated cost of providing street lighting plus related expenses for the ensuing year. (1989 (Reg. Sess., 1990), c. 923, s. 2.)

§ 153A-207: Reserved for future codification purposes.

§ 153A-208: Reserved for future codification purposes.

§ 153A-209: Reserved for future codification purposes.

§ 153A-210: Reserved for future codification purposes.

Article 9A.

Special Assessments for Critical Infrastructure Needs.

§ 153A-210.1. (Expires July 1, 2015) Purpose; sunset.

(a) Purpose. - This Article enables counties that face increased demands for infrastructure improvements as a result of rapid growth and development to issue revenue bonds payable from special assessments imposed under this Article on benefited property. This Article supplements the authority counties have in Article 9 of this Chapter. The provisions of Article 9 of this Chapter apply to this Article, to the extent they do not conflict with this Article.

(b) Sunset. - This Article expires July 1, 2015. The expiration does not affect the validity of assessments imposed or bonds issued or authorized under the provisions of this Article prior to the effective date of the expiration. (2008-165, s. 2; 2013-371, ss. 1(a), 3.)

§ 153A-210.2. (Expires July 1, 2015) Assessments.

(a) Projects. - The board of commissioners of a county may make special assessments as provided in this Article against benefited property within the county for the purpose of financing the capital costs of projects for which project development financing debt instruments may be issued under G.S. 159-103 or for the purpose of financing the installation of distributed generation renewable energy sources or energy efficiency improvements that are permanently fixed to residential, commercial, industrial, or other real property.

(b) Costs. - The board of commissioners must determine a project's total estimated cost. In addition to the costs allowed under G.S. 153A-193, the costs may include any expenses allowed under G.S. 159-84. A preliminary assessment roll may be prepared before the costs are incurred based on the estimated cost of the project.

(c) Method. - The board of commissioners must establish an assessment method that will most accurately assess each lot or parcel of land subject to the assessments according to the benefits conferred upon it by the project for which the assessment is made. In addition to other bases upon which assessments may be made under G.S. 153A-186, the board may select any other method designed to allocate the costs in accordance with benefits conferred. In doing so, the board may provide that the benefits conferred are measured on the basis of use being made on the lot or parcel of land and provide for adjustments of assessments upon a change in use, provided that the total amount of all assessments is sufficient to pay the costs of the project after the adjustments have been made. (2008-165, s. 2; 2008-187, s. 47.5(a); 2009-525, s. 1(a); 2013-371, ss. 1(b), 3.)

§ 153A-210.3. (Expires July 1, 2015) Petition required.

(a) Petition. - The board of commissioners may not impose a special assessment under this Article unless it receives a petition for the project to be financed by the assessment signed by (i) at least a majority of the owners of real property to be assessed and (ii) owners who represent at least sixty-six percent (66%) of the assessed value of all real property to be assessed. For purposes of determining whether the petition has been signed by a majority of owners, an owner who holds title to a parcel of real property alone shall be treated as having one vote each, and an owner who shares title to a parcel of real property with one or more other owners shall have a vote equal to one vote multiplied by a fraction, the numerator of which is one, and the denominator of which is the total number of owners of the parcel. For purposes of determining whether the assessed value represented by those signing the petition constitutes at least sixty-six percent (66%) of the assessed value of all real property to be assessed, an owner who holds title to a parcel of real property alone shall have the full assessed value of the parcel included in the calculation, and an owner who shares title to a parcel of real property with one or more other owners shall have their proportionate share of the full assessed value of the parcel included in the calculation. The petition must include the following:

(1) A statement of the project proposed to be financed in whole or in part by the imposition of an assessment under this Article.

(2) An estimate of the cost of the project.

(3) An estimate of the portion of the cost of the project to be assessed.

(b) Petition Withdrawn. - The board of commissioners must wait at least 10 days after the public hearing on the preliminary assessment resolution before adopting a final assessment resolution. A petition submitted under subsection (a) of this section may be withdrawn if notice of petition withdrawal is given in writing to the board signed by at least a majority of the owners who signed the petition submitted under subsection (a) of this section representing at least fifty percent (50%) of the assessed value of all real property to be assessed. The board may not adopt a final assessment resolution if it receives a timely notice of petition withdrawal.

(c) Validity of Assessment. - No right of action or defense asserting the invalidity of an assessment on grounds that the county did not comply with this section may be asserted except in an action or proceeding begun within 90 days after publication of the notice of adoption of the preliminary assessment resolution. (2008-165, s. 2; 2013-371, ss. 1(c), 3.)

§ 153A-210.4. (Expires July 1, 2015) Financing a project for which an assessment is imposed.

(a) Financing Sources. - A board of commissioners may provide for the payment of the cost of a project for which an assessment may be imposed under this Article from one or more of the financing sources listed in this subsection. The assessment resolution must include the estimated cost of the project and the amount of the cost to be derived from each respective financing source.

(1) Revenue bonds issued under G.S. 153A-210.6.

(2) Project development financing debt instruments issued under the North Carolina Project Development Financing Act, Article 6 of Chapter 159 of the General Statutes.

(3) General obligation bonds issued under the Local Government Bond Act, Article 4 of Chapter 159 of the General Statutes.

(4) General revenues.

(b) Assessments Pledged. - An assessment imposed under this Article may be pledged to secure revenue bonds under G.S. 153A-210.6 or as additional security for a project development financing debt instrument under G.S. 159-111. If an assessment imposed under this Article is pledged to secure financing, the board of commissioners must covenant to enforce the payment of the assessments. (2008-165, s. 2; 2009-525, s. 1(b); 2013-371, s. 3.)

§ 153A-210.5. (Expires July 1, 2015) Payment of assessments by installments.

An assessment imposed under this Article is payable in annual installments. The board of commissioners must set the number of annual installments, which may not be more than 30. The installments are due on the date that property taxes are due. (2008-165, s. 2; 2013-371, s. 3.)

§ 153A-210.6. (Expires July 1, 2015) Revenue bonds.

(a) Authorization. - A board of commissioners that imposes an assessment under this Article may issue revenue bonds under Article 5 of Chapter 159 of the General Statutes to finance the project for which the assessment is imposed and use the proceeds of the assessment imposed as revenues pertaining to the project.

(b) Modifications. - This Article specifically modifies the authority of a county to issue revenue bonds under Article 5 of Chapter 159 of the General Statutes by extending the authority in that Article to include a project for which an assessment may be imposed under this Article. In applying the provisions of Article 5, the following definitions apply:

(1) Revenue bond project. - Defined in G.S. 159-81(3). The term includes projects for which an assessment is imposed under this Article.

(2) Revenues. - Defined in G.S. 159-81(4). The term includes assessments imposed under this Article to finance a project allowed under this Article. (2008-165, s. 2; 2013-371, s. 3.)

§ 153A-210.7. (Effective July 1, 2015) Project implementation.

A county may act directly, through one or more contracts with other public agencies, through one or more contracts with private agencies, or by any combination thereof to implement the project financed in whole or in part by the imposition of an assessment imposed under this Article. If no more than twenty-five percent (25%) of the estimated cost of a project is to be funded from the proceeds of general obligation bonds or general revenue, a private agency that enters into a contract with a county for the implementation of all or part of the project is subject to the provisions of Article 8 of Chapter 143 of the General Statutes only to the extent specified in the contract. In the event any contract relating to construction a substantial portion of which is to be performed on publicly owned property is excluded from the provisions of Article 8 of Chapter 143, the county or any trustee or fiduciary responsible for disbursing funds shall obtain certification acceptable to the county in the amount due for work done or materials supplied for which payment will be paid from such disbursement. If the county or any trustee or fiduciary responsible for disbursing funds receives notice of a claim from any person who would be entitled to a mechanic's or materialman's lien but for the fact that the claim relates to work performed on or supplies provided to publicly owned property, then either no disbursement of funds may be made until the county, trustee, or fiduciary receives satisfactory proof of resolution of the claim or funds in the amount of the claim shall be set aside for payment thereof upon resolution of the claim. (2009-525, s. 1(c); 2013-371, s. 3.)

Article 10.

Law Enforcement and Confinement Facilities.

Part 1. Law Enforcement.

§ 153A-211. Training and development programs for law enforcement.

A county may plan and execute training and development programs for law-enforcement agencies, and for that purpose may:

(1) Contract with other counties, cities, and the State and federal governments and their agencies;

(2) Accept, receive, and disburse funds, grants, and services;

(3) Pursuant to the procedures and provisions of Chapter 160A, Article 20, Part 1, create joint agencies to act for and on behalf of the participating counties and cities;

(4) Apply for, receive, administer, and expend federal grant funds;

(5) Appropriate funds not otherwise limited as to use by law. (1969, c. 1145, s. 2; 1973, c. 822, s. 1.)

§ 153A-212. Cooperation in law-enforcement matters.

A county may cooperate with the State and other local governments in law-enforcement matters, as permitted by G.S. 160A-283 (joint auxiliary police), by G.S. 160A-288 (emergency aid), G.S. 160A-288.1 (assistance by State law-enforcement officers), and by Chapter 160A, Article 20, Part 1. (1973, c. 822, s. 1; 1979, c. 639, s. 2.)

§ 153A-212.1. Resources to protect the public.

Subject to the requirements of G.S. 7A-41, 7A-44.1, 7A-64, 7A-102, 7A-133, and 7A-498.7, a county may appropriate funds under contract with the State for the provision of services for the speedy disposition of cases involving drug offenses, domestic violence, or other offenses involving threats to public safety. Nothing in this section shall be construed to obligate the General Assembly to make any appropriation to implement the provisions of this section. Further, nothing in this section shall be construed to obligate the Administrative Office of the Courts or the Office of Indigent Defense Services to maintain positions or services initially provided for under this section. (1999-237, s. 17.17(b); 2000-67, s. 15.4(e); 2001-424, s. 22.11(e).)

§ 153A-212.2. Neighborhood crime watch programs.

A county may establish neighborhood crime watch programs within the county to encourage residents and business owners to promote citizen involvement in securing homes, businesses, and personal property against criminal activity and to report suspicious activities to law enforcement officials. (2006-181, s. 1.)

§ 153A-213. Reserved for future codification purposes.

§ 153A-214. Reserved for future codification purposes.

§ 153A-215. Reserved for future codification purposes.

Part 2. Local Confinement Facilities.

§ 153A-216. Legislative policy.

The policy of the General Assembly with respect to local confinement facilities is:

(1)   Local confinement facilities should provide secure custody of persons confined therein in order to protect the community and should be operated so as to protect the health and welfare of prisoners and provide for their humane treatment.

(2) Minimum statewide standards should be provided to guide and assist local governments in planning, constructing, and maintaining confinement facilities and in developing programs that provide for humane treatment of prisoners and contribute to the rehabilitation of offenders.

(3) The State should provide services to local governments to help improve the quality of administration and local confinement facilities. These services should include inspection, consultation, technical assistance, and other appropriate services.

(4) Adequate qualifications and training of the personnel of local confinement facilities are essential to improving the quality of these facilities. The State shall establish entry level employment standards for jailers and supervisory and administrative personnel of local confinement facilities to include training as a condition of employment in a local confinement facility pursuant to the provisions of Chapter 17C and Chapter 17E and the rules promulgated thereunder. (1967, c. 581, s. 2; 1973, c. 822, s. 1; 1983, c. 745, s. 4.)

§ 153A-217. Definitions.

Unless otherwise clearly required by the context, the words and phrases defined in this section have the meanings indicated when used in this Part:

(1) "Commission" means the Social Services Commission.

(2) "Secretary" means the Secretary of Health and Human Services.

(3) "Department" means the Department of Health and Human Services.

(4) "Governing body" means the governing body of a county or city or the policy-making body for a district or regional confinement facility.

(5) "Local confinement facility" includes a county or city jail, a local lockup, a regional or district jail, a juvenile detention facility, a detention facility for adults operated by a local government, and any other facility operated by a local government for confinement of persons awaiting trial or serving sentences except that it shall not include a county satellite jail/work release unit governed by Part 3 of Article 10 of Chapter 153A.

(6)   "Prisoner" includes any person, adult or juvenile, confined or detained in a confinement facility.

(7)   "Unit," "unit of local government," or "local government" means a county or city. (1967, c. 581, s. 2; 1969, c. 981, s. 1; 1973, c. 476, s. 138; c. 822, s. 1; 1987, c. 207, s. 2; 1997-443, s. 11A.118(a); 1998-202, s. 4(cc).)

§ 153A-218. County confinement facilities.

A county may establish, acquire, erect, repair, maintain, and operate local confinement facilities and may for these purposes appropriate funds not otherwise limited as to use by law. A juvenile detention facility may be located in the same facility as a county jail provided that the juvenile detention facility meets the requirements of this Article and G.S. 147-33.40. (1868, c. 20, s. 8; Code, s. 707; Rev., s. 1318; 1915, c. 140; C.S., s. 1297; 1973, c. 822, s. 1; 1998-202, s. 4(dd).)

§ 153A-219. District confinement facilities.

(a)   Two or more units of local government may enter into and carry out an agreement to establish, finance, and operate a district confinement facility. The units may construct such a facility or may designate an existing facility as a district confinement facility. In addition, two or more units of local government may enter into and carry out agreements under which one unit may use the local confinement facility owned and operated by another. In exercising the powers granted by this section, the units shall proceed according to the procedures and provisions of Chapter 160A, Article 20, Part 1.

(b)   If a district confinement facility is established, the units involved shall provide for a jail administrator for the facility. The administrator need not be the sheriff or any other official of a participating unit. The administrator and the other custodial personnel of a district confinement facility have the authority of law-enforcement officers for the purposes of receiving, maintaining custody of, and transporting prisoners.

(c) If a district confinement facility is established, or if one unit contracts to use the local confinement facility of another, the law-enforcement officers of the contracting units and the custodial personnel of the facility may transport prisoners to and from the facility.

(d) The Department shall provide technical and other assistance to units wishing to exercise any of the powers granted by this section. (1933, c. 201; 1967, c. 581, s. 2; 1969, c. 743; 1971, c. 341, s. 1; 1973, c. 822, s. 1.)

§ 153A-220. Jail and detention services.

The Commission has policy responsibility for providing and coordinating State services to local government with respect to local confinement facilities. The Department shall:

(1) Consult with and provide technical assistance to units of local government with respect to local confinement facilities.

(2) Develop minimum standards for the construction and operation of local confinement facilities.

(3) Visit and inspect local confinement facilities; advise the sheriff, jailer, governing board, and other appropriate officials as to deficiencies and recommend improvements; and submit written reports on the inspections to appropriate local officials.

(4) Review and approve plans for the construction and major modification of local confinement facilities.

(5) Repealed by Session Laws 1983, c. 745, s. 5, effective September 1, 1983.

(6) Perform any other duties that may be necessary to carry out the State's responsibilities concerning local confinement facilities. (1967, c. 581, s. 2; 1973, c. 476, s. 138; c. 822, s. 1; 1983, c. 745, s. 5.)

§ 153A-221. Minimum standards.

(a) The Secretary shall develop and publish minimum standards for the operation of local confinement facilities and may from time to time develop and publish amendments to the standards. The standards shall be developed with a view to providing secure custody of prisoners and to protecting their health and welfare and providing for their humane treatment. The standards shall provide for:

(1) Secure and safe physical facilities;

(2) Jail design;

(3) Adequacy of space per prisoner;

(4) Heat, light, and ventilation;

(5) Supervision of prisoners;

(6) Personal hygiene and comfort of prisoners;

(7) Medical care for prisoners, including mental health, mental retardation, and substance abuse services;

(8) Sanitation;

(9) Food allowances, food preparation, and food handling;

(10) Any other provisions that may be necessary for the safekeeping, privacy, care, protection, and welfare of prisoners.

(b) In developing the standards and any amendments thereto, the Secretary shall consult with organizations representing local government and local law enforcement, including the North Carolina Association of County Commissioners, the North Carolina League of Municipalities, the North Carolina Sheriffs' Association, and the North Carolina Police Executives' Association. The Secretary shall also consult with interested State departments and agencies, including the Division of Adult Correction of the Department of Public Safety, the Department of Health and Human Services, the Department of Insurance, and the North Carolina Criminal Justice Education and Training Standards Commission, and the North Carolina Sheriffs' Education and Training Standards Commission.

(c) Before the standards or any amendments thereto may become effective, they must be approved by the Commission and the Governor. Upon becoming effective, they have the force and effect of law.

(d) Notwithstanding any law or rule to the contrary, each dormitory in a county detention facility may house up to 64 inmates as long as the dormitory provides all of the following:

(1) A minimum floor space of 70 square feet per inmate, including both the sleeping and dayroom areas.

(2) One shower per eight inmates, one toilet per eight inmates, one sink with a security mirror per eight inmates, and one water fountain.

(3) A telephone jack or other telephone arrangement provided within the dormitory.

(4) Space designed to allow a variety of activities.

(5) Sufficient seating and tables for all inmates.

(6) A way for officers to observe the entire area from the entrance.

This subsection applies only to those counties that have a population in excess of 300,000, according to the most recent decennial federal census. (1967, c. 581, s. 2; 1973, c. 476, ss. 128, 133, 138; c. 822, s. 1; 1983, c. 745, s. 6; c. 768, s. 20; 1991, c. 237, s. 1; 1997-443, s. 11A.118(a); 2008-194, s. 10(a), (b); 2011-145, s. 19.1(h); 2011-324, s. 1.)

Part 2. Local Confinement Facilities.

§ 153A-221.1. Standards and inspections.

The legal responsibility of the Division of Juvenile Justice of the Department of Public Safety for State services to county juvenile detention homes under this Article is hereby confirmed and shall include the following: development of State standards under the prescribed procedures; inspection; consultation; technical assistance; and training.

The Secretary of Health and Human Services, in consultation with the Secretary of Public Safety, shall also develop standards under which a local jail may be approved as a holdover facility for not more than five calendar days pending placement in a juvenile detention home which meets State standards, providing the local jail is so arranged that any child placed in the holdover facility cannot converse with, see, or be seen by the adult population of the jail while in the holdover facility. The personnel responsible for the administration of a jail with an approved holdover facility shall provide close supervision of any child placed in the holdover facility for the protection of the child. (1973, c. 1230, s. 2; c. 1262, s. 10; 1975, c. 426, s. 2; 1983, c. 768, s. 21; 1997-443, s. 11A.118(a); 1998-202, s. 13(nn); 1999-423, s. 12; 2000-137, s. 4(hh); 2012-172, s. 2; 2013-360, s. 16D.7(c).)

§ 153A-222. Inspections of local confinement facilities.

Department personnel shall visit and inspect each local confinement facility at least semiannually. The purpose of the inspections is to investigate the conditions of confinement, the treatment of prisoners, the maintenance of entry level employment standards for jailers and supervisory and administrative personnel of local confinement facilities as provided for in G.S. 153A-216(4), and to determine whether the facilities meet the minimum standards published pursuant to G.S. 153A-221. The inspector shall make a written report of each inspection and submit it within 30 days after the day the inspection is completed to the governing body and other local officials responsible for the facility. The report shall specify each way in which the facility does not meet the minimum standards. The governing body shall consider the report at its first regular meeting after receipt of the report and shall promptly initiate any action necessary to bring the facility into conformity with the standards.
Notwithstanding the provisions of G.S. 8-53 or any other provision of law relating to the confidentiality of communications between physician and patient, the representatives of the Department of Health and Human Services who make these inspections may review any writing or other record in any recording medium which pertains to the admission, discharge, medication, treatment, medical condition, or history of persons who are or have been inmates of the facility being inspected. Physicians, psychologists, psychiatrists, nurses, and anyone else involved in giving treatment at or through a facility who may be interviewed by representatives of the Department may disclose to these representatives information related to an inquiry, notwithstanding the existence of the physician-patient privilege in G.S. 8-53 or any other rule of law; provided

the patient, resident or client has not made written objection to such disclosure. The facility, its employees, and any person interviewed during these inspections shall be immune from liability for damages resulting from the disclosure of any information to the Department. Any confidential or privileged information received from review of records or interviews shall be kept confidential by the Department and not disclosed without written authorization of the inmate or legal representative, or unless disclosure is ordered by a court of competent jurisdiction. The Department shall institute appropriate policies and procedures to ensure that this information shall not be disclosed without authorization or court order. The Department shall not disclose the name of anyone who has furnished information concerning a facility without the consent of that person. Neither the names of persons furnishing information nor any confidential or privileged information obtained from records or interviews shall be considered "public records" within the meaning of G.S. 132-1. Prior to releasing any information or allowing any inspections referred to in this section the patient, resident or client must be advised in writing that he has the right to object in writing to such release of information or review of his records and that by an objection in writing he may prohibit the inspection or release of his records. (1947, c. 915; 1967, c. 581, s. 2; 1973, c. 822, s. 1; 1981, c. 586, s. 6; 1983, c. 745, s. 7; 1997-443, s. 11A.118(a).)

§ 153A-223. Enforcement of minimum standards.

If an inspection conducted pursuant to G.S. 153A-222 discloses that the jailers and supervisory and administrative personnel of a local confinement facility do not meet the entry level employment standards established pursuant to Chapter 17C or Chapter 17E or that a local confinement facility does not meet the minimum standards published pursuant to G.S. 153A-221 and, in addition, if the Secretary determines that conditions in the facility jeopardize the safe custody, safety, health, or welfare of persons confined in the facility, the Secretary may order corrective action or close the facility, as provided in this section:

(1) The Secretary shall give notice of his determination to the governing body and each other local official responsible for the facility. The Secretary shall also send a copy of this notice, along with a copy of the inspector's report, to the senior resident superior court judge of the superior court district or set of districts as defined in G.S. 7A-41.1 in which the facility is located. Upon receipt of the Secretary's notice, the governing body shall call a public hearing to consider the report. The hearing shall be held within 20 days after the day the

Secretary's notice is received. The inspector shall appear at this hearing to advise and consult with the governing body concerning any corrective action necessary to bring the facility into conformity with the standards.

(2)   The governing body shall, within 30 days after the day the Secretary's notice is received, request a contested case hearing, initiate appropriate corrective action or close the facility. The corrective action must be completed within a reasonable time.

(3)   A contested case hearing, if requested, shall be conducted pursuant to G.S. 150B, Article 3. The issues shall be: (i) whether the facility meets the minimum standards; (ii) whether the conditions in the facility jeopardize the safe custody, safety, health, or welfare of persons confined therein; and (iii) the appropriate corrective action to be taken and a reasonable time to complete that action.

(4)   If the governing body does not, within 30 days after the day the Secretary's notice is received, or within 30 days after service of the final decision if a contested case hearing is held, either initiate corrective action or close the facility, or does not complete the action within a reasonable time, the Secretary may order that the facility be closed.

(5)   The governing body may appeal an order of the Secretary or a final decision to the senior resident superior court judge. The governing body shall initiate the appeal by giving by registered mail to the judge and to the Secretary notice of its intention to appeal. The notice must be given within 15 days after the day the Secretary's order or the final decision is received. If notice is not given within the 15-day period, the right to appeal is terminated.

(6)   The senior resident superior court judge shall hear the appeal. He shall cause notice of the date, time, and place of the hearing to be given to each interested party, including the Secretary, the governing body, and each other local official involved. The Office of Administrative Hearings, if a contested case hearing has been held, shall file the official record, as defined in G.S. 150B-37, with the senior resident superior court judge and shall serve a copy on each person who has been given notice of the hearing. The judge shall conduct the hearing without a jury. He shall consider the official record, if any, and may accept evidence from the Secretary, the governing body, and each other local official which he finds appropriate. The issue before the court shall be whether the facility continues to jeopardize the safe custody, safety, health, or welfare of persons confined therein. The court may affirm, modify, or reverse the

Secretary's order. (1947, c. 915; 1967, c. 581, s. 2; 1973, c. 476, s. 138; c. 822, s. 1; 1981, c. 614, ss. 20, 21; 1983, c. 745, s. 8; 1987, c. 827, s. 1; 1987 (Reg. Sess., 1988), c. 1037, s. 123; 2011-398, s. 55.)

§ 153A-224. Supervision of local confinement facilities.

(a)   No person may be confined in a local confinement facility unless custodial personnel are present and available to provide continuous supervision in order that custody will be secure and that, in event of emergency, such as fire, illness, assaults by other prisoners, or otherwise, the prisoners can be protected. These personnel shall supervise prisoners closely enough to maintain safe custody and control and to be at all times informed of the prisoners' general health and emergency medical needs.

(b)   In a medical emergency, the custodial personnel shall secure emergency medical care from a licensed physician according to the unit's plan for medical care. If a physician designated in the plan is not available, the personnel shall secure medical services from any licensed physician who is available. The unit operating the facility shall pay the cost of emergency medical services unless the inmate has third-party insurance, in which case the third-party insurer shall be the initial payor and the medical provider shall bill the third-party insurer. The county shall only be liable for costs not reimbursed by the third-party insurer, in which event the county may recover from the inmate the cost of the non-reimbursed medical services.

(c)   If a person violates any provision of this section, he is guilty of a Class 1 misdemeanor. (1967, c. 581, s. 2; 1973, c. 822, s. 1; 1993, c. 510, c. 539, s. 1061; 1994, Ex. Sess., c. 24, s. 14(c).)

§ 153A-225. Medical care of prisoners.

(a)   (Effective until July 1, 2014) Each unit that operates a local confinement facility shall develop a plan for providing medical care for prisoners in the facility. The plan

(1)   Shall be designed to protect the health and welfare of the prisoners and to avoid the spread of contagious disease;

(2)   Shall provide for medical supervision of prisoners and emergency medical care for prisoners to the extent necessary for their health and welfare;

(3)   Shall provide for the detection, examination and treatment of prisoners who are infected with tuberculosis or venereal diseases.

The unit shall develop the plan in consultation with appropriate local officials and organizations, including the sheriff, the county physician, the local or district health director, and the local medical society. The plan must be approved by the local or district health director after consultation with the area mental health, developmental disabilities, and substance abuse authority, if it is adequate to protect the health and welfare of the prisoners. Upon a determination that the plan is adequate to protect the health and welfare of the prisoners, the plan must be adopted by the governing body.

As a part of its plan, each unit may establish fees of not more than twenty dollars ($20.00) per incident for the provision of nonemergency medical care to prisoners and a fee of not more than ten dollars ($10.00) for a 30-day supply or less of a prescription drug. In establishing fees pursuant to this section, each unit shall establish a procedure for waiving fees for indigent prisoners.

(a)   (Effective July 1, 2014) Each unit that operates a local confinement facility shall develop a plan for providing medical care for prisoners in the facility. The plan:

(1)   Shall be designed to protect the health and welfare of the prisoners and to avoid the spread of contagious disease;

(2)   Shall provide for medical supervision of prisoners and emergency medical care for prisoners to the extent necessary for their health and welfare;

(3)   Shall provide for the detection, examination and treatment of prisoners who are infected with tuberculosis or venereal diseases; and

(4)   May utilize Medicaid coverage for inpatient hospitalization or for any other Medicaid services allowable for eligible prisoners, provided that the plan includes a reimbursement process which pays to the State the State portion of the costs, including the costs of the services provided and any administrative costs directly related to the services to be reimbursed, to the State's Medicaid program.

The unit shall develop the plan in consultation with appropriate local officials and organizations, including the sheriff, the county physician, the local or district health director, and the local medical society. The plan must be approved by the local or district health director after consultation with the area mental health, developmental disabilities, and substance abuse authority, if it is adequate to protect the health and welfare of the prisoners. Upon a determination that the plan is adequate to protect the health and welfare of the prisoners, the plan must be adopted by the governing body.

As a part of its plan, each unit may establish fees of not more than twenty dollars ($20.00) per incident for the provision of nonemergency medical care to prisoners and a fee of not more than ten dollars ($10.00) for a 30-day supply or less of a prescription drug. In establishing fees pursuant to this section, each unit shall establish a procedure for waiving fees for indigent prisoners.

(b)   If a prisoner in a local confinement facility dies, the medical examiner and the coroner shall be notified immediately. Within five days after the day of the death, the administrator of the facility shall make a written report to the local or district health director and to the Secretary of Health and Human Services. The report shall be made on forms developed and distributed by the Department of Health and Human Services.

(b1)   Whenever a local confinement facility transfers a prisoner from that facility to another local confinement facility, the transferring facility shall provide the receiving facility with any health information or medical records the transferring facility has in its possession pertaining to the transferred prisoner.

(c)   If a person violates any provision of this section (including the requirements regarding G.S. 130-97 and 130-121), he is guilty of a Class 1 misdemeanor. (1967, c. 581, s. 2; 1973, c. 476, ss. 128, 138; c. 822, s. 1; 1973, c. 1140, s. 3; 1989, c. 727, s. 204; 1991, c. 237, s. 2; 1993, c. 539, s. 1062; 1994, Ex. Sess., c. 24, s. 14(c); 1995, c. 385, s. 1; 1997-443, s. 11A.112; 2003-392, s. 1; 2004-199, s. 46(a); 2011-145, s. 31.26(f); 2011-192, s. 7(n); 2013-387, s. 2; 2013-389, s. 1.)

§ 153A-225.1. Duty of custodial personnel when prisoners are unconscious or semiconscious.

(a) Whenever a custodial officer of a local confinement facility takes custody of a prisoner who is unconscious, semiconscious, or otherwise apparently suffering from some disabling condition and unable to provide information on the causes of the condition, the officer should make a reasonable effort to determine if the prisoner is wearing a bracelet or necklace containing the Medic Alert Foundation's emergency alert symbol to indicate that the prisoner suffers from diabetes, epilepsy, a cardiac condition or any other form of illness which would cause a loss of consciousness. If such a symbol is found indicating that the prisoner suffers from one of those conditions, the officer must make a reasonable effort to have appropriate medical care provided.

(b) Failure of a custodial officer of a local confinement facility to make a reasonable effort to discover an emergency alert symbol as required by this section does not by itself establish negligence of the officer but may be considered along with other evidence to determine if the officer took reasonable precautions to ascertain the emergency medical needs of the prisoner in his custody.

(c) A prisoner who is provided medical care under the provisions of this section is liable for the reasonable costs of that care unless he is indigent.

(d) Repealed by Session Laws 1975, c. 818, s. 2. (1975, c. 306, s. 2; c. 818, s. 2.)

§ 153A-225.2. Payment of medical care of prisoners.

(a) Counties shall reimburse those providers and facilities providing requested or emergency medical care outside of the local confinement facility the lesser amount of either a rate of seventy percent (70%) of the provider's then-current prevailing charge or two times the then-current Medicaid rate for any given service. Each county shall have the right to audit any provider from whom the county has received a bill for services under this section but only to the extent necessary to determine the actual prevailing charge to ensure compliance with this section.

(b) Nothing in this section shall preclude a county from contracting with a provider for services at rates that provide greater documentable cost avoidance for the county than do the rates contained in subsection (a) of this subsection or at rates that are less favorable to the county but that will ensure the continued access to care.

(c) The county shall make reasonable efforts to equitably distribute prisoners among all hospitals or other appropriate health care facilities located within the same county and shall do so based upon the licensed acute care bed capacity at each of the hospitals located within the same county. Counties with more than one hospital or other appropriate health care facility shall provide semiannual reports conspicuously posted on the county's Web site that detail compliance with this section, including information on the distribution of prisoner health care services among different hospitals and health care facilities.

(d) For the purposes of this section, "requested or emergency medical care" shall include all medically necessary and appropriate care provided to an individual from the time that individual presents to the provider or facility in the custody of county law enforcement officers until the time that the individual is safely transferred back to the care of county law enforcement officers or medically discharged to another community setting, as appropriate. (2013-387, s. 1.)

§ 153A-226. Sanitation and food.

(a) The Commission for Public Health shall adopt rules governing the sanitation of local confinement facilities, including the kitchens and other places where food is prepared for prisoners. The rules shall address, but not be limited to, the cleanliness of floors, walls, ceilings, storage spaces, utensils, ventilation equipment, and other facilities; adequacy of lighting, water, lavatory facilities, bedding, food protection facilities, treatment of eating and drinking utensils, and waste disposal; methods of food preparation, handling, storage, and serving; and any other item necessary to the health of the prisoners or the public.

(b) The Commission for Public Health shall prepare a score sheet to be used by local health departments in inspecting local confinement facilities. The local health departments shall inspect local confinement facilities as often as may be required by the Commission for Public Health. If an inspector of the Department finds conditions that reflect hazards or deficiencies in the sanitation or food service of a local confinement facility, he shall immediately notify the local health department. The health department shall promptly inspect the facility. After making its inspection, the local health department shall forward a copy of its report to the Department of Health and Human Services and to the unit operating the facility, on forms prepared by the Department of Environment and Natural Resources. The report shall indicate whether the facility and its kitchen or other place for preparing food is approved or disapproved for public health purposes. If the facility is disapproved, the situation shall be rectified according to the procedures of G.S. 153A-223. (1967, c. 581, s. 2; 1973, c. 476, s. 128; c. 822, s. 1; 1989, c. 727, s. 205; 1993, c. 262, s. 5; 1997-443, ss. 11A.113, 11A.118(a); 2007-182, s. 2.)

§ 153A-227: Repealed by Session Laws 1983, c. 745, s. 9.

§ 153A-228. Separation of sexes.

Male and female prisoners shall be confined in separate facilities or in separate quarters in local confinement facilities. (1967, c. 581, s. 2; 1973, c. 822, s. 1.)

§ 153A-229. Jailers' report of jailed defendants.

The person having administrative control of a local confinement facility must furnish to the clerk of superior court a report listing such information reasonably at his disposal as is necessary to enable said clerk of superior court to comply with the provisions of G.S. 7A-109.1. (1973, c. 1286, s. 23; 1981, c. 522.)

Part 3. Satellite Jail/Work Release Units.

§ 153A-230. Legislative policy.

The policy of the General Assembly with respect to satellite jail/work release units is:

(1) To encourage counties to accept responsibility for incarcerated misdemeanants thereby relieving the State prison system of its misdemeanant population;

(2) To assist counties in providing suitable facilities for certain misdemeanants who receive active sentences;

(3) To allow more misdemeanants who are employed at the time of sentencing to retain their jobs by eliminating the time involved in processing persons through the State system;

(4) To enable misdemeanants to pay for their upkeep while serving time, to pay restitution, to continue to support their dependents, and to remain near the communities and families to which they will return after serving their time;

(5) To provide more appropriate, cost effective housing for certain minimum custody misdemeanants and to utilize vacant buildings where possible and suitable for renovation;

(6) To provide a rehabilitative atmosphere for non-violent misdemeanants who otherwise would face a substantial threat of imprisonment; and

(7) To encourage the use of alternative to incarceration programs. (1987, c. 207, s. 1.)

§ 153A-230.1. Definitions.

Unless otherwise clearly required by the context, the words and phrases defined in this section have the meanings indicated when used in this Part:

(1) "Office" means the Office of State Budget and Management.

(2) "Satellite Jail/Work Release Unit" means a building or designated portion of a building primarily designed, staffed, and used for the housing of misdemeanants participating in a work release program. These units shall house misdemeanants only, except that, if he so chooses, the Sheriff may accept responsibility from the Division of Adult Correction of the Department of Public Safety for the housing of felons who do not present security risks, who have achieved work release status, and who will be employed on work release, or for felons committed directly to his custody pursuant to G.S. 15A-1352(b). These units shall be operated on a full time basis, i.e., seven days/nights a week. (1987, c. 207, s. 1; 1987, (Reg. Sess., 1988), c. 1106, s. 1; 2000-140, s. 93.1(a); 2001-424, s. 12.2(b); 2011-145, s. 19.1(h).)

§ 153A-230.2. Creation of Satellite Jail/Work Release Unit Fund.

(a) There is created in the Office of State Budget and Management the County Satellite Jail/Work Release Unit Fund to provide State grant funds for counties or groups of counties for construction of satellite jail/work release units for certain misdemeanants who receive active sentences. A county or group of counties may apply to the Office for a grant under this section. The application shall be in a form established by the Office. The Office shall:

(1) Develop application and grant criteria based on the basic requirements listed in this Part,

(2) Provide all Boards of County Commissioners and Sheriffs with the criteria and appropriate application forms, technical assistance, if requested, and a proposed written agreement,

(3) Review all applications,

(4) Select grantees and award grants,

(5) Award no more than seven hundred fifty thousand dollars ($750,000) for any one county or group of counties except that if a group of counties agrees to jointly operate one unit for males and one unit for females, the maximum amount may be awarded for each unit,

(6) Take into consideration the potential number of misdemeanants and the percentage of the county's or counties' misdemeanant population to be diverted from the State prison system,

(7) Take into consideration the utilization of existing buildings suitable for renovation where appropriate,

(8) Take into consideration the timeliness with which a county proposes to complete and occupy the unit,

(9) Take into consideration the appropriateness and cost effectiveness of the proposal,

(10) Take into consideration the plan with which the county intends to coordinate the unit with other community service programs such as intensive supervision, community penalties, and community service.

When considering the items listed in subdivisions (6) through (10), the Office shall determine the appropriate weight to be given each item.

(b) A county or group of counties is eligible for a grant under this section if it agrees to abide by the basic requirements for satellite jail/work release units established in G.S. 153A-230.3. In order to receive a grant under this section, there must be a written agreement to abide by the basic requirements for satellite jail/work release units set forth in G.S. 153A-230.3. The written agreement shall be signed by the Chairman of the Board of County Commissioners, with approval of the Board of County Commissioners and after consultation with the Sheriff, and a representative of the Office of State Budget and Management. If a group of counties applies for the grant, then the agreement must be signed by the Chairman of the Board of County Commissioners of each county. Any variation from, including termination of, the original signed agreement must be approved by both the Office of State Budget and Management and by a vote of the Board of County Commissioners of the county or counties.

When the county or group of counties receives a grant under this section, the county or group of counties accepts ownership of the satellite jail/work release unit and full financial responsibility for maintaining and operating the unit, and for the upkeep of its occupants who comply with the eligibility criteria in G.S. 153A-230.3(a)(1). The county shall receive from the Division of Adult Correction of the Department of Public Safety the amount paid to local confinement facilities under G.S. 148-32.1 for prisoners which are in the unit, but do not meet the eligibility of requirements under G.S. 153A-230.3(a)(1). (1987, c. 207, s. 1; 1987 (Reg. Sess., 1988), c. 1106, ss. 2, 3; 1989, c. 761, s. 2; 2000-140, s. 93.1(a); 2001-424, s. 12.2(b); 2009-372, s. 7; 2011-145, s. 19.1(h).)

§ 153A-230.3. Basic requirements for satellite jail/work release units.

(a) Eligibility for Unit. - The following rules shall govern which misdemeanants are housed in a satellite jail/work release unit:

(1) Any convicted misdemeanant who:

a. Receives an active sentence in the county or group of counties operating the unit,

b. Is employed in the area or can otherwise earn his keep by working at the unit on maintenance and other jobs related to upkeep and operation of the unit or by assignment to community service work, and

c. Consents to placement in the unit under these conditions,

shall not be sent to the State prison system except by written findings of the sentencing judge that the misdemeanant is violent or otherwise a threat to the public and therefore unsuitable for confinement in the unit.

(2) The County shall offer work release programs to both male and female misdemeanants, through local facilities for both, or through a contractual agreement with another entity for either, provided that such arrangement is in reasonable proximity to the misdemeanant's workplace.

(3) The sentencing judge shall make a finding of fact as to whether the misdemeanant is qualified for occupancy in the unit pursuant to G.S. 15A-1352(a). If the sentencing judge determines that the misdemeanant is qualified for occupancy in the unit and the misdemeanant meets the requirements of subdivision (1), then the custodian of the local confinement facility may transfer the misdemeanant to the unit. If at any time either prior to or after placement of an inmate into the unit the Sheriff determines that there is an indication of violence, unsuitable behavior, or other threat to the public that could make the prisoner unsuitable for the unit, the Sheriff may place the prisoner in the county jail.

(4) The Sheriff may accept work release misdemeanants from other counties provided that those inmates agree to pay for their upkeep, that space is available, and that the Sheriff is willing to accept responsibility for the prisoner after screening.

(5) The Sheriff may accept work release misdemeanants or felons from the Division of Adult Correction of the Department of Public Safety provided that those inmates agree to pay for their upkeep, that space is available, and that the Sheriff is willing to accept responsibility for the prisoner after screening.

(a1) Non-eligible for unit. - If the sentencing judge finds that the misdemeanant does not meet the eligibility criteria set forth in G.S. 135A-230.3(a)(1)b, but is otherwise eligible for placement in the unit, then the Sheriff may transfer the misdemeanant from the local confinement facility to the unit if the misdemeanant meets the eligibility criteria at a later date. The Sheriff may also transfer prisoners who were placed in the unit pursuant to G.S. 148-32.1(b) to the local confinement facility when space becomes available.

(b) Operation of Satellite Jail/Work Release Unit. - A county or group of counties operating a satellite jail/work release unit shall comply with the following requirements concerning operation of the unit:

(1) The county shall make every effort to ensure that at least eighty percent (80%) of the unit occupants shall be employed and on work release, and that the remainder shall earn their keep by working at the unit on maintenance and other jobs related to the upkeep and operation of the unit or by assignment to community service work, and that alcohol and drug rehabilitation be available through community resources.

(2) The county shall require the occupants to give their earnings, less standard payroll deduction required by law and premiums for group health insurance coverage, to the Sheriff. The county may charge a per day charge from those occupants who are employed or otherwise able to pay from other resources available to the occupants. The per day charge shall be calculated based on the following formula: The charge shall be either the amount that the Division of Adult Correction of the Department of Public Safety deducts from a prisoner's work-release earnings to pay for the cost of the prisoner's keep or fifty percent (50%) of the occupant's net weekly income, whichever is greater, but in no event may the per day charge exceed an amount that is twice the amount that the Division of Adult Correction of the Department of Public Safety pays each local confinement facility for the cost of providing food, clothing, personal items, supervision, and necessary ordinary medical expenses. The per day charge may be adjusted on an individual basis where restitution and/or child support has been ordered, or where the occupant's salary or resources are insufficient to pay the charge.

The county also shall accumulate a reasonable sum from the earnings of the occupant to be returned to him when he is released from the unit. The county also shall follow the guidelines established for the Division of Adult Correction of the Department of Public Safety in G.S. 148-33.1(f) for determining the amount and order of disbursements from the occupant's earnings.

(3) Any and all proceeds from daily fees shall belong to the county's General Fund to aid in offsetting the operation and maintenance of the satellite unit.

(4) The unit shall be operated on a full-time basis, i.e., seven days/nights a week, but weekend leave may be granted by the Sheriff. In granting weekend leave, the Sheriff shall follow the policies and procedures of the Division of Adult Correction of the Department of Public Safety for granting weekend leave for Level 3 minimum custody inmates.

(5) Earned time shall be applied to these county prisoners in the same manner as prescribed in G.S. 15A-1340.20 and G.S. 148-13 for State prisoners.

(6) The Sheriff shall maintain complete and accurate records on each inmate. These records shall contain the same information as required for State prisoners that are housed in county local confinement facilities. (1987, c. 207, s. 1; 1987 (Reg. Sess., 1988), c. 1106, ss. 4, 5; 1989, c. 761, ss. 4, 7; 1993 (Reg. Sess., 1994), c. 767, s. 3; 2011-145, s. 19.1(h).)

§ 153A-230.4. Standards.

The county satellite jail/work release units for misdemeanants shall not be subject to the standards promulgated for local confinement facilities pursuant to G.S. 153A-221. The Secretary of Health and Human Services shall develop and enforce standards for satellite/work release units. The Secretary shall take into consideration that they are to house only screened misdemeanants most of whom are on work release and therefore occupy the premises only in their off-work hours. After consultation with the North Carolina Sheriff's Association, the North Carolina Association of County Commissioners, and the Joint Legislative Commission on Governmental Operations, the Secretary of Health and Human Services shall promulgate standards suitable for these units by January 1, 1988, and shall include these units in the Department's monitoring and inspection responsibilities. Further, the North Carolina Sheriffs' Education and Training Standards Commission shall include appropriate training for Sheriffs and other county law enforcement personnel in regard to the operation, management and guidelines for county work release centers pursuant to its authority under G.S. 17E-4. (1987, c. 207, s. 1; 1987 (Reg. Sess., 1988), c. 1106, s. 6; 1997-443, s. 11A.118(a).)

§ 153A-230.5. Satellite jails/work release units built with non-State funds.

(a) If a county is operating a satellite jail/work release unit prior to the enactment of this act, the county may apply to the Office of State Budget and Management for grant funds to recover any verifiable construction or renovation costs for those units and for improvement funds except that the total for reimbursement and improvement shall not exceed seven hundred fifty thousand dollars ($750,000). Any county accepting such a grant or any other State monies for county satellite jails must agree to all of the basic requirements listed in G.S. 153A-230.2 and G.S. 153A-230.3.

(b) If a county operates a non-State funded satellite jail/work release unit that does not comply with the basic requirements listed in G.S. 153A-230.2 and G.S. 153A-230.3, then the satellite jail shall be subject to the standards, rules, and regulations to be promulgated by the Secretary of Health and Human Services pursuant to Part 2 of Article 10 of Chapter 153A. If a county is reimbursed for the cost of a prisoner's keep from an inmate's work release earnings in an amount equal to or greater than that paid by the Division of Adult Correction of the Department of Public Safety to local confinement facilities under G.S. 148-32.1, the county may not receive additional payments from the Division for the cost of a prisoner's keep. However, if reimbursement to the county for the cost of a prisoner's keep is less than the amount allowed under G.S. 148-32.1, the county may receive from the Division of Adult Correction of the Department of Public Safety the difference in the amount received from work release earnings and the amount paid by the Division to local confinement facilities. The Division may promulgate rules regarding such payment arrangements. (1987, c. 207, s. 1; 1987 (Reg. Sess., 1988), c. 1106, s. 7; 1989, c. 761, s. 5; 1997-443, s. 11A.118(a); 2000-140, s. 93.1(a); 2001-424, s. 12.2(b); 2011-145, s. 19.1(h).)

§§ G.S. 153A-231 through 153A-232. Reserved for future codification purposes.

Article 11.

Fire Protection.

§ 153A-233. Fire-fighting and prevention services.

A county may establish, organize, equip, support, and maintain a fire department; may prescribe the duties of the fire department; may provide financial assistance to incorporated volunteer fire departments; may contract for fire-fighting or prevention services with one or more counties, cities, or other units of local government or with an agency of the State government, or with one or more incorporated volunteer fire departments; and may for these purposes appropriate funds not otherwise limited as to use by law. The county may also designate fire districts or parts of existing districts and prescribe the boundaries thereof for insurance grading purposes. (1945, c. 244; 1973, c. 822, s. 1; 1977, c. 158.)

§ 153A-234. Fire marshal.

A county may appoint a fire marshal and employ persons as his assistants. A county may also impose any duty that might be imposed on a fire marshal on any other officer or employee of the county. The board of commissioners shall set the duties of the fire marshal, which may include but are not limited to:

(1) Advising the board on improvements in the fire-fighting or fire prevention activities under the county's supervision or control.

(2) Coordinating fire-fighting and training activities under the county's supervision or control.

(3) Coordinating fire prevention activities under the county's supervision or control.

(4) Assisting incorporated volunteer fire departments in developing and improving their fire-fighting or fire prevention capabilities.

(5) Making fire prevention inspections, including the periodic inspections and reports of school buildings required by Chapter 115 and the inspections of child care facilities required by Chapter 110. A fire marshal shall not make electrical inspections unless he is qualified to do so under G.S. 153A-351. (1959, c. 290; 1969, c. 1064, s. 2; 1973, c. 822, s. 1; 1997-506, s. 62.)

§ 153A-235: Repealed by Session Laws 1989, c. 681, s. 14.

§ 153A-236. Honoring deceased or retiring firefighters.

A fire department established by a county pursuant to this Article may, in the discretion of the board of commissioners, award to a retiring firefighter or a surviving relative of a deceased firefighter, upon request, the fire helmet of the deceased or retiring firefighter, at a price determined in a manner authorized by the board. The price may be less than the fair market value of the helmet. (2003-145, s. 1.)

§ 153A-237. Reserved for future codification purposes.

Article 12.

Roads and Bridges.

§ 153A-238. Public road defined for counties.

(a) In this Article "public road" or "road" means any road, street, highway, thoroughfare, or other way of passage that has been irrevocably dedicated to the public or in which the public has acquired rights by prescription, without regard to whether it is open for travel, except that in G.S. 153A-239.1, the word "road" means both private roads and public roads.

(b) Repealed by Session Laws 1993, c. 62, s. 1. (1979, 2nd Sess., c. 1319, s. 1; 1981, c. 568; 1983, cc. 98, 299; 1987 (Reg. Sess., 1988), cc. 900, 906; 1989, c. 335, s. 1; 1989 (Reg. Sess., 1990), cc. 836, 854, 911; 1991, c. 9, s. 1; 1991 (Reg. Sess., 1992), c. 778, s. 1, c. 849, ss. 1, 2.1, c. 936, s. 1; 1993, c. 62, s. 1.)

§ 153A-239: Repealed by Session Laws 1993, c. 62, s. 2.

§ 153A-239.1. Naming roads and assigning street numbers in unincorporated areas for counties.

(a) A county may by ordinance name or rename any road within the county and not within a city, and may pursuant to a procedure established by ordinance assign or reassign street numbers for use on such a road. In naming or renaming a road, a county may not:

(1) Change the name, if any, given to the road by the Board of Transportation, unless the Board of Transportation agrees;

(2) Change the number assigned to the road by the Board of Transportation, but may give the road a name in addition to its number; or

(3) Give the road a name that is deceptively similar to the name of any other public road in the vicinity.

A county shall not name or rename a road or adopt an ordinance to establish a procedure to assign or reassign street numbers on a road until it has held a public hearing on the matter. At least 10 days before the day of the hearing to name or rename a road, the board of commissioners shall cause notice of the time, place and subject matter of the hearing to be prominently posted at the county courthouse, in at least two public places in the township or townships where the road is located, and shall publish a notice of such hearing in a newspaper of general circulation published in the county. At least 10 days before the day of the hearing to adopt an ordinance to establish a procedure to assign or reassign street numbers on a road, the board of commissioners shall publish a notice of such hearing in a newspaper of general circulation in the county. After naming or renaming a road, or assigning or reassigning street numbers on a road, a county shall cause notice of its action to be given to the local postmaster with jurisdiction over the road, to the Board of Transportation, and to any city within five miles of the road. Names may be initially assigned to new roads by recordation of an approved subdivision plat without following the procedure established by this section.

(b) Repealed by Session Laws 1993, c. 62, s. 3. (1979, 2nd Sess., c. 1319, s. 2; 1981, c. 568; 1983, cc. 98, 299; 1987 (Reg. Sess., 1988), cc. 900, 906; 1989, c. 335, s. 1; 1989 (Reg. Sess., 1990), cc. 836, 854, 911; 1991, c. 9, s. 2; 1991 (Reg. Sess., 1992), c. 778, s. 2; c. 849, ss. 2, 2.2; c. 936, s. 2; 1993, c. 62, s. 3; 2001-145, s. 1.)

§ 153A-240: Repealed by Session Laws 1993, c. 62, s. 4.

§ 153A-241. Closing public roads or easements.

A county may permanently close any public road or any easement within the county and not within a city, except public roads or easements for public roads under the control and supervision of the Department of Transportation. The board of commissioners shall first adopt a resolution declaring its intent to close the public road or easement and calling a public hearing on the question. The board shall cause a notice of the public hearing reasonably calculated to give full and fair disclosure of the proposed closing to be published once a week for three successive weeks before the hearing, a copy of the resolution to be sent by registered or certified mail to each owner as shown on the county tax records of property adjoining the public road or easement who did not join in the request to have the road or easement closed, and a notice of the closing and public hearing to be prominently posted in at least two places along the road or easement. At the hearing the board shall hear all interested persons who appear with respect to whether the closing would be detrimental to the public interest or to any individual property rights. If, after the hearing, the board of commissioners is satisfied that closing the public road or easement is not contrary to the public interest and (in the case of a road) that no individual owning property in the vicinity of the road or in the subdivision in which it is located would thereby be deprived of reasonable means of ingress and egress to his property, the board may adopt an order closing the road or easement. A certified copy of the order (or judgment of the court) shall be filed in the office of the register of deeds of the county.

Any person aggrieved by the closing of a public road or an easement may appeal the board of commissioners' order to the appropriate division of the General Court of Justice within 30 days after the day the order is adopted. The court shall hear the matter de novo and has jurisdiction to try the issues arising and to order the road or easement closed upon proper findings of fact by the trier of fact.

No cause of action founded upon the invalidity of a proceeding taken in closing a public road or an easement may be asserted except in an action or proceeding begun within 30 days after the day the order is adopted.

Upon the closing of a public road or an easement pursuant to this section, all right, title, and interest in the right-of-way is vested in those persons owning lots or parcels of land adjacent to the road or easement, and the title of each adjoining landowner, for the width of his abutting land, extends to the center line of the public road or easement. However, the right, title or interest vested in an adjoining landowner by this paragraph remains subject to any public utility use or facility located on, over, or under the road or easement immediately before its closing, until the landowner or any successor thereto pays to the utility involved the reasonable cost of removing and relocating the facility. (1949, c. 1208, ss. 1-3; 1957, c. 65, s. 11; 1965, cc. 665, 801; 1971, c. 595; 1973, c. 507, s. 5; c. 822, s. 1; 1977, c. 464, s. 34; 1995, c. 374, s. 1.)

§ 153A-242. Regulation or prohibition of fishing from bridges.

A county may by ordinance regulate or prohibit fishing from any bridge within the county and not within a city. In addition, the governing board of a city may by resolution permit a county to regulate or prohibit fishing from any bridge within the city. The city may by resolution withdraw its permission to the county ordinance. If it does so, the city shall give written notice to the county of its withdrawal of permission; 30 days after the date the county receives this notice the county ordinance ceases to be applicable within the city. An ordinance adopted pursuant to this section shall provide for signs to be posted on each bridge affected, summarizing the regulation or prohibition pertaining to that bridge.

No person may fish from the drawspan of a regularly attended bridge, and no county may permit any person to do so.

The authority granted by this section is subject to the authority of the Department of Transportation to prohibit fishing from any bridge on the State highway system. (1971, c. 690, ss. 1, 6; 1973, c. 507, s. 5; c. 822, s. 1; 1977, c. 464, s. 34.)

§ 153A-243. Authorizing bridges over navigable waters.

A county may grant to persons who between them own or occupy real property on both sides of a body of navigable water lying wholly within the county the right to construct and maintain across the body of water a bridge connecting the property. The board of commissioners shall first adopt a resolution declaring its intent to grant the right and calling a public hearing on the question. The board shall cause the resolution to be published once a week for four successive weeks before the hearing. At the hearing the board shall hear all interested persons who appear with respect to whether the grant would be in the public interest. If, after the hearing, the board finds that the grant is not contrary to the public interest, it may adopt an order granting the right to construct the bridge. The board may place reasonable terms and conditions, including time limitations, on the grant.

A person aggrieved by a grant may appeal the board of commissioners' order to the appropriate division of the General Court of Justice within 30 days after the day it is adopted. The court shall hear the matter de novo and has jurisdiction to try the issues arising and to grant the right to construct the bridge.

Before construction may be commenced on any bridge authorized pursuant to this section, the bridge's location and plans must be submitted to and approved by the Chief of Engineers of the United States Army and the Secretary of the Army. (Pub. Loc. 1191, c. 227; C.S., s. 1297; 1973, c. 822, s. 1.)

§ 153A-244. Railroad revitalization programs.

Any county is authorized to participate in State and federal railroad revitalization programs necessary to insure continued or improved rail service to the county, as are authorized in Article 2D of Chapter 136 of the General Statutes. County participation includes the authority to enter into contracts with the North Carolina Department of Transportation to provide for the nonfederal matching funds for railroad revitalization programs. Such funds may be comprised of State funds distributed to the counties under the provisions of G.S. 136-44.38 and of county funds. County governments are also authorized to levy local property tax for railroad revitalization programs subject to G.S. 153A-149(d). County funds for any project may not exceed ten percent (10%) of total project costs. (1979, c. 658, s. 4.)

§ 153A-245. Regulation of golf carts on streets, roads, and highways.

(a)   Notwithstanding the provisions of G.S. 20-50 and G.S. 20-54, a county may, by ordinance, regulate the operation of golf carts, as defined in G.S. 20-4.01(12a), on any public street, road, or highway where the speed limit is 35 miles per hour or less within the county that is located in any unincorporated areas of the county or on any property owned or leased by the county.

(b) By ordinance, a county may require the registration of golf carts, charge a fee for the registration, specify who is authorized to operate golf carts, and specify the required equipment, load limits, and the hours and methods of operation of golf carts. No person less than 16 years of age may operate a golf cart on a public street, road, or highway. (2009-459, s. 1.)

§ 153A-246. Reserved for future codification purposes.

Article 13.

Health and Social Services.

Part 1. Health Services.

§ 153A-247. Provision for public health and mental health.

A county may provide for and regulate the public health pursuant to Chapter 130A of the General Statutes and any other law authorizing local public health activities and may provide mental health[,] mental retardation, and substance abuse programs pursuant to Chapter 122C of the General Statutes. (1973, c. 822, s. 1; 1985, c. 589, s. 58.)

§ 153A-248. Health-related appropriations.

(a) A county may appropriate revenues not otherwise limited as to use by law:

(1) To a licensed facility for the mentally retarded, whether publicly or privately owned, to assist in maintaining and developing facilities and treatment, if the board of commissioners determines that the care offered by the facility is available to residents of the county. The facility need not be located within the county.

(2) To a sheltered workshop or other private, nonprofit, charitable organization offering work or training activities to the physically or mentally handicapped, and may otherwise assist such an organization.

(3) To an orthopedic hospital, whether publicly or privately owned, to assist in maintaining and developing facilities and treatment, if the board of commissioners determines that the care offered by the hospital is available to residents of the county. The hospital need not be located within the county.

(4) To a training center or other private, nonprofit, charitable organization offering education, treatment, rehabilitation, or developmental programs to the physically or mentally handicapped, and may otherwise assist such organizations; provided, however, such action shall be with the concurrence of the county board of education; and provided, further, that within 30 days after receipt of the request for concurrence, the county board of education shall notify the board of county commissioners whether it concurs, and should it fail to so notify the board of county commissioners within such period, it shall be deemed to have concurred.

(b) The ordinance making the appropriation shall state specifically what the appropriation is to be used for, and the board of commissioners shall require that the recipient account for the appropriation at the close of the fiscal year. (1967, cc. 464, 1074; 1969, c. 802; 1973, c. 822, s. 1; 1977, c. 474; 1979, c. 1074, s. 2.)

§ 153A-249. Hospital services.

A county may provide and support hospital services pursuant to Chapters 122C, 131 and 131E of the General Statutes. (1868, c. 20, s. 8; Code, s. 707; Rev., s. 1318; C.S., s. 1297; 1923, c. 81; 1973, c. 822, s. 1; 1985, c. 589, s. 59.)

§ 153A-250. Ambulance services.

(a) A county may by ordinance franchise ambulance services provided in the county to the public at large, whether the service is based inside or outside the county. The ordinance may:

(1) Grant franchises to ambulance operators on terms set by the board of commissioners;

(2) Make it unlawful to provide ambulance services or to operate an ambulance in the county without such a franchise;

(3) Limit the number of ambulances that may be operated within the county;

(4) Limit the number of ambulances that may be operated by each franchised operator;

(5) Determine the areas of the county that may be served by each franchised operator;

(6) Establish and from time to time revise a schedule of rates, fees, and charges that may be charged by franchised operators;

(7) Set minimum limits of liability insurance for each franchised operator;

(8) Establish other necessary regulations consistent with and supplementary to any statute or any Department of Health and Human Services regulation relating to ambulance services.

Before it may adopt an ordinance pursuant to this subsection, the board of commissioners must first hold a public hearing on the need for ambulance services. The board shall cause notice of the hearing to be published once a week for two successive weeks before the hearing. After the hearing the board may adopt an ordinance if it finds that to do so is necessary to assure the provision of adequate and continuing ambulance service and to preserve, protect, and promote the public health, safety, and welfare.

If a person, firm, or corporation is providing ambulance services in a county or any portion thereof on the effective date of an ordinance adopted pursuant to this subsection, the person, firm, or corporation is entitled to a franchise to continue to serve that part of the county in which the service is being provided. The board of commissioners shall determine whether the person, firm, or corporation so entitled to a franchise is in compliance with Chapter 131E, Article 7; and if that is the case, the board shall grant the franchise.

(b) In lieu of or in addition to adopting an ordinance pursuant to subsection (a) of this section, a county may operate or contract for ambulance services in all or a portion of the county. A county may appropriate for ambulance services any revenues not otherwise limited as to use by law, and may establish and from time to time revise schedules of rates, fees, charges, and penalties for the ambulance services. A county may operate its ambulance services as a line department or may create an ambulance commission and vest in it authority to operate the ambulance services.

(c)   A city may adopt an ordinance pursuant to and under the procedures of subsection (a) of this section and may operate or contract for ambulance services pursuant to subsection (b) of this section if (i) the county in which the city is located has adopted a resolution authorizing the city to do so or (ii) the county has not, within 180 days after being requested by the city to do so, provided for ambulance services within the city pursuant to this section. Any action taken by a city pursuant to this subsection shall apply only within the corporate limits of the city.

If a city is exercising a power granted by this subsection, the county in which the city is located may thereafter take action to provide for ambulance service within the city, either under subsection (a) or subsection (b) of this section, only after having given to the city 180 days' notice of the county's intention to take action. At the end of the 180 days, the city's authority under this subsection is preempted by the county.

(d)   A county or a city may contract with a franchised ambulance operator or with another county or city for ambulance service to be provided upon the call of a department or agency of the county or city. A county may contract with a franchised ambulance operator for transportation of indigents or persons certified by the county department of social services to be public assistance recipients.

(e)   Each county or city operating ambulance services is subject to the provisions of Chapter 131E, Article 7 ("Regulation of Emergency Medical Services"). (1967, c. 343, s. 5; 1969, c. 147; 1973, c. 476, s. 128; c. 822, s. 1; 1997-443, s. 11A.118(a); 2002-159, s. 51.)

§§ 153A-251 through 153A-254. Reserved for future codification purposes.

Part 2. Social Service Provisions.

§ 153A-255. Authority to provide social service programs.

Each county shall provide social service programs pursuant to Chapter 108A and Chapter 111 and may otherwise undertake, sponsor, organize, engage in, and support other social service programs intended to further the health, welfare, education, employment, safety, comfort, and convenience of its citizens. (1868, c. 20, s. 8; Code, s. 707; Rev., s. 1318; C.S., s. 1297; 1973, c. 822, s. 1; 1981, c. 562, s. 12; 1997-443, s. 12.13.)

§ 153A-256. County home.

A county may establish, erect, acquire, lease as lessor or lessee, equip, support, operate, and maintain a county home for aged and infirm persons and may appropriate funds for these purposes.

The superintendent of each county home shall make an annual report on its operation to the board of commissioners of the county operating the home and to the Department of Health and Human Services. The report shall contain any information that the board of commissioners and the Department of Health and Human Services, respectively, require, and the Department may provide forms for this report. (1876-7, c. 277, s. 3; Code, ss. 3541, 3543; 1891, c. 138; Rev., ss. 1328, 1329; 1919, c. 72; C.S., ss. 1336, 1337, 1338; 1961, c. 139, s. 1; 1973, c. 476, s. 138; c. 822, s. 1; 1997-443, s. 11A.118(a).)

§ 153A-257. Legal residence for social service purposes.

(a) Legal residence in a county determines which county is responsible (i) for financial support of a needy person who meets the eligibility requirements for a public assistance or medical care program offered by the county or (ii) for other social services required by the person.

Legal residence in a county is determined as follows:

(1) Except as modified below, a person has legal residence in the county in which he resides.

(2) If a person is in a hospital, mental institution, nursing home, boarding home, confinement facility, or similar institution or facility, he does not, solely

because of that fact, have legal residence in the county in which the institution or facility is located.

(3)   A minor has the legal residence of the parent or other relative with whom he resides. If the minor does not reside with a parent or relative and is not in a foster home, hospital, mental institution, nursing home, boarding home, educational institution, confinement facility, or similar institution or facility, he has the legal residence of the person with whom he resides. Any other minor has the legal residence of his mother, or if her residence is not known then the legal residence of his father; if his mother's or father's residence is not known, the minor is a legal resident of the county in which he is found.

(b)   A legal residence continues until a new one is acquired, either within or outside this State. When a new legal residence is acquired, all former legal residences terminate.

(c)   This section is intended to replace the law defining "legal settlement." Therefore any general law or local act that refers to "legal settlement" is deemed to refer to this section and the rules contained herein.

(d)   If two or more county departments of social services disagree regarding the legal residence of a minor in a child abuse, neglect, or dependency case, any one of the county departments of social services may refer the issue to the Department of Health and Human Services, Division of Social Services, for resolution. The Director of the Division of Social Services or the Director's designee shall review the pertinent background facts of the case and shall determine which county department of social services shall be responsible for providing protective services and financial support for the minor in question. (1777, c. 117, s. 16, P.R.; R.C., c. 86, s. 12; Code, s. 3544; Rev., s. 1333; C.S., s. 1342; 1931, c. 120; 1943, c. 753, s. 2; 1959, c. 272; 1973, c. 822, s. 1; 2003-304, s. 7.)

§ 153A-258. Reserved for future codification purposes.

Part 3. Health and Social Services Contracts.

§ 153A-259. Counties authorized to contract with other entities for health and social services.

A county is authorized to contract with any governmental agency, person, association, or corporation for the provision of health or social services provided that the expenditure of funds pursuant to such contracts shall be for the purpose for which the funds were appropriated and is not otherwise prohibited by law. (1979, 2nd Sess., c. 1094, s. 2.)

§ 153A-260. Reserved for future codification purposes.

Article 14.

Libraries.

§ 153A-261. Declaration of State policy.

The General Assembly recognizes that the availability of adequate, modern library services and facilities is in the general interest of the people of North Carolina and a proper concern of the State and of local governments. Therefore it is the policy of the State of North Carolina to promote the establishment and development of public library services throughout the State. (1973, c. 822, s. 1.)

§ 153A-262. Library materials defined.

For purposes of this Article, the phrase "library materials" includes, without limitation, books, plates, pictures, engravings, maps, magazines, pamphlets, newspapers, manuscripts, films, transparencies, microforms, recordings, or other specimens, works of literature, or objects of art, historical significance, or curiosity. (1953, c. 721; 1963, c. 945; 1971, c. 698, s. 3; 1973, c. 822, s. 1.)

§ 153A-263. Public library systems authorized.

A county or city may:

(1)   Establish, operate, and support public library systems;

(2) Set apart lands and buildings for a public library system;

(3) Acquire real property for a public library system by gift, grant, purchase, lease, exercise of the power of eminent domain, or any other lawful method. If a library board of trustees is appointed, a county or city shall, before acquiring real property by purchase, lease, or exercise of the power of eminent domain, seek the recommendations of the board of trustees regarding the proposed acquisition;

(4) Provide, acquire, construct, equip, operate, and maintain buildings and other structures for a public library system;

(5) Acquire library materials by purchase, exchange, devise, gift, or any other lawful method;

(6) Appropriate funds to carry out the provisions of this Article;

(7) Accept any gift, grant, lease, loan, exchange, or devise of real or personal property for a public library system. Devises, grants, and gifts may be accepted and held subject to any term or condition that may be imposed by the grantor or trustor, except that no county or city may accept or administer any term or condition that requires it to discriminate among its citizens on the basis of race, sex, or religion. (1953, c. 721; 1963, c. 945; 1971, c. 698, s. 3; 1973, c. 822, s. 1; 2011-284, s. 107.)

§ 153A-264. Free library services.

If a county or city, pursuant to this Article, operates or makes contributions to the support of a library, any resident of the county or city, as the case may be, is entitled to the free use of the library. (1953, c. 721; 1963, c. 945; 1971, c. 698, s. 3; 1973, c. 822, s. 1.)

§ 153A-265. Library board of trustees.

The governing body of a county or city may appoint a library board of trustees. The governing body shall determine the number of members of the board of trustees (which may not be more than 12), the length of their terms, the manner of filling vacancies, and the amount, if any, of their compensation and allowances. The governing body may remove a trustee at any time for incapacity, unfitness, misconduct, or neglect of duty. (1953, c. 721; 1963, c. 945; 1971, c. 698, s. 1; 1973, c. 822, s. 1.)

§ 153A-266. Powers and duties of trustees.

If a board of trustees is appointed, it shall elect a chairman and may elect other officers. The governing body may delegate to the board of trustees any of the following powers:

(1)   To formulate and adopt programs, policies, and regulations for the government of the library;

(2)   To make recommendations to the governing body concerning the construction and improvement of buildings and other structures for the library system;

(3)   To supervise and care for the facilities of the library system;

(4)   To appoint a chief librarian or director of library services and, with his advice, to appoint other employees of the library system. If some other body or official is to appoint the chief librarian or director of library services, to advise that body or official concerning that appointment;

(5)   To establish, a schedule of fines and charges for late return of, failure to return, damage to, and loss of library materials, and to take other measures to protect and regulate the use of such materials;

(6)   To participate in preparing the annual budget of the library system;

(7)   To extend the privileges and use of the library system to nonresidents of the county or city establishing or supporting the system, on any terms or conditions the board may prescribe.

(8)   To otherwise advise the board of commissioners on library matters.

The board of trustees shall make an annual report on the operations of the library to the governing body of the county or city and shall make an annual report to the Department of Cultural Resources as required by G.S. 125-5. If no board of trustees is established, the governing body shall make the annual report to the Department. (1953, c. 721; 1963, c. 945; 1969, c. 488; 1971, c. 698, s. 3; 1973, c. 476, s. 84; c. 822, s. 1.)

§ 153A-267. Qualifications of chief librarian; library employees.

(a) To be eligible for appointment and service as chief administrative officer of a library system (whether designated chief librarian, director of library services, or some other title), a person must have a professional librarian certificate issued by the Secretary of Cultural Resources, pursuant to G.S. 125-9, under regulations for certification of public librarian as established by the North Carolina Public Librarian Certification Commission pursuant to the provisions of G.S. 143B-67.

(b) The employees of a county or city library system are, for all purposes, employees of the county or city, as the case may be. (1953, c. 721; 1963, c. 945; 1969, c. 488; 1971, c. 698, s. 3; 1973, c. 476, s. 53; c. 822, s. 1; 1975, c. 516.)

§ 153A-268. Financing library systems.

A county or city may appropriate for library purposes any funds not otherwise limited as to use by law. (1973, c. 822, s. 1.)

§ 153A-269. Title to library property.

The title to all property acquired by a county or city for library purposes shall be in the name of the county or city. If property is given, granted, devised, or otherwise conveyed to the board of trustees of a county or city library system, it shall be deemed to have been conveyed to the county or city and shall be held in the name of the county or city. (1953, c. 721; 1963, c. 945; 1971, c. 698, s. 3; 1973, c. 822, s. 1; 2011-284, s. 108.)

§ 153A-270. Joint libraries; contracts for library services.

Two or more counties or cities or counties and cities may establish a joint library system or contract for library services, according to the procedures and provisions of Chapter 160A, Article 20, Part 1. (1953, c. 721; 1963, c. 945; 1971, c. 698, s. 3; 1973, c. 822, s. 1.)

§ 153A-271. Library systems operated under local acts brought under this Article.

If a county or city operates a library system pursuant to a local act, the governing body of the county or city may by ordinance provide that the library system is to be operated pursuant to this Article. (1973, c. 822, s. 1.)

§ 153A-272. Designation of library employees to register voters.

The governing body of each public library with four or more employees shall designate at least one employee of the library to be appointed by the county board of elections to register voters pursuant to G.S. 163-80(a)(6). With the approval of the board of elections, additional employees may also be designated for this purpose by the governing body. (1983, c. 588, s. 1.)

§ 153A-273. Reserved for future codification purposes.

Article 15.

Public Enterprises.

Part 1. General Provisions.

§ 153A-274. Public enterprise defined.

As used in this Article, "public enterprise" includes:

(1)   Water supply and distribution systems.

(2)   Wastewater collection, treatment, and disposal systems of all types, including septic tank systems or other on-site collection or disposal facilities or systems.

(3)   Solid waste collection and disposal systems and facilities.

(4)   Airports.

(5)   Off-street parking facilities.

(6)   Public transportation systems.

(7)   Stormwater management programs designed to protect water quality by controlling the level of pollutants in, and the quantity and flow of, stormwater and structural and natural stormwater and drainage systems of all types. (1965, c. 370; 1957, c. 266, s. 3; 1961, c. 514, s. 1; c. 1001, s. 1; 1971, c. 568; 1973, c. 822, s. 1; c. 1214; 1977, c. 514, s. 1; 1979, c. 619, s. 1; 1989, c. 643, s. 2; 1991 (Reg. Sess., 1992), c. 944, s. 13; 2000-70, s. 1.)

§ 153A-275. Authority to operate public enterprises.

(a)   A county may acquire, lease as lessor or lessee, construct, establish, enlarge, improve, extend, maintain, own, operate, and contract for the operation of public enterprises in order to furnish services to the county and its citizens. A county may acquire, construct, establish, enlarge, improve, maintain, own, and operate outside its borders any public enterprise.

(b)   A county may adopt adequate and reasonable rules to protect and regulate a public enterprise belonging to or operated by it. The rules shall be adopted by ordinance, shall apply to the public enterprise system both within and outside the county, and may be enforced with the remedies available under any provision of law. (1955, c. 370; 1957, c. 266, s. 3; 1961, c. 514, s. 1; c. 1001, s. 1; 1967, c. 462; 1971, c. 568; 1973, c. 822, s. 1; 1991 (Reg. Sess., 1992), c. 836, s. 2.)

§ 153A-276. Financing public enterprises.

Subject to the restrictions, limitations, procedures, and regulations otherwise provided by law, a county may finance the cost of a public enterprise by levying taxes, borrowing money, and appropriating any other revenues, and by accepting and administering gifts and grants from any source. (1973, c. 822, s. 1.)

§ 153A-277. Authority to fix and enforce rates.

(a) A county may establish and revise from time to time schedules of rents, rates, fees, charges, and penalties for the use of or the services furnished by a public enterprise. Schedules of rents, rates, fees, charges, and penalties may vary for the same class of service in different areas of the county and may vary according to classes of service, and different schedules may be adopted for services provided outside of the county. A county may include a fee relating to subsurface discharge wastewater management systems and services on the property tax bill for the real property where the system for which the fee is imposed is located.

(a1) (1) Before it establishes or revises a schedule of rates, fees, charges, or penalties for stormwater management programs and structural and natural stormwater and drainage systems under this section, the board of commissioners shall hold a public hearing on the matter. A notice of the hearing shall be given at least once in a newspaper having general circulation in the area, not less than seven days before the public hearing. The hearing may be held concurrently with the public hearing on the proposed budget ordinance.

(2) The fees established under this subsection must be made applicable throughout the area of the county outside municipalities. Schedules of rates, fees, charges, and penalties for providing stormwater management programs and structural and natural stormwater and drainage system service may vary according to whether the property served is residential, commercial, or industrial property, the property's use, the size of the property, the area of impervious surfaces on the property, the quantity and quality of the runoff from the property, the characteristics of the watershed into which stormwater from the property drains, and other factors that affect the stormwater drainage system. Rates, fees, and charges imposed under this subsection may not exceed the county's cost of providing a stormwater management program and a structural and

natural stormwater and drainage system. The county's cost of providing a stormwater management program and a structural and natural stormwater and drainage system includes any costs necessary to assure that all aspects of stormwater quality and quantity are managed in accordance with federal and State laws, regulations, and rules.

(3)   No stormwater utility fee may be levied under this subsection whenever two or more units of local government operate separate stormwater management programs or separate structural and natural stormwater and drainage system services in the same area within a county. However, two or more units of local government may allocate among themselves the functions, duties, powers, and responsibilities for jointly operating a stormwater management program and structural and natural stormwater and drainage system service in the same area within a county, provided that only one unit may levy a fee for the service within the joint service area. For purposes of this subsection, a unit of local government shall include a regional authority providing stormwater management programs and structural and natural stormwater and drainage system services.

(b)   A county may collect delinquent accounts by any remedy provided by law for collecting and enforcing private debts, and may specify by ordinance the order in which partial payments are to be applied among the various enterprise services covered by a bill for the services. A county may also discontinue service to a customer whose account remains delinquent for more than 10 days. If a delinquent customer is not the owner of the premises to which the services are delivered, the payment of the delinquent account may not be required before providing services at the request of a new and different tenant or occupant of the premises. If water or sewer services are discontinued for delinquency, it is unlawful for a person other than a duly authorized agent or employee of the county to reconnect the premises to the water or sewer system.

(b1)   A county shall not do any of the following in its debt collection practices:

(1)   Suspend or disconnect service to a customer because of a past-due and unpaid balance for service incurred by another person who resides with the customer after service has been provided to the customer's household, unless one or more of the following apply:

a.   The customer and the person were members of the same household at a different location when the unpaid balance for service was incurred.

b. The person was a member of the customer's current household when the service was established, and the person had an unpaid balance for service at that time.

c. The person is or becomes responsible for the bill for the service to the customer.

(2) Require that in order to continue service, a customer must agree to be liable for the delinquent account of any other person who will reside in the customer's household after the customer receives the service, unless one or more of the following apply:

a. The customer and the person were members of the same household at a different location when the unpaid balance for service was incurred.

b. The person was a member of the customer's current household when the service was established, and the person had an unpaid balance for service at that time.

(b2) Notwithstanding the provisions of subsection (b1) of this section, if a customer misrepresents his or her identity in a written or verbal agreement for service or receives service using another person's identity, the county shall have the power to collect a delinquent account using any remedy provided by subsection (b) of this section from that customer.

(c) Rents, rates, fees, charges, and penalties for enterprisory services are in no case a lien upon the property or premises served and, except as provided in subsection (d) of this section, are legal obligations of the person contracting for them, provided that no contract shall be necessary in the case of structural and natural stormwater and drainage systems.

(d) Rents, rates, fees, charges, and penalties for enterprisory services are legal obligations of the owner of the property or premises served when:

(1) The property or premises is leased or rented to more than one tenant and services rendered to more than one tenant are measured by the same meter; or

(2) Charges made for use of a sewerage system are billed separately from charges made for the use of a water distribution system. (1961, c. 1001, s. 1;

1973, c. 822, s. 1; 1991, c. 591, s. 2; 1991 (Reg. Sess., 1992), c. 932, s. 3; c. 1007, s. 45; 2000-70, s. 2; 2009-302, s. 2.)

§ 153A-278. Joint provision of enterprisory services.

Two or more counties, cities, or other units of local government may cooperate in the exercise of any power granted by this Article according to the procedures and provisions of Chapter 160A, Article 20, Part 1. (1961, c. 1001, s. 1; 1973, c. 822, s. 1.)

§ 153A-279. Limitations on rail transportation liability.

(a) As used in this section:

(1) "Claim" means a claim, action, suit, or request for damages, whether compensatory, punitive, or otherwise, made by any person or entity against:

a. The County, a railroad, or an operating rights railroad; or

b. An officer, director, trustee, employee, parent, subsidiary, or affiliated corporation as defined in G.S. 105-130.2, or agent of: the County, a railroad, or an operating rights railroad.

(2) "Operating rights railroad" means a railroad corporation or railroad company that, prior to January 1, 2001, was granted operating rights by a State-Owned Railroad Company or operated over the property of a State-owned railroad company under a claim of right over or adjacent to facilities used by or on behalf of the County.

(3) "Passenger rail services" means the transportation of rail passengers by or on behalf of the County and all services performed by a railroad pursuant to a contract with the County in connection with the transportation of rail passengers, including, but not limited to, the operation of trains; the use of right-of-way, trackage, public or private roadway and rail crossings, equipment, or station areas or appurtenant facilities; the design, construction, reconstruction, operation, or maintenance of rail-related equipment, tracks, and any appurtenant facilities; or the provision of access rights over or adjacent to lines

owned by the County or a railroad, or otherwise occupied by the County or a railroad, pursuant to charter grant, fee-simple deed, lease, easement, license, trackage rights, or other form of ownership or authorized use.

(4) "Railroad" means a railroad corporation or railroad company, including a State-Owned Railroad Company as defined in G.S. 124-11, that has entered into any contracts or operating agreements of any kind with the County concerning passenger rail services.

(b) Contracts Allocating Financial Responsibility Authorized. - The County may contract with any railroad to allocate financial responsibility for passenger rail services claims, including, but not limited to, the execution of indemnity agreements, notwithstanding any other statutory, common law, public policy, or other prohibition against same, and regardless of the nature of the claim or the conduct giving rise to such claim.

(c) Insurance Required. -

(1) If the County enters into any contract authorized by subsection (b) of this section, the contract shall require the County to secure and maintain, upon and after the commencement of the operation of trains by or on behalf of the county, a liability insurance policy covering the liability of the parties to the contract, a State-Owned Railroad Company as defined in G.S. 124-11 that owns or claims an interest in any real property subject to the contract, and any operating rights railroad for all claims for property damage, personal injury, bodily injury, and death arising out of or related to passenger rail services. The policy shall name the parties to the contract, a State-Owned Railroad Company as defined in G.S. 124-11 that owns or claims an interest in any real property subject to the contract, and any operating rights railroad as named insureds and shall have policy limits of not less than two hundred million dollars ($200,000,000) per single accident or incident, and may include a self-insured retention in an amount of not more than five million dollars ($5,000,000).

(2) If the County does not enter into any contract authorized by subsection (b) of this section, upon and after the commencement of the operation of trains by or on behalf of the County, the County shall secure and maintain a liability insurance policy, with policy limits and a self-insured retention consistent with subdivision (1) of this subsection, for all claims for property damage, personal injury, bodily injury, and death arising out of or related to passenger rail services.

(d) Liability Limit. - The aggregate liability of the County, the parties to the contract or contracts authorized by subsection (b) of this section, a State-Owned Railroad Company as defined in G.S. 124-11, and any operating rights railroad for all claims arising from a single accident or incident related to passenger rail services for property damage, personal injury, bodily injury, and death is limited to two hundred million dollars ($200,000,000) per single accident or incident or to any proceeds available under any insurance policy secured pursuant to subsection (c) of this section, whichever is greater.

(e) Effect on Other Laws. - This section shall not affect the damages that may be recovered under the Federal Employers' Liability Act, 45 U.S.C. § 51, et seq., (1908); or under Article 1 of Chapter 97 of the General Statutes.

(f) Applicability. - This section shall apply only to counties that have entered into a transit governance interlocal agreement with, among other local governments, a city with a population of more than 500,000 persons. (2002-78, s. 2; 2012-79, s. 1.14(e).)

§ 153A-280. Public enterprise improvements.

(a) Authorization. - A county may contract with a developer or property owner, or with a private party who is under contract with the developer or property owner, for public enterprise improvements that are adjacent or ancillary to a private land development project. Such a contract shall allow the county to reimburse the private party for costs associated with the design and construction of improvements that are in addition to those required by the county's land development regulations. Such a contract is not subject to Article 8 of Chapter 143 of the General Statutes if the public cost will not exceed two hundred fifty thousand dollars ($250,000) and the county determines that: (i) the public cost will not exceed the estimated cost of providing for those improvements through either eligible force account qualified labor or through a public contract let pursuant to Article 8 of Chapter 143 of the General Statutes; or (ii) the coordination of separately constructed improvements would be impracticable. A county may enact ordinances and policies setting forth the procedures, requirements, and terms for agreements authorized by this section.

(b) Property Acquisition. - The improvements may be constructed on property owned or acquired by the private party or on property owned or acquired by the county. The private party may assist the county in obtaining easements in favor of the county from private property owners on those properties that will be involved in or affected by the project. The contract between the county and the private party may be entered into before the acquisition of any real property necessary to the project. (2005-426, s. 8(e).)

§ 153A-281. Reserved for future codification purposes.

§ 153A-282. Reserved for future codification purposes.

Part 2. Special Provisions for Water and Sewer Services.

§ 153A-283. Nonliability for failure to furnish water or sewer services.

In no case may a county be held liable for damages for failure to furnish water or sewer services. (1961, c. 1001, s. 1; 1973, c. 822, s. 1.)

§ 153A-284. Power to require connections.

A county may require the owner of developed property on which there are situated one or more residential dwelling units or commercial establishments located so as to be served by a water line or sewer collection line owned, leased as lessee, or operated by the county or on behalf of the county to connect the owner's premises with the water or sewer line and may fix charges for these connections. In the case of improved property that would qualify for the issuance of a building permit for the construction of one or more residential dwelling units or commercial establishments and where the county has installed water or sewer lines or a combination thereof directly available to the property, the county may require payment of a periodic availability charge, not to exceed the minimum periodic service charge for properties that are connected. (1963, c. 985, s. 1; 1965, c. 969, s. 2; 1973, c. 822, s. 1; 1979, c. 619, s. 13; 1995, c. 511, s. 3.)

§ 153A-284.1. Notes or deeds of trust to reserve wastewater treatment capacity unenforceable if capacity unused.

No note or deed of trust granted to a county for the purpose of securing or reserving wastewater treatment capacity is valid or enforceable if that capacity is not utilized by the maker or grantor. (2013-386, s. 6.)

§ 153A-285: Repealed by Session Laws 1993, c. 348, s. 4.

§ 153A-286. Law with respect to riparian rights not changed.

Nothing in this Article changes or modifies existing common or statute law with respect to the relative rights of riparian owners or others concerning the use of or disposal of water in the streams of North Carolina. (1961, c. 1001, s. 1; 1973, c. 822, s. 1.)

§ 153A-287: Repealed by Session Laws 1993, c. 348, s. 5.

§ 153A-288. Venue for actions by riparian owners.

Any riparian owner alleging injury as a result of an act taken pursuant to this Article by a county or city acting jointly or by a joint agency may maintain an action for relief against the act (i) in the county where the land of the riparian owner lies, (ii) in the county taking the action, or (iii) in any county in which the city or joint agency is located or operates. (1961, c. 1001, s. 1; 1973, c. 822, s. 1.)

§ 153A-289. Reserved for future codification purposes.

§ 153A-290. Reserved for future codification purposes.

Part 3. Special Provisions for Solid Waste Collection and Disposal.

§ 153A-291. Cooperation between the Department of Transportation and any county in establishing or operating solid waste disposal facilities.

A county and the Department of Transportation may enter into an agreement under which the Department of Transportation will make available to the county the use of equipment and prison and other labor in order to establish or operate solid waste disposal facilities within the county. The county shall reimburse the Department of Transportation for the cost of providing the equipment and labor. The agreement shall specify the work to be done thereunder and shall set forth the basis for reimbursement. (1967, c. 707; 1973, c. 507, s. 5; c. 822, s. 1; 1977, c. 464, s. 34.)

Part 3. Special Provisions for Solid Waste Collection and Disposal.

§ 153A-292. County collection and disposal facilities.

(a) The board of county commissioners of any county may establish and operate solid waste collection and disposal facilities in areas outside the corporate limits of a city. The board may by ordinance regulate the use of a disposal facility provided by the county, the nature of the solid wastes disposed of in a facility, and the method of disposal. The board may contract with any city, individual, or privately owned corporation to collect and dispose of solid waste in the area. Counties and cities may establish and operate joint collection and disposal facilities. A joint agreement shall be in writing and executed by the governing bodies of the participating units of local government.

(b) The board of county commissioners may impose a fee for the collection of solid waste. The fee may not exceed the costs of collection.

The board of county commissioners may impose a fee for the use of a disposal facility provided by the county. Except as provided in this subsection, the fee for use may not exceed the cost of operating the facility. The fee may exceed those costs if the county enters into a contract with another local government located within the State to accept the other local government's solid waste and the county by ordinance levies a surcharge on the fee. The fee authorized by this paragraph may only be used to cover the costs of operating the facility. The surcharge authorized by this paragraph may be used for any purpose for which the county may appropriate funds. A fee under this paragraph may be imposed only on those who use the facility. The fee for use may vary based on the amount, characteristics, and form of recyclable materials present in solid waste brought to the facility for disposal. A county may not impose a fee for the use of a disposal facility on a city located in the county or a contractor or resident of the city unless the fee is based on a schedule that applies uniformly throughout the county.

The board of county commissioners may impose a fee for the availability of a disposal facility provided by the county. A fee for availability may not exceed the cost of providing the facility and may be imposed on all improved property in the county that benefits from the availability of the facility. A county may not impose an availability fee on property whose solid waste is collected by a county, a city, or a private contractor for a fee if the fee imposed by a county, a city, or a private contractor for the collection of solid waste includes a charge for the availability and use of a disposal facility provided by the county. Property served by a private contractor who disposes of solid waste collected from the property in a disposal facility provided by a private contractor that provides the same services as those provided by the county disposal facility is not considered to benefit from a disposal facility provided by the county and is not subject to a fee imposed by the county for the availability of a disposal facility provided by the county. To the extent that the services provided by the county disposal facility differ from the services provided by the disposal facility provided by a private contractor in the same county, the county may charge an availability fee to cover the costs of the additional services provided by the county disposal facility.

In determining the costs of providing and operating a disposal facility, a county may consider solid waste management costs incidental to a county's handling and disposal of solid waste at its disposal facility, including the costs of the methods of solid waste management specified in G.S. 130A-309.04(a) of the Solid Waste Management Act of 1989. A fee for the availability or use of a disposal facility may be based on the combined costs of the different disposal facilities provided by the county.

(c)   The board of county commissioners may use any suitable vacant land owned by the county for the site of a disposal facility, subject to the permit requirements of Article 9 of Chapter 130A of the General Statutes. If the county does not own suitable vacant land for a disposal facility, it may acquire suitable land by purchase or condemnation. The board may erect a gate across a highway that leads directly to a disposal facility operated by the county. The gate may be erected at or in close proximity to the boundary of the disposal facility. The county shall pay the cost of erecting and maintaining the gate.

(d),   (e) Repealed by Session Laws 1991, c. 652, s. 1.

(f)   This section does not prohibit a county from providing aid to low-income persons to pay all or part of the cost of solid waste management services for those persons. (1961, c. 514, s. 1; 1971, c. 568; 1973, c. 535; c. 822, s. 2;

1981, c. 919, s. 22; 1989 (Reg. Sess., 1990), c. 1009, s. 3; 1991, c. 652, s. 1; 1995 (Reg. Sess., 1996), c. 594, s. 27; 2007-550, s. 10(a); 2013-413, s. 59.4(a).)

§ 153A-293. (See editor's note) Collection of fees for solid waste disposal facilities and solid waste collection services.

A county may adopt an ordinance providing that any fee imposed under G.S. 153A-292 may be billed with property taxes, may be payable in the same manner as property taxes, and, in the case of nonpayment, may be collected in any manner by which delinquent personal or real property taxes can be collected. If an ordinance states that delinquent fees can be collected in the same manner as delinquent real property taxes, the fees are a lien on the real property described on the bill that includes the fee. (1989, c. 591; 1989 (Reg. Sess., 1990), c. 905, c. 938, c. 940, c. 974, c. 1017; 1991, c. 652, s. 2; 1991 (Reg. Sess., 1992), c. 1007, s. 26.)

§ 153A-294. Solid waste defined.

As used in this Article, "solid waste" means nonhazardous solid waste, that is, solid waste as defined in G.S. 130A-290 but not including hazardous waste. (1991 (Reg. Sess., 1992), c. 1013, s. 4.)

§§ G.S. 153A-295 through 153A-299. Reserved for future codification purposes.

Part 4. Long Term Contracts for Disposal of Soild Waste.

§§ 153A-299.1 through 153A-299.6: Repealed by Session Laws 1991 (Regular Session, 1992), c. 1013, 5.

Article 16.

County Service Districts; County Research and Production Service Districts; County Economic Development and Training Districts.

Part 1. County Service Districts.

§ 153A-300. Title; effective date.

This Article may be cited as "The County Service District Act of 1973," and is enacted pursuant to Article V, Sec. 2(4) of the Constitution of North Carolina, effective July 1, 1973. (1973, c. 489, s. 1; c. 822, s. 2.)

§ 153A-301. Purposes for which districts may be established.

(a) The board of commissioners of any county may define any number of service districts in order to finance, provide, or maintain for the districts one or more of the following services, facilities and functions in addition to or to a greater extent than those financed, provided or maintained for the entire county:

(1) Beach erosion control and flood and hurricane protection works.

(2) Fire protection.

(3) Recreation.

(4) Sewage collection and disposal systems of all types, including septic tank systems or other on-site collection or disposal facilities or systems.

(5) Solid waste collection and disposal systems.

(6) Water supply and distribution systems.

(7) Ambulance and rescue.

(8) Watershed improvement projects, including but not limited to watershed improvement projects as defined in Chapter 139 of the General Statutes; drainage projects, including but not limited to the drainage projects provided for by Chapter 156 of the General Statutes; and water resources development projects, including but not limited to the federal water resources development projects provided for by Article 21 of Chapter 143 of the General Statutes.

(9) Cemeteries.

(10) Law enforcement if all of the following apply:

a. The population of the county is (i) over 900,000 according to the most recent federal decennial census, and (ii) less than ten percent (10%) of the population of the county is in an unincorporated area according to the most recent federal decennial census.

b. The county has an interlocal agreement or agreements with a municipality or municipalities for the provision of law enforcement services in the unincorporated area of the county.

c. Repealed by Session Laws 2008-134, s. 76(c), effective July 28, 2008.

(11) Services permitted under Article 24 of this Chapter if the district is subject to G.S. 153A-472.1.

(b) The General Assembly finds that coastal-area counties have a special problem with lack of maintenance of platted rights-of-way, resulting in ungraded sand travelways deviating from the original rights-of-way and encroaching on private property, and such cartways exhibit poor drainage and are blocked by junk automobiles.

(c) To address the problem described in subsection (b), the board of commissioners of any coastal-area county as defined by G.S. 113A-103(2) may define any number of service districts in order to finance, provide, or maintain for the districts one or more of the following services, facilities and functions in addition to or to a greater extent than those financed, provided or maintained for the entire county:

(1) Removal of junk automobiles; and

(2) Street maintenance.

(d) The board of commissioners of a county that contains a protected mountain ridge, as defined by G.S. 113A-206(6), may define any number of service districts, composed of subdivision lots within one or more contiguous subdivisions that are served by common public roads, to finance for the district the maintenance of such public roads that are either located in the district or provide access to some or all lots in the district from a State road, where some portion of those roads is not subject to compliance with the minimum standards of the Board of Transportation set forth in G.S. 136-102.6. The service district or districts created shall include only subdivision lots within the subdivision, and one or more additional contiguous subdivisions, where the property owners' association, whose purpose is to represent these subdivision lots, agrees to be included in the service district. For subdivision lots in an additional contiguous subdivision or for other adjacent or contiguous property to be annexed according to G.S. 153A-303, the property owners' association representing the subdivision or property to be annexed must approve the annexation. For the purposes of this subsection: (i) "subdivision lots" are defined as either separate tracts appearing of record upon a recorded plat, or other lots, building sites, or divisions of land for sale or building development for residential purposes; and (ii) "public roads" are defined as roads that are in actual open use as public vehicular areas, or dedicated or offered for dedication to the public use as a road, highway, street, or avenue, by a deed, grant, map, or plat, and that have been constructed and are in use by the public, but that are not currently being maintained by any public authority.

(e) The board of commissioners of a county that adjoins or contains a lake, river, or tributary of a river or lake that has an identified noxious aquatic weed problem may define any number of noxious aquatic weed control service districts composed of property that is contiguous to the water or that provides direct access to the water through a shared, certified access site to the water. As used in this subsection, the term "noxious aquatic weed" is any plant organism identified by the Secretary of Environment and Natural Resources under G.S. 113A-222 or regulated as a plant pest by the Commissioner of Agriculture under Article 36 of Chapter 106 of the General Statutes. (1973, c. 489, s. 1; c. 822, s. 2; c. 1375; 1979, c. 595, s. 1; c. 619, s. 6; 1983 (Reg. Sess., 1984), c. 1078, s. 1; 1989, c. 620; 1993, c. 378, s. 1; 1995, c. 354, s. 1; c. 434, s. 1; 1997-456, s. 24; 2005-433, s. 10(b); 2005-440, s. 1; 2008-134, s. 76(c); 2011-100, s. 1.)

§ 153A-302. Definition of service districts.

(a) Standards. - In determining whether to establish a proposed service district, the board of commissioners shall consider all of the following:

(1) The resident or seasonal population and population density of the proposed district.

(2) The appraised value of property subject to taxation in the proposed district.

(3) The present tax rates of the county and any cities or special districts in which the district or any portion thereof is located.

(4) The ability of the proposed district to sustain the additional taxes necessary to provide the services planned for the district.

(5) If it is proposed to furnish water, sewer, or solid waste collection services in the district, the probable net revenues of the projects to be financed and the extent to which the services will be self-supporting.

(6) Any other matters that the commissioners believe to have a bearing on whether the district should be established.

(a1) Findings. - The board of commissioners may establish a service district if, upon the information and evidence it receives, the board finds that all of the following apply:

(1) There is a demonstrable need for providing in the district one or more of the services listed in G.S. 153A-301.

(2) It is impossible or impracticable to provide those services on a countywide basis.

(3) It is economically feasible to provide the proposed services in the district without unreasonable or burdensome annual tax levies.

(4) There is a demonstrable demand for the proposed services by persons residing in the district.

Territory lying within the corporate limits of a city or sanitary district may not be included unless the governing body of the city or sanitary district agrees by resolution to such inclusion.

(b) Report. - Before the public hearing required by subsection (c), the board of commissioners shall cause to be prepared a report containing:

(1) A map of the proposed district, showing its proposed boundaries;

(2) A statement showing that the proposed district meets the standards set out in subsection (a); and

(3) A plan for providing one or more of the services listed in G.S. 153A-301 to the district.

The report shall be available for public inspection in the office of the clerk to the board for at least four weeks before the date of the public hearing.

(c) Hearing and Notice. - The board of commissioners shall hold a public hearing before adopting any resolution defining a new service district under this section. Notice of the hearing shall state the date, hour, and place of the hearing and its subject, and shall include a map of the proposed district and a statement that the report required by subsection (b) is available for public inspection in the office of the clerk to the board. The notice shall be published at least once not less than one week before the date of the hearing. In addition, it shall be mailed at least four weeks before the date of the hearing by any class of U.S. mail which is fully prepaid to the owners as shown by the county tax records as of the preceding January 1 (and at the address shown thereon) of all property located within the proposed district. The person designated by the board to mail the notice shall certify to the board that the mailing has been completed and his certificate is conclusive in the absence of fraud.

(d) Effective Date. - The resolution defining a service district shall take effect at the beginning of a fiscal year commencing after its passage, as determined by the board of commissioners.

(e) Exceptions For Countywide District. - The following requirements do not apply to a board of commissioners that proposes to create a law enforcement service district pursuant to G.S. 153A-301(a)(10) that covers the entire unincorporated area of the county:

(1) The requirement that the district cannot be created unless the board makes the finding in subdivision (a1)(2) of this section.

(2) The requirement in subsection (c) of this section to notify each property owner by mail, if the board publishes a notice of its proposal to establish the district, once a week for four successive weeks before the date of the hearing required by that subsection.

(f) Exceptions for Article 24 District. - The following requirements do not apply to a board of commissioners that proposes to create a service district pursuant to G.S. 153A-301(a)(11) that covers the entire unincorporated area of the county:

(1) The requirement that the district cannot be created unless the board makes the finding in subdivision (a1)(2) of this section.

(2) The requirement in subsection (c) of this section to notify each property owner by mail, if the board publishes a notice of its proposal to establish the district, once a week for two successive weeks before the date of the hearing required by that subsection. (1973, c. 489, s. 1; c. 822, s. 2; 1981, c. 53, s. 1; 1995, c. 354, s. 2; 2005-433, s. 10(c).)

§ 153A-303. Extension of service districts.

(a) Standards. - The board of commissioners may by resolution annex territory to any service district upon finding that:

(1) The area to be annexed is contiguous to the district, with at least one eighth of the area's aggregate external boundary coincident with the existing boundary of the district; and

(2) That the area to be annexed requires the services of the district.

(b) Annexation by Petition. - The board of commissioners may also by resolution extend by annexation the boundaries of any service district when one hundred percent (100%) of the real property owners of the area to be annexed have petitioned the board for annexation to the service district.

(c) Territory lying within the corporate limits of a city or sanitary district may not be annexed to a service district unless the governing body of the city or sanitary district agrees by resolution to such annexation.

(d) Report. - Before the public hearing required by subsection (e), the board shall cause to be prepared a report containing:

(1) A map of the service district and the adjacent territory, showing the present and proposed boundaries of the district;

(2) A statement showing that the area to be annexed meets the standards and requirements of subsections (a), (b), and (c); and

(3) A plan for extending services to the area to be annexed.

The report shall be available for public inspection in the office of the clerk to the board for at least two weeks before the date of the public hearing.

(e) Hearing and Notice. - The board shall hold a public hearing before adopting any resolution extending the boundaries of a service district. Notice of the hearing shall state the date, hour and place of the hearing and its subject, and shall include a statement that the report required by subsection (d) is available for inspection in the office of the clerk to the board. The notice shall be published at least once not less than one week before the date of the hearing. In addition, the notice shall be mailed at least four weeks before the date of the hearing to the owners as shown by the county tax records as of the preceding January 1 of all property located within the area to be annexed. The notice may be mailed by any class of U.S. mail which is fully prepaid. The person designated by the board to mail the notice shall certify to the board that the mailing has been completed, and his certificate shall be conclusive in the absence of fraud.

(f) Effective Date. - The resolution extending the boundaries of the district shall take effect at the beginning of a fiscal year commencing after its passage, as determined by the board. (1973, c. 489, s. 1; c. 822, s. 2; 1981, c. 53, s. 2.)

§ 153A-303.1. Removal of territory from service districts.

(a) Standards. - A board of commissioners may by resolution remove territory from a service district upon finding that:

(1) One hundred percent (100%) of the owners of real property in the territory to be removed have petitioned for removal.

(2) The territory to be removed no longer requires the services, facilities, or functions financed, provided, or maintained for the district.

(3) The service district was created only to provide the services listed in G.S. 153A-301(a)(4) or G.S. 153A-301(a)(6) or both.

(4) The service district does not have any obligation or expense related to the issuance of bonds.

(b) Report. - Before the public hearing required by subsection (c) of this section, the board shall cause to be prepared a report containing:

(1) A map of the district highlighting the territory proposed to be removed, showing the present and proposed boundaries of the district; and

(2) A statement showing that the territory to be removed meets the standards and requirements of subsection (a) of this section.

The report shall be available for public inspection in the office of the clerk to the board for at least 10 days before the date of the public hearing.

(c) Hearing and Notice. - The board shall hold a public hearing before adopting any resolution reducing the boundaries of a district. Notice of the hearing shall state the date, hour, and place of the hearing and its subject and shall include a statement that the report required by subsection (b) of this section is available for inspection in the office of the clerk to the board. The notice shall be published at least once not less than seven days before the hearing. In addition, the notice shall be mailed at least two weeks before the date of the hearing by any class of U.S. mail which is fully prepaid to the owners as shown by the county tax records as of the preceding January 1 (and at the address shown thereon) of all property located within the territory to be removed. The person designated by the board to mail the notice shall certify to the board that the mailing has been completed, and the certificate shall be conclusive in the absence of fraud.

(d) Effective Date. - The resolution reducing the boundaries of the district shall take effect at the beginning of a fiscal year commencing after its passage, as determined by the board. (2013-402, s. 1.)

§ 153A-304. Consolidation of service districts.

(a) The board of commissioners may by resolution consolidate two or more service districts upon finding that:

(1) The districts are contiguous or are in a continuous boundary;

(2) The services provided in each of the districts are substantially the same; or

(3) If the services provided are lower for one of the districts, there is a need to increase those services for that district to the level of that enjoyed by the other districts.

(b) Report. - Before the public hearing required by subsection (c), the board of commissioners shall cause to be prepared a report containing:

(1) A map of the districts to be consolidated;

(2) A statement showing the proposed consolidation meets the standards of subsection (a); and

(3) If necessary, a plan for increasing the services for one of the districts so that they are substantially the same throughout the consolidated district.

The report shall be available in the office of the clerk to the board for at least two weeks before the public hearing.

(c) Hearing and Notice. - The board of commissioners shall hold a public hearing before adopting any resolution consolidating service districts. Notice of the hearing shall state the date, hour, and place of the hearing and its subject, and shall include a statement that the report required by subsection (b) is available for inspection in the office of the clerk to the board. The notice shall be published at least once not less than one week before the date of the hearing. In addition, the notice shall be mailed at least four weeks before the hearing to the owners as shown by the county tax records as of the preceding January 1 of all property located within the consolidated district. The notice may be mailed by any class of U.S. mail which is fully prepaid. The person designated by the board to mail the notice shall certify to the board that the mailing has been completed, and his certificate shall be conclusive in the absence of fraud.

(d) Effective Date. - The consolidation of service districts shall take effect at the beginning of a fiscal year commencing after passage of the resolution of consolidation, as determined by the board. (1973, c. 489, s. 1; c. 822, s. 2; 1981, c. 53, s. 2.)

§ 153A-304.1. Reduction in district after annexation.

(a)   When the whole or any portion of a county service district organized for fire protection purposes under G.S. 153A-301(2) has been annexed by a municipality furnishing fire protection to its citizens, and the municipality had not agreed to allow territory within it to be within the county service district under G.S. 153A-302(a), then such county service district or the portion thereof so annexed shall immediately thereupon cease to be a county service district or a portion of a county service district; and such district or portion thereof so annexed shall no longer be subject to G.S. 153A-307 authorizing the board of county commissioners to levy and collect a tax in such district for the purpose of furnishing fire protection therein.

(b)   Nothing in this section prevents the board of county commissioners from levying and collecting taxes for fire protection in the remaining portion of a county service district not annexed by a municipality.

(c)   When all or part of a county service district is annexed, and the effective date of the annexation is a date other than a date in the month of June, the amount of the county service district tax levied on property in the district for the fiscal year in which municipal taxes are prorated under G.S. 160A-58.10 shall be multiplied by the following fraction: the denominator shall be 12 and the numerator shall be the number of full calendar months remaining in the fiscal year following the day on which the annexation becomes effective. For each owner, the product of the multiplication is the prorated fire protection payment. The finance officer of the city shall obtain from the assessor or tax collector of the county where the annexed territory was located a list of the owners of property on which fire protection district taxes were levied in the territory being annexed, and the city shall, no later than 90 days after the effective date of the annexation, pay the amount of the prorated fire protection district payment to the owners of that property. Such payments shall come from any funds not otherwise restricted by law.

(d)   Whenever a city is required to make fire protection district tax payments by subsection (c) of this section, and the city has paid or has contracted to pay to a rural fire department funds under G.S. 160A-37.1 or G.S. 160A-58.57, the county shall pay to the city from funds of the county service district an amount equal to the amount paid by the city (or to be paid by the city) to a rural fire department under G.S. 160A-37.1 or G.S. 160A-58.57 on account of annexation of territory in the county service district for the number of months in that fiscal year used in calculating the numerator under subsection (c) of this section; provided that the required payments by the county to the city shall not exceed the total of fire protection district payments made to taxpayers in the district on account of that annexation. (1987, c. 711, s. 1; 2008-134, s. 76(b).)

§ 153A-304.2. Reduction in district after annexation to Chapter 69 fire district.

(a) When the whole or any portion of a county service district organized for fire protection purposes under G.S. 153A-301(2) has been annexed into a fire protection district created under Chapter 69 of the General Statutes, then such county service district or the portion thereof so annexed shall immediately thereupon cease to be a county service district or a portion of a county service district; and such district or portion thereof so annexed shall no longer be subject to G.S. 153A-307 authorizing the board of county commissioners to levy and collect a tax in such district for the purpose of furnishing fire protection therein.

(b) Nothing in this section prevents the board of county commissioners from levying and collecting taxes for fire protection in the remaining portion of a county service district not annexed into a fire protection district. This section does not affect the rights or liabilities of the county, a taxpayer, or other person concerning taxes previously levied. (1989, c. 622.)

§ 153A-304.3. Changes in adjoining service districts.

(a) Changes. - The board of county commissioners may by resolution relocate the boundary lines between adjoining county service districts if the districts were established for substantially similar purposes. The boundary lines may be changed in accordance with a petition from landowners or may be changed in any manner the board deems appropriate. Upon receipt of a request to change service district boundaries, the board of county commissioners shall set a date and time for a public hearing on the request prior to taking action on the request.

(b)   Report. - Before the public hearing required by subsection (a) of this section, the board of county commissioners shall cause to be prepared a report containing all of the following:

(1)   A map of the service district and the adjacent territory showing the current and proposed boundaries of the district.

(2)   A statement indicating that the proposed boundary relocation meets the requirements of subsection (a) of this section.

(3)   A plan for providing service to the area affected by the relocation of district boundaries.

(4)   The effect that the changes in the amount of taxable property will have on the ability of the district to provide services or to service any debt.

The report shall be available for public inspection in the office of the clerk of the board for at least two weeks before the date of the public hearing.

(c)   Notice and Hearing. - The board shall hold a public hearing before adopting any resolution relocating the boundaries of a service district. Notice of the hearing shall state the date, hour, and place of the hearing and its subject, and shall include a statement that the report required by subsection (b) of this section is available for inspection in the office of the clerk to the board. The notice shall be published at least once not less than one week before the date of the hearing.

(d)   Effective Date. - The resolution changing the boundaries of the districts shall take effect at the beginning of a fiscal year commencing after its passage, as determined by the board. (2005-136, s. 1.)

§ 153A-304.4. Reduction in law enforcement service district after annexation.

When any portion of a county law enforcement service district organized under G.S. 153A-301(10) is annexed by a municipality, and the effective date of the annexation is a date other than a date in the month of June, the amount of the county law enforcement service district tax levied on each parcel of real property in the district for the fiscal year in which municipal taxes are prorated under G.S.

160A-58.10 shall be multiplied by the following fraction: the denominator shall be 12 and the numerator shall be the number of full calendar months remaining in the fiscal year following the day on which the annexation becomes effective. For each parcel of real property in the portion of the district that is annexed, the product of the multiplication is the amount of the law enforcement service district tax to be refunded if the taxes have been paid, or released if the taxes have not been paid. The finance officer of the county shall obtain from the assessor or tax collector of the county a list of the owners of the real property on which law enforcement service district taxes were levied in the territory annexed, and the county shall pay the refund amount, if applicable, to the owner as shown on the records of the tax assessor of the real property as of the January 1 immediately preceding the date of the refund. Refund payments shall come from any funds not otherwise restricted by law. (2008-134, s. 76(a).)

§ 153A-305. Required provision or maintenance of services.

(a) New District. - When a county defines a new service district, it shall provide, maintain, or let contracts for the services for which the residents of the district are being taxed within a reasonable time, not to exceed one year, after the effective date of the definition of the district.

(b) Extended District. - When a county annexes territory to a service district, it shall provide, maintain, or let contracts for the services provided or maintained throughout the district to the residents of the area annexed to the district within a reasonable time, not to exceed one year, after the effective date of the annexation.

(c) Consolidated District. - When a county consolidates two or more service districts, one of which has had provided or maintained a lower level of services, it shall increase the services within that district (or let contracts therefor) to a level comparable to those provided or maintained elsewhere in the consolidated district within a reasonable time, not to exceed one year, after the effective date of the consolidation. (1973, c. 489, s. 1; c. 822, s. 2.)

§ 153A-306. Abolition of service districts.

Upon finding that there is no longer a need for a particular service district and that there are no outstanding bonds or notes issued to finance projects in the district, the board of commissioners may by resolution abolish that district. The board shall hold a public hearing before adopting a resolution abolishing a district. Notice of the hearing shall state the date, hour and place of the hearing, and its subject, and shall be published at least once not less than one week before the date of the hearing. The abolition of any service district shall take effect at the end of a fiscal year following passage of the resolution, as determined by the board. (1973, c. 489, s. 1; c. 822, s. 2.)

§ 153A-307. Taxes authorized; rate limitation.

A county may levy property taxes within defined service districts in addition to those levied throughout the county, in order to finance, provide or maintain for the districts services provided therein in addition to or to a greater extent than those financed, provided or maintained for the entire county. In addition, a county may allocate to a service district any other revenues whose use is not otherwise restricted by law.

Property subject to taxation in a newly established district or in an area annexed to an existing district is that subject to taxation by the county as of the preceding January 1.

Property taxes may not be levied within any district established pursuant to this Article in excess of a rate on each one hundred dollars ($100.00) value of property subject to taxation which, when added to the rate levied countywide for purposes subject to the rate limitation, would exceed the rate limitation established in G.S. 153A-149(c), unless the portion of the rate in excess of this limitation is submitted to and approved by a majority of the qualified voters residing within the district. Any referendum held pursuant to this paragraph shall be held and conducted as provided in G.S. 153A-149. (1973, c. 489, s. 1; c. 822, s. 2.)

§ 153A-308. Bonds authorized.

A county may issue its general obligation bonds under the Local Government Bond Act to finance services, facilities, or functions provided within a service district. If a proposed bond issue is required by law to be submitted to and approved by the voters of the county, and if the proceeds of the proposed bond issue are to be used in connection with a service that is or, if the bond issue is approved, will be provided only for one or more service districts or at a higher level in service districts than countywide, the proposed bond issue must be approved concurrently by a majority of those voting throughout the entire county and by a majority of the total of those voting in all of the affected or to-be-affected service districts. (1973, c. 489, s. 1; c. 822, s. 2.)

§ 153A-309. EMS services in fire protection districts.

(a) If a service district is established under this Article for fire protection purposes under G.S. 153A-301(2), (including a district established with a rate limitation under G.S. 153A-309.2), and it was not also established under this Article for ambulance and rescue purposes under G.S. 153A-301(7), the board of county commissioners may, by resolution, permit the service district to provide emergency medical, rescue, and/or ambulance services, and may levy property taxes for such purposes under G.S. 153A-307, but if the district was established under G.S. 153A-309.2, the rate limitation established under that section shall continue to apply.

(b) The resolution expanding the purposes of the district under this section shall take effect at the beginning of a fiscal year commencing after its passage. (1983, c. 642; 1989, c. 559.)

§ 153A-309.1. Reserved for future codification purposes.

§ 153A-309.2. Rate limitation in certain districts - Alternative procedure for fire protection service districts.

(a) In connection with the establishment of a service district for fire protection as provided by G.S. 153A-301(2) [G.S. 153A-301(a)(2)], if the board of commissioners adopts a resolution within 90 days prior to the public hearing required by G.S. 153A-302(c) but prior to the first publication of notice required by subsection (b) of this section, which resolution states that property taxes within a district may not be levied in excess of a rate of fifteen cents (15¢) on each one hundred dollars ($100.00) of property subject to taxation, then property taxes may not be levied in that service district in excess of that rate.

(b) Whenever a service district is established under this section, instead of the procedures for hearing and notice under G.S. 153A-302(c), the board of commissioners shall hold a public hearing before adopting any resolution defining a new service district under this section. Notice of the hearing shall state the date, hour and place of the hearing and its subject, and shall include a map of the proposed district and a statement that the report required by G.S. 153A-302(b) is available for public inspection in the office of the clerk to the board. The notice shall be published at least twice, with one publication not less than two weeks before the hearing, and the other publication on some other day not less than two weeks before the hearing. (1985, c. 724.)

§ 153A-309.3. Rate limitation in certain districts - Fire protection service districts for industrial property.

(a) Any area in a service district for fire protection established pursuant to G.S. 153A-301(a)(2) may be removed from that district by resolution of the county board of commissioners and a new service district simultaneously created for the area so removed if the area is an industrial facility (and appurtenant land and structures):

(1) Subject to a contract not to annex by a municipality under which the owner of the industrial property is obligated to make payments in lieu of taxes equal to or in excess of fifty percent (50%) of the taxes such industry would pay if it were annexed and is current in making such payments.

(2) Actively served by an industrial fire brigade which meets the standards of the National Fire Protection Association and the requirements of the North Carolina Occupational Safety and Health Standards for General Industry (Title 29 Code of Federal Regulations Part 1910 incorporated by reference in 13 NCAC 07F.0101) for industrial fire brigades.

(b) Prior to removing such area from the service district and simultaneously creating a new district of that same area, the board shall hold a public hearing. Notice of the hearing shall state the date, hour, and place of the hearing and its subject. The notice shall be published at least once not less than one week before the date of the hearing. In addition, the notice shall be mailed at least two weeks before the date of the hearing to the owners as shown by the county tax records as of the preceding January 1 of all property located within the area to be removed and a new district created. The notice may be mailed by any class of U.S. mail which is fully prepaid. The person designated by the board to mail the notice shall certify to the board that the mailing has been completed, and his certificate shall be conclusive in the absence of fraud.

(c)   In any district created under this section from area removed from an existing district, the county may not levy or collect property taxes for the purpose of financing fire protection pursuant to this Article in excess of a rate of three and one-half cents (3.5¢) on each one hundred dollars ($100.00) of property valuation subject to taxation.

(d)   If any district established under this section ceases to meet the tests established by subdivisions (a)(1) and (a)(2) of this section, the board of commissioners may by resolution abolish that district and annex that territory to the district from which it was removed after a public hearing under the same provisions as set out in subsection (b) of this section.

(e)   Any resolutions adopted under this section become effective the first day of July following their adoption. (2005-281, s. 1.)

§ 153A-310. Rate limitation in certain districts - Alternative procedure for ambulance and rescue districts.

(a)   In connection with the establishment of a service district for ambulance and rescue as provided by G.S. 153A-301(7) [G.S. 153A-301(a)(7)], if the board of commissioners adopts a resolution within 90 days prior to the public hearing required by G.S. 153A-302(c) but prior to the first publication of notice required by subsection (b) of this section, which resolution states that property taxes within a district may not be levied in excess of a rate of five cents (5¢) on each one hundred dollars ($100.00) of property subject to taxation, then property taxes may not be levied in that service district in excess of that rate.

(b)   Whenever a service district is established under this section, instead of the procedures for hearing and notice under G.S. 153A-302(c), the board of commissioners shall hold a public hearing before adopting any resolution defining a new service district under this section. Notice of the hearing shall state the date, hour and place of the hearing and its subject, and shall include a map of the proposed district and a statement that the report required by G.S. 153A-302(b) is available for public inspection in the office of the clerk to the board. The notice shall be published at least twice, with one publication not less than two weeks before the hearing, and the other publication on some other day not less than two weeks before the hearing. (1985, c. 430, s. 1.)

Part 2. County Research and Production Service Districts and Urban Research Service Districts.

§ 153A-311. Purposes for which districts may be established.

The board of commissioners of any county may define a county research and production service district in order to finance, provide, and maintain for the district any service, facility, or function that a county or a city is authorized by general law to provide, finance, or maintain. Such a service, facility, or function shall be financed, provided, or maintained in the district either in addition to or to a greater extent than services, facilities, or functions are financed, provided, or maintained for the entire county. (1985, c. 435, s. 1.)

§ 153A-312. Definition of research and production service district.

(a) Standards. - The board of commissioners may by resolution establish a research and production service district for any area of the county that, at the time the resolution is adopted, meets the following standards:

(1) All (i) real property in the district is being used for or is subject to covenants that limit its use to research; or scientifically-oriented production, technology, education; or associated commercial, residential, or institutional purposes; or for other purposes specifically authorized pursuant to the terms and conditions of the covenants, or (ii) if all the real property in the district is part of a multijurisdictional industrial park that satisfies the criteria of G.S. 143B-437.08(h), all such real property in the district is subject to covenants that limit its use to research or scientifically oriented production, associated commercial or institutional purposes, or other industrial and associated commercial and institutional uses.

(2) The district (i) contains at least 4,000 acres or (ii) satisfies the criteria of G.S. 143B-437.08(h).

(3) The district (i) includes research and production facilities that in combination employ at least 5,000 persons or (ii) satisfies the criteria of G.S. 143B-437.08(h).

(4) Repealed by Session Laws 2012-73, s.1, effective June 26, 2012.

(5) A petition requesting creation of the district signed by at least fifty percent (50%) of the owners of real property in the district who own at least fifty percent (50%) of total area of the real property in the district has been presented to the board of commissioners. In determining the total area of real property in the district and the number of owners of real property, there shall be excluded (1) real property exempted from taxation and real property classified and excluded from taxation and (2) the owners of such exempted or classified and excluded property.

(6) Repealed by Session Laws 2012-73, s.1, effective June 26, 2012.

(7) There exists in the district an association of owners and tenants, to which at least seventy-five percent (75%) of the owners of nonresidential real property belong, which association can make the recommendations provided for in G.S. 153A-313. This subdivision shall not apply to a research and production service district that satisfies the criteria of G.S. 143B-437.08(h).

(8) There exist deed-imposed conditions, covenants, restrictions, and reservations that apply to all real property in the district, provided that the covenants, restrictions, and reservations shall not be effective against the United States as long as it owns or leases property in the district but shall apply to any subsequent owner or lessee of such property.

(9) No part of the district lies within the boundaries of any incorporated city or town.

The Board of Commissioners may establish a research and production service district if, upon the information and evidence it receives, the Board finds that:

(1) The proposed district meets the standards set forth in this subsection; and

(2) It is impossible or impracticable to provide on a countywide basis the additional or higher levels of services, facilities, or functions proposed for the district; and

(3) It is economically feasible to provide the proposed services, facilities, or functions to the district without unreasonable or burdensome tax levies.

(a1) Additional Uses. - A developer of a research and production service district established prior to June 1, 2012, may amend the covenants that limit the use of real property in the district to include any of the following uses: research; or scientifically-oriented production, technology, education; or associated commercial, residential, or institutional purposes; or for other purposes specifically authorized pursuant to the terms and conditions of the covenants. A research and production service district is presumed to be in compliance with the standards in subsection (a) of this section if the district met the standards in subsection (a) of this section, as that subsection was enacted at the time of the establishment of the district.

(b) Multi-County Districts. - If an area that meets the standards for creation of a research and production service district lies in more than one county, the boards of commissioners of those counties may adopt concurrent resolutions establishing a district, even if that portion of the district lying in any one of the counties does not by itself meet the standards. Each of the county boards of commissioners shall follow the procedure set out in this section for creation of a district.

If a multi-county district is established, as provided in this subsection, the boards of commissioners of the counties involved shall jointly determine whether the same appraisal and assessment standards apply uniformly throughout the district, or, in the case of a multijurisdictional industrial park that satisfies the criteria of G.S. 143B-437.08(h), whether there is a current need in each participating county to levy a tax, which determination shall be made by each participating county's board of commissioners. This determination shall be set out in concurrent resolutions of the boards. If the same appraisal and assessment standards apply uniformly throughout the district, the boards of commissioners of all the counties shall levy the same rate of tax for the district, so that a uniform rate of tax is levied for district purposes throughout the district. If the boards determine that the same standards do not apply uniformly throughout the district, the boards shall agree on the extent of divergence between the counties and on the resulting adjustments of tax rates that will be necessary in order that an effectively uniform rate of tax is levied for district purposes throughout the district. In the event that one or more of the boards of commissioners in one or more of the counties participating in a multijurisdictional industrial park that satisfies the criteria of G.S. 143B-437.08(h) determines that there is no current need to levy a tax for all or part of the property meeting said requirements within its jurisdictional boundaries, then that county or those counties shall be under no obligation to do so. That county or those counties participating in a multijurisdictional industrial park that satisfies the criteria of G.S. 143B-437.08(h) that choose to levy a tax for all or part of the property meeting said requirements within its jurisdictional boundaries may do so without setting an effectively uniform rate of tax as described above, provided such rate shall not exceed the rate allowed in G.S. 143B-317(b).

The boards of commissioners of the counties establishing a multi-county district pursuant to this subsection may, by concurrent resolution, provide for the administration of services within the district by one or more counties on behalf of all the establishing counties.

(c)   Report. - Before the public hearing required by subsection (d), the board of commissioners shall cause to be prepared a report containing:

(1)   A map of the proposed district, showing its proposed boundaries;

(2)   A statement showing that the proposed district meets the standards set out in subsection (a); and

(3)   A plan for providing one or more services, facilities, or functions to the district.

The report shall be available for public inspection in the office of the clerk to the board for at least four weeks before the date of the public hearing.

(d)   Hearing and Notice. - The board of commissioners shall hold a public hearing before adopting any resolution defining a district under this section. Notice of the hearing shall state the date, hour, and place of the hearing and its subject, and shall include a map of the proposed district and a statement that the report required by subsection (c) is available for public inspection in the office of the clerk to the board. The notice shall be published at least once not less than one week before the date of the hearing. In addition, it shall be mailed at least four weeks before the date of the hearing by any class of U.S. mail which is fully prepaid to the owners as shown by the county tax records as of the preceding January 1 (and at the address shown thereon) of all property located within the proposed district. The person designated by the board to mail the notice shall certify to the board that the mailing has been completed and his certificate is conclusive in the absence of fraud.

(e)   Effective Date. - The resolution defining a district shall take effect at the beginning of a fiscal year commencing after its passage, as determined by the board of commissioners. (1985, c. 435, s. 1; 2009-523, s. 3(a); 2012-73, s. 1.)

§ 153A-313. Research and production service district advisory committee.

(a)   The board or boards of commissioners, in the resolution establishing a research and production service district, shall also provide for an advisory committee for the district. Such a committee shall have at least 10 members, serving terms as set forth in the resolution; one member shall be the representative of the developer of the research and production park established as a research and production service district. The resolution shall provide for the appointment or designation of a chair. The board of commissioners or, in the case of a multi-county district, the boards of commissioners shall appoint the members of the advisory committee. If a multi-county district is established, the concurrent resolutions establishing the district shall provide how many members of the advisory committee are to be appointed by each board of commissioners. Before making the appointments, the appropriate board shall request the association of owners and tenants, required by G.S. 153A-312(a), to submit a list of persons to be considered for appointment to the committee; the association shall submit at least two names for each appointment to be made. Except as provided in the next two sentences, the board of commissioners shall make the appointments to the committee from the list of persons submitted. In addition, the developer of the research and production park shall appoint one person to the advisory committee as the developer's representative on the committee. In addition, in a single county district, the board of commissioners may make two additional appointments of such other persons as the board of commissioners deems appropriate, and in a multi-county district, each board of county commissioners may make one additional appointment of such other person as that board of commissioners deems appropriate. Whenever a vacancy occurs on the committee in a position filled by appointment by the board of commissioners, the appropriate board, before filling the vacancy, shall request the association to submit the names of at least two persons to be considered for the vacancy; and the board shall fill the vacancy by appointing one of the persons so submitted, except that if the vacancy is in a position appointed by the board of commissioners under the preceding sentence of this section, the board of commissioners making that appointment shall fill the vacancy with such person as that board of commissioners deems appropriate.

Each year, before adopting the budget for the district and levying the tax for the district, the board or boards of commissioners shall request recommendations from the advisory committee as to the level of services, facilities, or functions to be provided for the district for the ensuing year. The board or boards of commissioners shall, to the extent permitted by law, expend the proceeds of any tax levied for the district in the manner recommended by the advisory committee.

(b)   In the event that the research and production service district satisfies the criteria of G.S. 143B-437.08(h), the board of directors for the nonprofit corporation which owns the industrial park shall serve as the advisory committee described in subsection (a) of this section. (1985, c. 435, s. 1; 2009-523, s. 3(b); 2012-73, s. 1.)

§ 153A-314. Extension of service districts.

(a)   Standards. - A board of commissioners may by resolution annex territory to a research and production service district upon finding that:

(1)   The conditions, covenants, restrictions, and reservations required by G.S. 153A-312(a)(8) that apply to all real property in the district also apply or will apply to the property to be annexed, provided that the covenants, restrictions, and reservations shall not be effective against the United States as long as it owns or leases property in the district but shall apply to any subsequent owner or lessee of such property.

(2)   One hundred percent (100%) of the owners of real property in the area to be annexed have petitioned for annexation.

(3)   The district, following the annexation, will continue to meet the standards set out in G.S. 153A-312(a).

(4)   The area to be annexed requires the services, facilities, or functions financed, provided, or maintained for the district.

(5)   The area to be annexed is contiguous to the district.

(b)   Report. - Before the public hearing required by subsection (c), the board shall cause to be prepared a report containing:

(1)   A map of the district and the adjacent territory proposed to be annexed, showing the present and proposed boundaries of the district; and

(2)   A statement showing that the area to be annexed meets the standards and requirements of subsection (a) of this section.

The report shall be available for public inspection in the office of the clerk to the board for at least four weeks before the date of the public hearing.

(c)   Hearing and Notice. - The board shall hold a public hearing before adopting any resolution extending the boundaries of a district. Notice of the hearing shall state the date, hour and place of the hearing and its subject, and shall include a statement that the report required by subsection (b) of this section is available for inspection in the office of the clerk to the board. The notice shall be published at least once not less than four weeks before the hearing. In addition, the notice shall be mailed at least four weeks before the date of the hearing by any class of U.S. mail which is fully prepaid to the owners as shown by the county tax records as of the preceding January 1 (and at the address shown thereon) of all property located within the area to be annexed. The person designated by the board to mail the notice shall certify to the board that the mailing has been completed, and the certificate shall be conclusive in the absence of fraud.

(d)   Effective Date. - The resolution extending the boundaries of the district shall take effect at the beginning of a fiscal year commencing after its passage, as determined by the board. (1985, c. 435, s. 1; 2012-73, s. 1.)

§ 153A-314.1. Removal of territory from districts.

(a)   Standards. - A board of commissioners may by resolution remove territory from a research and production service district upon finding that:

(1)   The removal has been recommended by a vote of two-thirds of the eligible votes of the owners and tenants association.

(2) One hundred percent (100%) of the owners of real property in the territory to be removed have petitioned for removal.

(3) The territory to be removed no longer requires the services, facilities, or functions financed, provided, or maintained for the district.

(b) Report. - Before the public hearing required by subsection (c) of this section, the board shall cause to be prepared a report containing:

(1) A map of the district highlighting the territory proposed to be removed, showing the present and proposed boundaries of the district; and

(2) A statement showing that the territory to be removed meets the standards and requirements of subsection (a) of this section.

The report shall be available for public inspection in the office of the clerk to the board for at least 10 days before the date of the public hearing.

(c) Hearing and Notice. - The board shall hold a public hearing before adopting any resolution reducing the boundaries of a district. Notice of the hearing shall state the date, hour, and place of the hearing and its subject and shall include a statement that the report required by subsection (b) of this section is available for inspection in the office of the clerk to the board. The notice shall be published at least once not less than seven days before the hearing. In addition, the notice shall be mailed at least two weeks before the date of the hearing by any class of U.S. mail which is fully prepaid to the owners as shown by the county tax records as of the preceding January 1 (and at the address shown thereon) of all property located within the territory to be removed. The person designated by the board to mail the notice shall certify to the board that the mailing has been completed, and the certificate shall be conclusive in the absence of fraud.

(d) Municipal Annexation Allowed Under General Law. - The general law concerning annexation, Article 4A of Chapter 160A of the General Statutes, shall apply to any territory removed from the district under this section, notwithstanding any local act to the contrary.

(e) Effective Date. - The resolution reducing the boundaries of the district shall take effect at the beginning of a fiscal year commencing after its passage, as determined by the board. (2003-187, s. 1; 2012-73, s. 1.)

§ 153A-315. Required provision or maintenance of services.

(a) New District. - When a county or counties define a research and production service district, it or they shall provide, maintain, or let contracts for the services for which the district is being taxed within a reasonable time, not to exceed one year, after the effective date of the definition of the district.

(b) Extended District. - When a territory is annexed to a research and production service district, the county or counties shall provide, maintain, or let contracts for the services provided or maintained throughout the district to property in the area annexed to the district within a reasonable time, not to exceed one year, after the effective date of the annexation. (1985, c. 435, s. 1.)

§ 153A-316. Abolition of districts.

A board or boards of county commissioners may by resolution abolish a research and production service district upon finding that (i) a petition requesting abolition, signed by at least fifty percent (50%) of the owners of nonresidential real property in the district who own at least fifty percent (50%) of the total area of nonresidential real property in the district, has been submitted to the board or boards; and (ii) there is no longer a need for such district. In determining the total area of nonresidential real property in the district and the number of owners of nonresidential real property, there shall be excluded (1) real property exempted from taxation and real property classified and excluded from taxation and (2) the owners of such exempted or classified and excluded property. The board or boards shall hold a public hearing before adopting a resolution abolishing a district. Notice of the hearing shall state the date, hour, and place of the hearing, and its subject, and shall be published at least once not less than one week before the date of the hearing. The abolition of any district shall take effect at the end of a fiscal year following passage of the resolution, as determined by the board or boards. If a multi-county district is established, it may be abolished only by concurrent resolution of the board of commissioners of each county in which the district is located. (1985, c. 435, s. 1; 2012-73, s. 1.)

§ 153A-316.1. Urban research service district (URSD).

(a) Standards. - The board of commissioners of a county may establish one or more urban research service districts ("URSD" as used in this Part) that meets the following standards:

(1) The URSD is wholly within a county research and production service district located partly within that county.

(2) The URSD is located wholly within that county.

(3) The URSD is not contained within another URSD.

(4) A petition requesting creation of the URSD signed by at least fifty percent (50%) of the owners of real property in the URSD who own at least fifty (50%) of total area of the real property in the URSD has been presented to the board of commissioners.

(b) Report. - Before the public hearing required by subsection (c) of this section, the board of commissioners shall cause to be prepared and adopted by it a report. The report shall be available for public inspection in the office of the clerk to the board for at least four weeks before the date of the public hearing. The report shall contain the following:

(1) A map of the proposed URSD, showing its proposed boundaries.

(2) A statement showing that the proposed URSD is for the purpose of providing urban services, facilities, or functions to a greater extent than (i) in the entire county and (ii) in the county research and production service district.

(3) A plan for providing one or more services, facilities, or functions to the URSD.

(c) Hearing and Notice. - The board of commissioners shall hold a public hearing before adopting any resolution defining a URSD under this section. Notice of the hearing shall state the date, hour, and place of the hearing and its subject, and shall include a map of the proposed URSD and a statement that the report required by subsection (b) of this section is available for public inspection in the office of the clerk to the board. The notice shall be published at least once not less than one week before the date of the hearing. In addition, it shall be mailed at least four weeks before the date of the hearing by any class of U.S. mail that is fully prepaid to the owners, as shown by the county tax records as of the preceding January 1, of all property located within the proposed URSD. The person designated by the board to mail the notice shall certify to the board that the mailing has been completed, and the designated person's certificate is conclusive in the absence of fraud.

(d) Effective Date. - The resolution defining a URSD shall take effect at the beginning of a fiscal year commencing after its passage, as determined by the board of commissioners. (2012-73, s. 1; 2012-194, s. 62.5.)

§ 153A-316.2. URSD advisory committee.

(a) Members. - The board of commissioners, in the resolution establishing a URSD, shall also provide for an advisory committee for the URSD. The committee shall have at least 10 members, serving terms as set forth in the resolution. The resolution shall provide for the appointment or designation of a chairperson. The board of commissioners shall appoint the members of the USRD [URSD] advisory committee. Before making the appointments, the board shall request the association of owners and tenants, required by G.S. 153A-312(a), to submit a list of persons to be considered for appointment to the committee. The association shall submit at least two names for each appointment to be made. Except as provided in subsection (b) of this section, the board of commissioners shall make the appointments to the committee from the list of persons submitted.

(b) Additional Members. - In addition to the members provided in subsection (a) of this section, the developer of the research and production park established as a research and production service district shall appoint one person to the URSD advisory committee as the developer's representative on the committee. The board of commissioners may make two additional appointments of such other persons as the board of commissioners deems appropriate.

(c) Vacancy. - Whenever a vacancy occurs on the committee in a position filled by appointment by the board of commissioners, the board, before filling the vacancy, shall request the association to submit the names of at least two persons to be considered for the vacancy, and the board shall fill the vacancy by appointing one of the persons so submitted, except that if the vacancy is in a position appointed by the board of commissioners under subsection (b) of this section, the board of commissioners making that appointment shall fill the vacancy with such person as the board of commissioners deems appropriate.

(d) Advisory Role. - Each year, before adopting the budget for the URSD and levying the tax for the URSD, the board of commissioners shall request recommendations from the URSD advisory committee as to the level of services, facilities, or functions to be provided for the URSD for the ensuing year. The board of commissioners shall, to the extent permitted by law, expend the proceeds of any tax levied for the URSD in the manner recommended by the URSD advisory committee. (2012-73, s. 1.)

§ 153A-316.3. Extension of URSD.

(a) Standards. - A board of commissioners may by resolution annex territory to a URSD upon finding that:

(1) The conditions, covenants, restrictions, and reservations required by G.S. 153A-312(a)(8) that apply to all real property in the URSD also apply or will apply to the property to be annexed, provided that such covenants, restrictions, and reservations shall not be effective against the United States as long as it owns or leases property in the URSD but shall apply to any subsequent owner or lessee of such property.

(2) One hundred percent (100%) of the owners of real property in the area to be annexed have petitioned for annexation.

(3) The URSD, following the annexation, will continue to meet the standards set out in G.S. 153A-316.1(a).

(4) The area to be annexed requires the services, facilities, or functions financed, provided, or maintained for the URSD.

(5) The area to be annexed is contiguous to the URSD.

(b) Report. - Before the public hearing required by subsection (c) of this section, the board shall cause to be prepared a report. The report shall be available for public inspection in the office of the clerk to the board for at least four weeks before the date of the public hearing. The report shall contain the following:

(1) A map of the URSD and the adjacent territory proposed to be annexed, showing the present and proposed boundaries of the URSD.

(2) A statement showing that the area to be annexed meets the standards and requirements of subsection (a) of this section.

(c) Hearing and Notice. - The board shall hold a public hearing before adopting any resolution extending the boundaries of a URSD. Notice of the hearing shall state the date, hour, and place of the hearing and its subject, and shall include a statement that the report required by subsection (b) of this section is available for inspection in the office of the clerk to the board. The notice shall be published at least once not less than four weeks before the hearing. In addition, the notice shall be mailed at least four weeks before the date of the hearing by any class of U.S. mail that is fully prepaid to the owners, as shown by the county tax records as of the preceding January 1, of all property located within the area to be annexed. The person designated by the board to mail the notice shall certify to the board that the mailing has been completed, and the certificate shall be conclusive in the absence of fraud.

(d) Effective Date. - The resolution extending the boundaries of the URSD shall take effect at the beginning of a fiscal year commencing after its passage, as determined by the board. (2012-73, s. 1.)

§ 153A-316.4. Removal of territory from URSD.

(a) Standards. - A board of commissioners may by resolution remove territory from a URSD upon finding that:

(1) The removal has been recommended by a vote of two-thirds of the eligible voters of the owners and tenants association.

(2) One hundred percent (100%) of the owners of real property in the territory to be removed have petitioned for removal.

(3) The territory to be removed no longer requires the services, facilities, or functions financed, provided, or maintained for the URSD.

(4) The county has not financed any project for which taxes levied on the URSD provide debt service pursuant to G.S. 153A-317.1(c).

(b) Report. - Before the public hearing required by subsection (c) of this section, the board shall cause to be prepared a report. The report shall be available for public inspection in the office of the clerk to the board for at least 10 days before the date of the public hearing. The report shall contain the following:

(1) A map of the URSD highlighting the territory proposed to be removed, showing the present and proposed boundaries of the URSD.

(2) A statement showing that the territory to be removed meets the standards and requirements of subsection (a) of this section.

(c) Hearing and Notice. - The board shall hold a public hearing before adopting any resolution reducing the boundaries of the URSD. Notice of the hearing shall state the date, hour, and place of the hearing and its subject, and shall include a statement that the report required by subsection (b) of this section is available for inspection in the office of the clerk to the board. The notice shall be published at least once not less than seven days before the hearing. In addition, the notice shall be mailed at least two weeks before the date of the hearing by any class of U.S. mail that is fully prepaid to the owners, as shown by the county tax records as of the preceding January 1, of all property located within the territory to be removed. The person designated by the board to mail the notice shall certify to the board that the mailing has been completed, and the certificate shall be conclusive in the absence of fraud.

(d) Effective Date. - The resolution reducing the boundaries of the URSD shall take effect at the beginning of a fiscal year commencing after its passage, as determined by the board. (2012-73, s. 1.)

§ 153A-316.5. Required provision or maintenance of services in URSD.

(a) New URSD. - When a county defines a URSD, it shall provide, maintain, or let contracts for the services for which the URSD is being taxed within a reasonable time, not to exceed one year, after the effective date of the definition of the URSD. When a county defines a URSD, it may designate the developer of the research and development park established as a research and production service district in which the URSD is located as an agent that may contract with any local government for the provision of services within the URSD.

(b) Extended URSD. - When a territory is annexed to a URSD, the county shall provide, maintain, or let contracts for the services provided or maintained throughout the URSD to property in the area annexed to the URSD within a reasonable time, not to exceed one year, after the effective date of the annexation. (2012-73, s. 1.)

§ 153A-316.6. Abolition of URSD.

A county board of commissioners may by resolution abolish a URSD upon finding that (i) a petition requesting abolition, signed by at least fifty percent (50%) of the owners of nonresidential real property in the URSD who own at least fifty percent (50%) of the total area of nonresidential real property in the URSD, has been submitted to the board or boards; (ii) there is no longer a need for such URSD; and (iii) the county has not financed any project for which there is outstanding debt serviced by tax revenues levied within the URSD. In determining the total area of nonresidential real property in the URSD and the number of owners of nonresidential real property, there shall be excluded (i) real property exempted from taxation and real property classified and excluded from taxation and (ii) the owners of such exempted or classified and excluded property. The board or boards shall hold a public hearing before adopting a resolution abolishing a URSD. Notice of the hearing shall state the date, hour, and place of the hearing and its subject, and shall be published at least once not less than one week before the date of the hearing. The abolition of any URSD shall take effect at the end of a fiscal year following passage of the resolution, as determined by the board. (2012-73, s. 1.)

§ 153A-317. Research and production service district taxes authorized; rate limitation.

(a) Tax Authorized. - A county, upon recommendation of the advisory committee established pursuant to G.S. 153A-313, may levy property taxes within a research and production service district in addition to those levied throughout the county, in order to finance, provide, or maintain for the district services provided therein in addition to or to a greater extent than those financed, provided, or maintained for the entire county. In addition, a county may allocate to a district any other revenues whose use is not otherwise restricted by law. The proceeds of taxes only within a district may be expended only for services provided for the district.

Property subject to taxation in a newly established district or in an area annexed to an existing district is that subject to taxation by the county as of the preceding January 1.

(b) Limit. - Such additional property taxes may not be levied within any district established pursuant to this Article in excess of a rate of ten cents (10¢) on each one hundred dollars ($100.00) value of property subject to taxation or, in the event that the research and production service district satisfies the criteria of G.S. 143B-437.08(h), such additional property taxes may not be levied within said district in excess of a rate of twenty cents (20¢) on each one hundred dollars ($100.00) value of property subject to taxation.

(c) Public Transportation. - For the purpose of constructing, maintaining, or operating public transportation as defined by G.S. 153A-149(c)(27), in addition to the additional property taxes levied under subsections (a) and (b) of this section, a county, upon recommendation of the advisory committee established pursuant to G.S. 153A-313, may levy additional property taxes within any district established pursuant to this Article not in excess of a rate of ten cents (10¢) on each one hundred dollars ($100.00) value of property subject to taxation. Such property taxes for public transportation may only be used within the district, or to provide for public transportation from the district to other public transportation systems or to other places outside the district including airports. (1985, c. 435, s. 1; 2009-523, s. 3(c); 2009-527, s. 6; 2012-73, s. 1.)

§ 153A-317.1. Urban research service district taxes authorized; rate.

(a) Tax Authorized. - A county, upon recommendation of the advisory committee established pursuant to G.S. 153A-316.2, may levy property taxes within a URSD in addition to those levied throughout the county, and in addition to those levied throughout the county research and production service district, in order to finance, provide, or maintain for the URSD services provided therein in addition to or to a greater extent than those financed, provided, or maintained both for the entire county and for the county research and production service district. Only those services that cities are authorized by law to provide may be provided. In addition, a county may allocate to a URSD any other revenue not otherwise restricted by law.

(b) Rate. - Property subject to taxation in a newly established URSD or in an area annexed to an existing URSD is that subject to taxation by the county as of the preceding January. The maximum tax rate set forth in G.S. 153A-317 shall not apply to the URSD. The additional property taxes within any URSD may not be levied in excess of the rate levied in the prior year by a city that:

(1) Is the largest city in population that is contiguous to the county research and production service district where the URSD is located.

(2) Is located primarily within the same county the URSD is located.

(c) Use. - The proceeds of taxes levied within a URSD may be expended only for the benefit of the URSD. The taxes levied for the URSD may be used for debt service on any debt issued by the county that is used wholly or partly for capital projects located within the URSD, but not in greater proportion than expense of projects located within the URSD bear to the entire expense of capital projects financed by that borrowing of the county. For the purpose of this subsection, "debt" includes (i) general obligation bonds and notes issued under Chapter 159 of the General Statutes, (ii) revenue bonds issued under Chapter 159 of the General Statutes, (iii) financing agreements under Article 8 of Chapter 159 of the General Statutes, and (iv) special obligation bonds issued by the county. (2012-73, s. 1.)

§ 153A-317.2: Reserved for future codification purposes.

§ 153A-317.3: Reserved for future codification purposes.

§ 153A-317.4: Reserved for future codification purposes.

§ 153A-317.5: Reserved for future codification purposes.

§ 153A-317.6: Reserved for future codification purposes.

§ 153A-317.7: Reserved for future codification purposes.

§ 153A-317.8: Reserved for future codification purposes.

§ 153A-317.9: Reserved for future codification purposes.

§ 153A-317.10: Reserved for future codification purposes.

Part 3. Economic Development and Training Districts.

§ 153A-317.11. Purpose and nature of districts.

The board of commissioners of any county may define a county economic development and training district, as provided in this Part, to finance, provide, and maintain for the district a skills training center in cooperation with its community college branch in or for the county to prepare residents of the county to perform manufacturing, research and development, and related service and support jobs in the pharmaceutical, biotech, life sciences, chemical, telecommunications, and electronics industries, and allied, ancillary, and subordinate industries, to provide within the district any of the education, training, and related services, facilities, or functions that a county or a city is authorized by general law to provide, finance, or maintain, and to promote economic development in the county. The skills training center and related services shall be financed, provided, or maintained in the district either in addition to or to a greater extent than training facilities and services are financed, provided, or maintained in the entire county. A district created under this Part is a special tax area under Section 2(4) of Article V of the North Carolina Constitution. (2003-418, s. 1; 2004-170, s. 38.)

§ 153A-317.12. Definition of economic development and training district.

(a) Standards. - The board of commissioners may by resolution establish an economic development and training district for an area or areas of the county that, at the time the resolution is adopted, meet the following standards:

(1) All of the real property in the district primarily is being used for, or is subject to, a declaration of covenants, conditions, and restrictions that limits its use primarily to biotech processing, chemical manufacturing, pharmaceutical manufacturing, electronics manufacturing, telecommunications manufacturing, and any allied, ancillary, or subordinate uses including, without limitation, any research and development facility, headquarters or office, temporary lodging facility, restaurant, warehouse, or transportation or distribution facility.

(2) The district includes at least two pharmaceuticals manufacturing or bioprocessing facilities occupying sites in the district containing in the aggregate at least 425 acres owned by publicly held corporations.

(3) The bioprocessing and pharmaceuticals manufacturing facilities in the district employ in the aggregate at least 1,600 persons.

(4) The district includes an industrial park consisting of at least 60 acres within a noncontiguous parcel of at least 625 acres now or formerly owned by an airport authority.

(5) The district's zoning classifications permit the uses listed in this section.

(6) All real property in the district is either zoned for or is being used primarily for pharmaceutical, biotech, life sciences, chemical, telecommunications, or electronics manufacturing or processing or allied, ancillary, or subordinate uses.

(7) The district shall include a skills training center situated on a tract containing not less than eight acres, which facility shall be designed and staffed to provide relevant training to prepare existing or prospective employees of targeted industries for jobs in one or more of the pharmaceutical, biotech, life sciences, chemical, telecommunications, and electronics industries and allied, ancillary, or subordinate industries. The training center shall be completed within a reasonable period after the creation of the district.

(8) At the date of creation, no part of the district lies within the boundaries of any incorporated city or town.

(9) There exists a uniform set of covenants, conditions, restrictions, and reservations that applies to all real property in the district other than property owned by the federal, State, or local government.

(10) There exists in the district an association of owners and tenants to which owners of real property representing at least fifty percent (50%) of the assessed value of real property in the district belong, which association can make the recommendations provided for in G.S. 153A-317.13.

(11) A petition requesting creation of the district signed by owners of real property in the district who own real and personal property representing at least fifty percent (50%) of the total assessed value of the real and personal property

in the district has been presented to the board of commissioners. In determining the assessed value of real and personal property in the district and the owners of real property, there shall be excluded: (i) real property exempted from taxation and real property classified and excluded from taxation and (ii) the owners of such exempted or classified and excluded property. Assessed value shall mean the most recent values determined by the county for the imposition of taxes on real and personal property.

(b) Findings. - The board of commissioners may establish an economic development and training district if, upon the information and evidence it receives, the board determines that:

(1) The proposed district meets the standards set forth in subsection (a) of this section;

(2) Economic development of the county will be served by providing selected skills training in a facility designed specifically to address the needs of targeted industries such as pharmaceuticals, biotech processing, telecommunications, electronics, and allied, ancillary, or subordinate supplies or services to induce existing industries and targeted industries to improve and expand their facilities and new industries to locate facilities in the district, thereby providing employment opportunities for the residents of the county;

(3) It is impossible or impractical to provide training facilities and services on a countywide basis to all existing and future employers in the county to the same extent as such training services are intended to be furnished within the district; and

(4) It is economically feasible to provide the proposed training facilities and services in the district without unreasonable or burdensome tax levies.

(c) Report. - Before the public hearing required by subsection (d) of this section, the board of commissioners shall cause to be prepared a report containing all of the following:

(1) A map of the proposed district showing its proposed boundaries.

(2) A statement showing that the proposed district meets the standards set out in subsection (a) of this section.

(3)   A plan for providing the skills training center and training services to the district.

The report shall be available for public inspection in the office of the clerk to the board for at least four weeks before the date of the public hearing.

(d)   Hearing and Notice. - The board of commissioners shall hold a public hearing before adopting any resolution defining a district under this section. Notice of the hearing shall state the date, hour, and place of the hearing and its subject and shall include a map of the proposed district and a statement that the report required by subsection (c) of this section is available for public inspection in the office of the clerk to the board. The notice shall be published at least once not less than one week before the date of the hearing. In addition, it shall be mailed at least four weeks before the date of the hearing by any class of U.S. mail which is fully prepaid to the owners as shown by the county tax records as of the preceding January 1 (and at the address shown thereon) of all property located within the proposed district. The person designated by the board to mail the notice shall certify to the board that the mailing has been completed, and the certificate shall be conclusive in the absence of fraud.

(e)   Effective Date. - The resolution creating a district shall take effect at the beginning of the fiscal year commencing after its passage or such other date as shall be determined by the board of commissioners. (2003-418, s. 1.)

§ 153A-317.13. Advisory committee.

(a)   Creation. - The board of commissioners, in the resolution establishing an economic development and training district, shall also provide for an advisory committee for the district. The committee shall consist of five members, serving terms as set forth in the resolution. The resolution shall provide for the appointment or designation of a chair. The board of commissioners shall appoint the members of the advisory committee as provided in this section.

(b)   Membership. - Three of the five committee members shall represent the association of owners and tenants, as required by G.S. 153A-317.12(a)(10), and two members shall represent the county. Before making the appointments representing the association, the board of commissioners shall request the association to submit a list of persons to be considered for appointment to the committee. The association of owners and tenants shall submit at least two names for each appointment to be made and the board of commissioners shall make the appointments to the committee representing the association from the list of persons submitted to it by the association. Whenever a vacancy occurs on the committee in a position filled by an appointment by the board of commissioners representing the association of owners and tenants, the board, before filling the vacancy, shall request the association to submit the names of at least two persons to be considered for the vacancy, and the board shall fill the vacancy by appointing one of the persons so submitted.

(c)   Advisory Duties. - Each year, before adopting the budget for the district and levying the tax for the district, the board shall request recommendations from the advisory committee as to the type and level of services, facilities, or functions to be provided for the district for the ensuing years. The board of commissioners shall, to the extent permitted by law, expend the proceeds of any tax levied for the district in the manner recommended by the advisory committee. (2003-418, s. 1.)

§ 153A-317.14. Extension of economic development and training districts.

(a)   Standards. - A board of commissioners may by resolution annex territory to an economic development and training district upon finding that:

(1)   The conditions, covenants, restrictions, and reservations required by G.S. 153A-317.12(a)(1) that apply to all real property in the district, other than property owned by the federal, State, or local government, also apply or will apply to the property, other than property owned by the federal government, to be annexed.

(2)   One hundred percent (100%) of the owners of real property in the area to be annexed have petitioned for annexation.

(3)   The district, following the annexation, will continue to meet the standards set out in G.S. 153A-317.12(a).

(4)   The reasonably anticipated training needs of the existing companies in the area to be annexed and of new companies that may locate within the expanded area can be met by the skills training facility located in the district.

(5)   The area to be annexed is either contiguous to a lot, parcel, or tract of land in the district or at least 500 acres in the aggregate counting all parcels proposed for annexation. A property shall, for purposes of this section, be

deemed to be contiguous notwithstanding that it may be separated from other property by a street, road, highway, right-of-way, or easement.

(6) If any of the area proposed to be annexed to the district is wholly or partially within the extraterritorial jurisdiction of a municipality, then it shall be necessary to first obtain the affirmative vote of a majority of the members of the governing body of the municipality before the area can be annexed.

(b) Report. - Before the public hearing required by subsection (c) of this section, the board shall cause to be prepared a report containing all of the following:

(1) A map of the district and the territory proposed to be annexed showing the present and proposed boundaries of the district.

(2) A statement that the area to be annexed meets the standards and requirements of subsection (a) of this section.

The report shall be available for public inspection in the office of the clerk to the board for at least four weeks before the date of the public hearing.

(c) Hearing and Notice. - The board shall hold a public hearing before adopting any resolution extending the boundaries of a district. Notice of the hearing shall state the date, hour, and place of the hearing and its subject and shall include a statement that the report required by subsection (b) of this section is available for inspection in the office of the clerk to the board. The notice shall be published at least once not less than four weeks before the hearing. In addition, the notice shall be mailed at least four weeks before the date of the hearing by any class of U.S. mail which is fully prepaid to the owners as shown by the county tax records as of the preceding January 1 (and at the address shown thereon) of all property located within the area to be annexed. The person designated by the board to mail the notice shall certify to the board that the mailing has been completed, and the certificate shall be conclusive in the absence of fraud.

(d) Effective Date. - The resolution extending the boundaries of the district shall take effect at the beginning of the fiscal year commencing after its passage or such other date as shall be determined by the board. (2003-418, s. 1.)

§ 153A-317.15. Required provision or maintenance of skills training center.

(a) New District. - When a county creates a district, it shall provide, maintain, or let contracts for the skills training center for which the district is being taxed within a reasonable time, not to exceed one year, after the effective date of the creation of the district.

(b) Extended District. - When a territory is annexed to a district, the county shall provide, maintain, or let contracts for any necessary additions to the skills training center to provide the same training provided throughout the district to existing and new industries in the area annexed to the district within a reasonable time, not to exceed one year, after the effective date of the annexation. (2003-418, s. 1.)

§ 153A-317.16. Abolition of economic development and training districts.

A board of county commissioners may by resolution abolish a district upon finding that a petition requesting abolition, signed by at least fifty percent (50%) of the owners of real property in the district who own at least fifty percent (50%) of the real and personal property in the district based upon the most recent valuation thereof, has been submitted to the board and that there is no longer a need for such district. In determining the total real and personal property in the district and the number of owners of real and personal property, there shall be excluded: (i) property exempted from taxation and property classified and excluded from taxation and (ii) the owners of such exempted or classified and excluded property. The board shall hold a public hearing before adopting a resolution abolishing a district. Notice of the hearing shall state the date, hour, and place of the hearing and its subject and shall be published at least once not less than one week before the date of the hearing. The abolition of any district shall take effect at the end of a fiscal year following passage of the resolution, as determined by the board. (2003-418, s. 1.)

§ 153A-317.17. Taxes authorized; rate limitation.

A county may levy property taxes within an economic development and training district, in addition to those levied throughout the county, for the purposes listed in G.S. 153A-317.11 within the district in addition to or to a greater extent than the same purposes provided for the entire county. In addition, a county may allocate to a district any other revenues whose use is not otherwise restricted by law. The proceeds of taxes within a district may be expended only to pay annual debt service on up to one million two hundred thousand dollars ($1,200,000) of the capital costs of a skills training center provided for the district and any other services or facilities provided by a county in response to a recommendation of an advisory committee.

Property subject to taxation in a newly established district or in an area annexed to an existing district is subject to taxation by the county as of the preceding January 1.

Such additional property taxes may not be levied within any district established pursuant to this Article in excess of a rate of eight cents (8¢) on each one hundred dollars ($100.00) value of property subject to taxation. (2003-418, s. 1; 2004-170, s. 39.)

Article 17.

Reserved.

§ 153A-318. Reserved for future codification purposes.

§ 153A-319. Reserved for future codification purposes.

Article 18.

Planning and Regulation of Development.

Part 1. General Provisions.

§ 153A-320. Territorial jurisdiction.

Each of the powers granted to counties by this Article and by Article 19 of Chapter 160A of the General Statutes may be exercised throughout the county except as otherwise provided in G.S. 160A-360. (1959, c. 1006, s. 1; c. 1007; 1965, c. 194, s. 2; c. 195; 1969, c. 1066, s. 1; 1973, c. 822, s. 1; 2011-326, s. 9.)

§ 153A-321. Planning boards.

A county may by ordinance create or designate one or more boards or commissions to perform the following duties:

(1) Make studies of the county and surrounding areas;

(2) Determine objectives to be sought in the development of the study area;

(3) Prepare and adopt plans for achieving these objectives;

(4) Develop and recommend policies, ordinances, administrative procedures, and other means for carrying out plans in a coordinated and efficient manner;

(5) Advise the board of commissioners concerning the use and amendment of means for carrying out plans;

(6) Exercise any functions in the administration and enforcement of various means for carrying out plans that the board of commissioners may direct;

(7) Perform any other related duties that the board of commissioners may direct.

A board or commission created or designated pursuant to this section may include but shall not be limited to one or more of the following:

(1) A planning board or commission of any size (with not fewer than three members) or composition considered appropriate, organized in any manner considered appropriate;

(2) A joint planning board created by two or more local governments according to the procedures and provisions of Chapter 160A, Article 20, Part 1. (1945, c. 1040, s. 1; 1955, c. 1252; 1957, c. 947; 1959, c. 327, s. 1; c. 390; 1973, c. 822, s. 1; 1979, c. 611, s. 6; 1997-309, s. 5; 2004-199, s. 41(c).)

§ 153A-322. Supplemental powers.

(a) A county or its designated planning board may accept, receive, and disburse in furtherance of its functions funds, grants, and services made available by the federal government or its agencies, the State government or its agencies, any local government or its agencies, and private or civic sources. A county, or its designated planning board with the concurrence of the board of commissioners, may enter into and carry out contracts with the State or federal governments or any agencies of either under which financial or other planning assistance is made available to the county and may agree to and comply with any reasonable conditions that are imposed upon the assistance.

(b) A county, or its designated planning board with the concurrence of the board of commissioners, may enter into and carry out contracts with any other county, city, regional council, or planning agency under which it agrees to furnish technical planning assistance to the other local government or planning agency. A county, or its designated planning board with the concurrence of the board of commissioners, may enter into and carry out contracts with any other county, city, regional council, or planning agency under which it agrees to pay the other local government or planning board for technical planning assistance.

(c) A county may make any appropriations that may be necessary to carry out an activity or contract authorized by this Article, by Chapter 157A, or by Chapter 160A, Article 19 or to support, and compensate members of, any planning board that it may create or designate pursuant to this Article.

(d) A county may elect to combine any of the ordinances authorized by this Article into a unified ordinance. Unless expressly provided otherwise, a county may apply any of the definitions and procedures authorized by law to any or all aspects of the unified ordinance and may employ any organizational structure, board, commission, or staffing arrangement authorized by law to any or all aspects of the ordinance. (1945, c. 1040, s. 1; 1955, c. 1252; 1957, c. 947; 1959, c. 327, s. 1; c. 390; 1973, c. 822, s. 1; 1983, c. 377, s. 8; 2004-199, s. 41(d); 2005-418, s. 1(b).)

§ 153A-323. Procedure for adopting, amending, or repealing ordinances under this Article and Chapter 160A, Article 19.

(a) Before adopting, amending, or repealing any ordinance authorized by this Article or Chapter 160A, Article 19, the board of commissioners shall hold a public hearing on the ordinance or amendment. The board shall cause notice of the hearing to be published once a week for two successive calendar weeks. The notice shall be published the first time not less than 10 days nor more than 25 days before the date fixed for the hearing. In computing such period, the day of publication is not to be included but the day of the hearing shall be included.

(b) If the adoption or modification of the ordinance would result in any of the changes listed in this subsection and those changes would be located five miles or less from the perimeter boundary of a military base, the board of commissioners shall provide written notice of the proposed changes by certified mail, or by any other written means reasonably designed to provide actual notice, to the commander of the military base or the commander's designee not less than 10 days nor more than 25 days before the date fixed for the public hearing. Prior to the date of the public hearing, the military may provide comments or analysis to the board regarding the compatibility of the proposed changes with military operations at the base. If the board does not receive a response within 30 days of the notice, the military is deemed to waive the comment period. If the military provides comments or analysis regarding the compatibility of the proposed ordinance or amendment with military operations at the base, the board of commissioners shall take the comments and analysis into consideration before making a final determination on the ordinance. The proposed changes requiring notice are:

(1) Changes to the zoning map.

(2) Changes that affect the permitted uses of land.

(3) Changes relating to telecommunications towers or windmills.

(4) Changes to proposed new major subdivision preliminary plats.

(5) An increase in the size of an approved subdivision by more than fifty percent (50%) of the subdivision's total land area including developed and undeveloped land. (1959, c. 1006, s. 1; c. 1007; 1973, c. 822, s. 1; 1981, c. 891, ss. 2, 9; 2004-75, s. 1; 2005-426, s. 1(b); 2013-59, s. 1.)

§ 153A-324. Enforcement of ordinances.

(a) In addition to the enforcement provisions of this Article and subject to the provisions of the ordinance, any ordinance adopted pursuant to this Article, to Chapter 157A, or to Chapter 160A, Article 19 may be enforced by any remedy provided by G.S. 153A-123.

(b) If the county is found to have illegally exacted a tax, fee, or monetary contribution for development or a development permit not specifically authorized by law, the county shall return the tax, fee, or monetary contribution plus interest of six percent (6%) per annum. (1959, c. 1006, s. 1; 1961, c. 414; 1973, c. 822, s. 1; 2007-371, s. 1.)

§ 153A-325. Submission of statement concerning improvements.

A county may by ordinance require that when a property owner improves property at a cost of more than twenty-five hundred dollars ($2,500) but less than five thousand dollars ($5,000), the property owner must, within 14 days after the completion of the work, submit to the county assessor a statement setting forth the nature of the improvement and the total cost thereof. (1983, c. 614, s. 4; 1987, c. 45, s. 1.)

§ 153A-326. Building setback lines.

Counties shall have the same authority to regulate building setback lines as is provided for cities in G.S. 160A-306. (1987, c. 747, s. 15.)

§ 153A-327. Reserved for future codification purposes.

§ 153A-328. Reserved for future codification purposes.

§ 153A-329. Reserved for future codification purposes.

Part 2. Subdivision Regulation.

§ 153A-330. Subdivision regulation.

A county may by ordinance regulate the subdivision of land within its territorial jurisdiction. If a county, pursuant to G.S. 153A-342, has adopted a zoning ordinance that applies only to one or more designated portions of its territorial jurisdiction, it may adopt subdivision regulations that apply only within the areas so zoned and need not regulate the subdivision of land in the rest of its jurisdiction. In addition to final plat approval, the ordinance may include provisions for review and approval of sketch plans and preliminary plats. The ordinance may provide for different review procedures for differing classes of subdivisions. The ordinance may be adopted as part of a unified development ordinance or as a separate subdivision ordinance. Decisions on approval or denial of preliminary or final plats may be made only on the basis of standards explicitly set forth in the subdivision or unified development ordinance. Whenever the ordinance includes criteria for decision that require application of judgment, those criteria must provide adequate guiding standards for the entity charged with plat approval. (1959, c. 1007; 1965, c. 195; 1973, c. 822, s. 1; 2005-418, s. 2(b).)

§ 153A-331. Contents and requirements of ordinance.

(a) A subdivision control ordinance may provide for the orderly growth and development of the county; for the coordination of transportation networks and utilities within proposed subdivisions with existing or planned streets and highways and with other public facilities; for the dedication or reservation of recreation areas serving residents of the immediate neighborhood within the subdivision and of rights-of-way or easements for street and utility purposes including the dedication of rights-of-way pursuant to G.S. 136-66.10 or G.S. 136-66.11; and for the distribution of population and traffic in a manner that will avoid congestion and overcrowding and will create conditions that substantially promote public health, safety, and the general welfare.

(b) The ordinance may require that a plat be prepared, approved, and recorded pursuant to the provisions of the ordinance whenever any subdivision of land takes place. The ordinance may include requirements that the final plat show sufficient data to determine readily and reproduce accurately on the ground the location, bearing, and length of every street and alley line, lot line, easement boundary line, and other property boundaries, including the radius and other data for curved property lines, to an appropriate accuracy and in conformity with good surveying practice.

(c) A subdivision control ordinance may provide that a developer may provide funds to the county whereby the county may acquire recreational land or areas to serve the development or subdivision, including the purchase of land that may be used to serve more than one subdivision or development within the immediate area.

The ordinance may provide that in lieu of required street construction, a developer may provide funds to be used for the development of roads to serve the occupants, residents, or invitees of the subdivision or development. All funds received by the county under this section shall be transferred to the municipality to be used solely for the development of roads, including design, land acquisition, and construction. Any municipality receiving funds from a county under this section is authorized to expend such funds outside its corporate limits for the purposes specified in the agreement between the municipality and the county. Any formula adopted to determine the amount of funds the developer is to pay in lieu of required street construction shall be based on the trips generated from the subdivision or development. The ordinance may require a combination of partial payment of funds and partial dedication of constructed streets when the governing body of the county determines that a combination is in the best interest of the citizens of the area to be served.

The ordinance may provide for the more orderly development of subdivisions by requiring the construction of community service facilities in accordance with county plans, policies, and standards. To assure compliance with these and other ordinance requirements, the ordinance may provide for performance guarantees to assure successful completion of required improvements. If a performance guarantee is required, the county shall provide a range of options of types of performance guarantees, including, but not limited to, surety bonds or letters of credit, from which the developer may choose. For any specific development, the type of performance guarantee from the range specified by the county shall be at the election of the developer.

The ordinance may provide for the reservation of school sites in accordance with comprehensive land use plans approved by the board of commissioners or the planning board. For the authorization to reserve school sites to be effective, the board of commissioners or planning board, before approving a comprehensive land use plan, shall determine jointly with the board of education with jurisdiction over the area the specific location and size of each school site to be reserved, and this information shall appear in the plan. Whenever a subdivision that includes part or all of a school site to be reserved under the plan is submitted for approval, the board of commissioners or the planning board shall immediately notify the board of education. The board of education shall promptly decide whether it still wishes the site to be reserved and shall notify the board of commissioners or planning board of its decision. If the board of education does not wish the site to be reserved, no site may be reserved. If the board of education does wish the site to be reserved, the subdivision may not be approved without the reservation. The board of education must acquire the site within 18 months after the date the site is reserved, either by purchase or by exercise of the power of eminent domain. If the board of education has not purchased the site or begun proceedings to condemn the site within the 18 months, the subdivider may treat the land as freed of the reservation. (1959, c. 1007; 1973, c. 822, s. 1; 1975, c. 231; 1987, c. 747, ss. 10, 17; 2005-426, s. 2(b).)

§ 153A-332. Ordinance to contain procedure for plat approval; approval prerequisite to plat recordation; statement by owner.

A subdivision ordinance adopted pursuant to this Part shall contain provisions setting forth the procedures to be followed in granting or denying approval of a subdivision plat before its registration.

The ordinance shall provide that the following agencies be given an opportunity to make recommendations concerning an individual subdivision plat before the plat is approved:

(1)   The district highway engineer as to proposed State streets, State highways, and related drainage systems;

(2)   The county health director or local public utility, as appropriate, as to proposed water or sewerage systems;

(3)   Any other agency or official designated by the board of commissioners.

The ordinance may provide that final decisions on preliminary plats and final plats are to be made by:

(1)   The board of commissioners,

(2)   The board of commissioners on recommendation of a designated body, or

(3)   A designated planning board, technical review committee, or other designated body or staff person.

From the effective date of a subdivision ordinance that is adopted by the county, no subdivision plat of land within the county's jurisdiction may be filed or recorded until it has been submitted to and approved by the appropriate board or agency, as specified in the subdivision ordinance, and until this approval is entered in writing on the face of the plat by an authorized representative of the county. The Review Officer, pursuant to G.S. 47-30.2, shall not certify a plat of a subdivision of land located within the territorial jurisdiction of the county that has not been approved in accordance with these provisions, and the clerk of superior court may not order or direct the recording of a plat if the recording would be in conflict with this section. (1959, c. 1007; 1973, c. 822, s. 1; 1997-309, s. 6; 2005-418, s. 3(b).)

§ 153A-333. Effect of plat approval on dedications.

The approval of a plat does not constitute or effect the acceptance by the county or the public of the dedication of any street or other ground, public utility line, or other public facility shown on the plat and shall not be construed to do so. (1959, c. 1007; 1973, c. 822, s. 1.)

§ 153A-334. Penalties for transferring lots in unapproved subdivisions.

(a)   If a person who is the owner or the agent of the owner of any land located within the territorial jurisdiction of a county that has adopted a subdivision regulation ordinance subdivides his land in violation of the ordinance or transfers or sells land by reference to, exhibition of, or any other use of a plat showing a subdivision of the land before the plat has been properly approved under the ordinance and recorded in the office of the appropriate register of deeds, he is guilty of a Class 1 misdemeanor. The description by metes and bounds in the instrument of transfer or other document used in the process of selling or transferring land does not exempt the transaction from this penalty. The county may bring an action for injunction of any illegal subdivision, transfer, conveyance, or sale of land, and the court shall, upon appropriate findings, issue an injunction and order requiring the offending party to comply with the subdivision ordinance. Building permits required pursuant to G.S. 153A-357 may be denied for lots that have been illegally subdivided. In addition to other remedies, a county may institute any appropriate action or proceedings to prevent the unlawful subdivision of land, to restrain, correct, or abate the violation, or to prevent any illegal act or conduct.

(b) The provisions of this section shall not prohibit any owner or its agent from entering into contracts to sell or lease by reference to an approved preliminary plat for which a final plat has not yet been properly approved under the subdivision ordinance or recorded with the register of deeds, provided the contract does all of the following:

(1) Incorporates as an attachment a copy of the preliminary plat referenced in the contract and obligates the owner to deliver to the buyer a copy of the recorded plat prior to closing and conveyance.

(2) Plainly and conspicuously notifies the prospective buyer or lessee that a final subdivision plat has not been approved or recorded at the time of the contract, that no governmental body will incur any obligation to the prospective buyer or lessee with respect to the approval of the final subdivision plat, that changes between the preliminary and final plats are possible, and that the contract or lease may be terminated without breach by the buyer or lessee if the final recorded plat differs in any material respect from the preliminary plat.

(3) Provides that if the approved and recorded final plat does not differ in any material respect from the plat referred to in the contract, the buyer or lessee may not be required by the seller or lessor to close any earlier than five days after the delivery of a copy of the final recorded plat.

(4) Provides that if the approved and recorded final plat differs in any material respect from the preliminary plat referred to in the contract, the buyer or lessee may not be required by the seller or lessor to close any earlier than 15 days after the delivery of the final recorded plat, during which 15-day period the buyer or lessee may terminate the contract without breach or any further obligation and may receive a refund of all earnest money or prepaid purchase price.

(c) The provisions of this section shall not prohibit any owner or its agent from entering into contracts to sell or lease land by reference to an approved preliminary plat for which a final plat has not been properly approved under the subdivision ordinance or recorded with the register of deeds where the buyer or lessee is any person who has contracted to acquire or lease the land for the purpose of engaging in the business of construction of residential, commercial, or industrial buildings on the land, or for the purpose of resale or lease of the land to persons engaged in that kind of business, provided that no conveyance of that land may occur and no contract to lease it may become effective until after the final plat has been properly approved under the subdivision ordinance and recorded with the register of deeds. (1959, c. 1007; 1973, c. 822, s. 1; 1977, c. 820, s. 1; 1993, c. 539, s. 1063; 1994, Ex. Sess., c. 24, s. 14(c); 2005-426, s. 3(b).)

§ 153A-335. "Subdivision" defined.

(a) For purposes of this Part, "subdivision" means all divisions of a tract or parcel of land into two or more lots, building sites, or other divisions when any one or more of those divisions are created for the purpose of sale or building development (whether immediate or future) and includes all division of land involving the dedication of a new street or a change in existing streets; however, the following is not included within this definition and is not subject to any regulations enacted pursuant to this Part:

(1) The combination or recombination of portions of previously subdivided and recorded lots if the total number of lots is not increased and the resultant lots are equal to or exceed the standards of the county as shown in its subdivision regulations.

(2) The division of land into parcels greater than 10 acres if no street right-of-way dedication is involved.

(3) The public acquisition by purchase of strips of land for widening or opening streets or for public transportation system corridors.

(4) The division of a tract in single ownership the entire area of which is no greater than two acres into not more than three lots, if no street right-of-way dedication is involved and if the resultant lots are equal to or exceed the standards of the county as shown by its subdivision regulations.

(b) A county may provide for expedited review of specified classes of subdivisions. (1959, c. 1007; 1973, c. 822, s. 1; 1979, c. 611, s. 2; 2003-284, s. 29.23(b); 2005-426, s. 4(b).)

§ 153A-336. Appeals of decisions on subdivision plats.

(a) When a subdivision ordinance adopted under this Part provides that the decision whether to approve or deny a preliminary or final subdivision plat is to be made by a board of commissioners or a planning board, other than a planning board comprised solely of members of a county planning staff, and the ordinance authorizes the board of commissioners or planning board to make a quasi-judicial decision in deciding whether to approve the subdivision plat, then that quasi-judicial decision of the board of commissioners or planning board shall be subject to review by the superior court by proceedings in the nature of certiorari. The provisions of G.S. 153A-340(f), 160A-388(e2)(2), and 153A-349 shall apply to those appeals.

(b) When a subdivision ordinance adopted under this Part provides that a board of commissioners, planning board, or staff member is authorized to make only an administrative or ministerial decision in deciding whether to approve a preliminary or final subdivision plat, then any party aggrieved by that administrative or ministerial decision may seek to have the decision reviewed by filing an action in superior court seeking appropriate declaratory or equitable relief. Such an action must be filed within the time frame specified in G.S. 153A-340(f) for petitions in the nature of certiorari.

(c) For purposes of this section, an ordinance shall be deemed to authorize a quasi-judicial decision if the board of commissioners or planning board is authorized to decide whether to approve or deny the plat based not only upon whether the application complies with the specific requirements set forth in the ordinance, but also on whether the application complies with one or more generally stated standards requiring a discretionary decision to be made by the board of commissioners or planning board. (2009-421, s. 2(b); 2013-126, s. 7.)

§ 153A-337. Reserved for future codification purposes.

§ 153A-338. Reserved for future codification purposes.

§ 153A-339. Reserved for future codification purposes.

Part 3. Zoning.

§ 153A-340. Grant of power.

(a)   For the purpose of promoting health, safety, morals, or the general welfare, a county may adopt zoning and development regulation ordinances. These ordinances may be adopted as part of a unified development ordinance or as a separate ordinance. A zoning ordinance may regulate and restrict the height, number of stories and size of buildings and other structures, the percentage of lots that may be occupied, the size of yards, courts and other open spaces, the density of population, and the location and use of buildings, structures, and land for trade, industry, residence, or other purposes. The ordinance may provide density credits or severable development rights for dedicated rights-of-way pursuant to G.S. 136-66.10 or G.S. 136-66.11.

(b)   (1)   These regulations may affect property used for bona fide farm purposes only as provided in subdivision (3) of this subsection. This subsection does not limit regulation under this Part with respect to the use of farm property for nonfarm purposes.

(2)   Except as provided in G.S. 106-743.4 for farms that are subject to a conservation agreement under G.S. 106-743.2, bona fide farm purposes include the production and activities relating or incidental to the production of crops, grains, fruits, vegetables, ornamental and flowering plants, dairy, livestock, poultry, and all other forms of agriculture, as defined in G.S. 106-581.1. For purposes of this subdivision, "when performed on the farm" in G.S. 106-581.1(6) shall include the farm within the jurisdiction of the county and any other farm owned or leased to or from others by the bona fide farm operator, no matter where located. For purposes of this subdivision, the production of a nonfarm product that the Department of Agriculture and Consumer Services recognizes as a "Goodness Grows in North Carolina" product that is produced on a farm subject to a conservation agreement under G.S. 106-743.2 is a bona fide farm purpose. For purposes of determining whether a property is being used for bona fide farm purposes, any of the following shall constitute sufficient evidence that the property is being used for bona fide farm purposes:

a.   A farm sales tax exemption certificate issued by the Department of Revenue.

b.   A copy of the property tax listing showing that the property is eligible for participation in the present use value program pursuant to G.S. 105-277.3.

c.   A copy of the farm owner's or operator's Schedule F from the owner's or operator's most recent federal income tax return.

d. A forest management plan.

e. A Farm Identification Number issued by the United States Department of Agriculture Farm Service Agency.

(3) The definitions set out in G.S. 106-802 apply to this subdivision. A county may adopt zoning regulations governing swine farms served by animal waste management systems having a design capacity of 600,000 pounds steady state live weight (SSLW) or greater provided that the zoning regulations may not have the effect of excluding swine farms served by an animal waste management system having a design capacity of 600,000 pounds SSLW or greater from the entire zoning jurisdiction.

(c) The regulations may provide that a board of adjustment may determine and vary their application in harmony with their general purpose and intent and in accordance with general or specific rules therein contained, provided no change in permitted uses may be authorized by variance.

(c1) The regulations may also provide that the board of adjustment, the planning board, or the board of commissioners may issue special use permits or conditional use permits in the classes of cases or situations and in accordance with the principles, conditions, safeguards, and procedures specified therein and may impose reasonable and appropriate conditions and safeguards upon these permits. Where appropriate, the conditions may include requirements that street and utility rights-of-way be dedicated to the public and that recreational space be provided. When deciding special use permits or conditional use permits, the board of county commissioners or planning board shall follow quasi-judicial procedures. Notice of hearings on special or conditional use permit applications shall be as provided in G.S. 160A-388(a2). No vote greater than a majority vote shall be required for the board of county commissioners or planning board to issue such permits. For the purposes of this section, vacant positions on the board and members who are disqualified from voting on a quasi-judicial matter shall not be considered "members of the board" for calculation of the requisite majority. Every such decision of the board of county commissioners or planning board shall be subject to review of the superior court in the nature of certiorari consistent with G.S. 160A-388.

(d) A county may regulate the development over estuarine waters and over lands covered by navigable waters owned by the State pursuant to G.S. 146-12, within the bounds of that county.

(e) For the purpose of this section, the term "structures" shall include floating homes.

(f) Repealed by Session Laws 2005-426, s. 5(b), effective January 1, 2006.

(g) A member of the board of county commissioners shall not vote on any zoning map or text amendment where the outcome of the matter being considered is reasonably likely to have a direct, substantial, and readily identifiable financial impact on the member. Members of appointed boards providing advice to the board of county commissioners shall not vote on recommendations regarding any zoning map or text amendment where the outcome of the matter being considered is reasonably likely to have a direct, substantial, and readily identifiable financial impact on the member.

(h) As provided in this subsection, counties may adopt temporary moratoria on any county development approval required by law. county development approval required by law, except for the purpose of developing and adopting new or amended plans or ordinances as to residential uses. The duration of any moratorium shall be reasonable in light of the specific conditions that warrant imposition of the moratorium and may not exceed the period of time necessary to correct, modify, or resolve such conditions. Except in cases of imminent and substantial threat to public health or safety, before adopting an ordinance imposing a development moratorium with a duration of 60 days or any shorter period, the board of commissioners shall hold a public hearing and shall publish a notice of the hearing in a newspaper having general circulation in the area not less than seven days before the date set for the hearing. A development moratorium with a duration of 61 days or longer, and any extension of a moratorium so that the total duration is 61 days or longer, is subject to the notice and hearing requirements of G.S. 153A-323. Absent an imminent threat to public health or safety, a development moratorium adopted pursuant to this section shall not apply to any project for which a valid building permit issued pursuant to G.S. 153A-357 is outstanding, to any project for which a conditional use permit application or special use permit application has been accepted, to development set forth in a site-specific or phased development plan approved pursuant to G.S. 153A-344.1, to development for which substantial expenditures have already been made in good faith reliance on a prior valid administrative or quasi-judicial permit or approval, or to preliminary or final subdivision plats that have been accepted for review by the county prior to the call for public hearing to adopt the moratorium. Any preliminary subdivision plat accepted for review by the county prior to the call for public hearing, if subsequently approved, shall be allowed to proceed to final plat approval without being subject to the moratorium.

Any ordinance establishing a development moratorium must expressly include at the time of adoption each of the following:

(1)   A clear statement of the problems or conditions necessitating the moratorium and what courses of action, alternative to a moratorium, were considered by the county and why those alternative courses of action were not deemed adequate.

(2)   A clear statement of the development approvals subject to the moratorium and how a moratorium on those approvals will address the problems or conditions leading to imposition of the moratorium.

(3)   An express date for termination of the moratorium and a statement setting forth why that duration is reasonably necessary to address the problems or conditions leading to imposition of the moratorium.

(4)   A clear statement of the actions, and the schedule for those actions, proposed to be taken by the county during the duration of the moratorium to address the problems or conditions leading to imposition of the moratorium.

No moratorium may be subsequently renewed or extended for any additional period unless the city shall have taken all reasonable and feasible steps proposed to be taken by the county in its ordinance establishing the moratorium to address the problems or conditions leading to imposition of the moratorium and unless new facts and conditions warrant an extension. Any ordinance renewing or extending a development moratorium must expressly include, at the time of adoption, the findings set forth in subdivisions (1) through (4) of this subsection, including what new facts or conditions warrant the extension.

Any person aggrieved by the imposition of a moratorium on development approvals required by law may apply to the appropriate division of the General Court of Justice for an order enjoining the enforcement of the moratorium, and the court shall have jurisdiction to issue that order. Actions brought pursuant to this section shall be set down for immediate hearing, and subsequent proceedings in those actions shall be accorded priority by the trial and appellate courts. In any such action, the county shall have the burden of showing compliance with the procedural requirements of this subsection.

(i) In order to encourage construction that uses sustainable design principles and to improve energy efficiency in buildings, a county may charge reduced building permit fees or provide partial rebates of building permit fees for buildings that are constructed or renovated using design principles that conform to or exceed one or more of the following certifications or ratings:

(1) Leadership in Energy and Environmental Design (LEED) certification or higher rating under certification standards adopted by the U.S. Green Building Council.

(2) A One Globe or higher rating under the Green Globes program standards adopted by the Green Building Initiative.

(3) A certification or rating by another nationally recognized certification or rating system that is equivalent or greater than those listed in subdivisions (1) and (2) of this subsection.

(j) An ordinance adopted pursuant to this section shall not prohibit single-family detached residential uses constructed in accordance with the North Carolina State Building Code on lots greater than 10 acres in size in zoning districts where more than fifty percent (50%) of the land is in use for agricultural or silvicultural purposes, except that this restriction shall not apply to commercial or industrial districts where a broad variety of commercial or industrial uses are permissible. An ordinance adopted pursuant to this section shall not require that a lot greater than 10 acres in size have frontage on a public road or county-approved private road, or be served by public water or sewer lines, in order to be developed for single-family residential purposes.

(k) A zoning or unified development ordinance may not differentiate in terms of the regulations applicable to fraternities or sororities between those fraternities or sororities that are approved or recognized by a college or university and those that are not. (1959, c. 1006, s. 1; 1967, c. 1208, s. 4; 1973, c. 822, s. 1; 1981, c. 891, s. 6; 1983, c. 441; 1985, c. 442, s. 2; 1987, c. 747, s. 12; 1991, c. 69, s. 1; 1997-458, s. 2.1; 2005-390, s. 6; 2005-426, s. 5(b); 2006-259, s. 26(a); 2007-381, s. 1; 2011-286, s. 1; 2011-363, s. 1; 2011-384, s. 5; 2013-126, ss. 5, 8; 2013-347, s. 1; 2013-413, s. 6(a).)

§ 153A-341. Purposes in view.

Zoning regulations shall be made in accordance with a comprehensive plan. Prior to adopting or rejecting any zoning amendment, the governing board shall adopt a statement describing whether its action is consistent with an adopted comprehensive plan and explaining why the board considers the action taken to be reasonable and in the public interest. That statement is not subject to judicial review.

The planning board shall advise and comment on whether the proposed amendment is consistent with any comprehensive plan that has been adopted and any other officially adopted plan that is applicable. The planning board shall provide a written recommendation to the board of county commissioners that addresses plan consistency and other matters as deemed appropriate by the planning board, but a comment by the planning board that a proposed amendment is inconsistent with the comprehensive plan shall not preclude consideration or approval of the proposed amendment by the governing board.

Zoning regulations shall be designed to promote the public health, safety, and general welfare. To that end, the regulations may address, among other things, the following public purposes: to provide adequate light and air; to prevent the overcrowding of land; to avoid undue concentration of population; to lessen congestion in the streets; to secure safety from fire, panic, and dangers; and to facilitate the efficient and adequate provision of transportation, water, sewerage, schools, parks, and other public requirements. The regulations shall be made with reasonable consideration as to, among other things, the character of the district and its peculiar suitability for particular uses, and with a view to conserving the value of buildings and encouraging the most appropriate use of land throughout the county. In addition, the regulations shall be made with reasonable consideration to expansion and development of any cities within the county, so as to provide for their orderly growth and development. (1959, c. 1006, s. 1; 1973, c. 822, s. 1; 2005-426, s. 7(b).)

§ 153A-341.1. Zoning regulations for manufactured homes.

The provisions of G.S. 160A-383.1 shall apply to counties. (1987, c. 805, s. 2.)

§ 153A-341.2. Reasonable accommodation of amateur radio antennas.

A county ordinance based on health, safety, or aesthetic considerations that regulates the placement, screening, or height of the antennas or support structures of amateur radio operators must reasonably accommodate amateur radio communications and must represent the minimum practicable regulation necessary to accomplish the purpose of the county. A county may not restrict antennas or antenna support structures of amateur radio operators to heights of 90 feet or lower unless the restriction is necessary to achieve a clearly defined health, safety, or aesthetic objective of the county. (2007-147, s. 2.)

§ 153A-342. Districts; zoning less than entire jurisdiction.

(a) A county may divide its territorial jurisdiction into districts of any number, shape, and area that it may consider best suited to carry out the purposes of this Part. Within these districts a county may regulate and restrict the erection, construction, reconstruction, alteration, repair, or use of buildings, structures, or land. Such districts may include, but shall not be limited to, general use districts, in which a variety of uses are permissible in accordance with general standards; overlay districts, in which additional requirements are imposed on certain properties within one or more underlying general or special use districts; special use districts or conditional use districts, in which uses are permitted only upon the issuance of a special use permit or a conditional use permit and conditional zoning districts, in which site plans and individualized development conditions are imposed.

(b) Property may be placed in a special use district, conditional use district, or conditional district only in response to a petition by the owners of all the property to be included. Specific conditions applicable to the districts may be proposed by the petitioner or the county or its agencies, but only those conditions mutually approved by the county and the petitioner may be incorporated into the zoning regulations or permit requirements. Conditions and site-specific standards imposed in a conditional district shall be limited to those that address the conformance of the development and use of the site to county ordinances and an officially adopted comprehensive or other plan and those that address the impacts reasonably expected to be generated by the development or use of the site.

A statement analyzing the reasonableness of the proposed rezoning shall be prepared for each petition for a rezoning to a special or conditional use district, or a conditional district, or other small-scale rezoning.

(c) Except as authorized by the foregoing, all regulations shall be uniform for each class or kind of building throughout each district, but the regulations in one district may differ from those in other districts.

(d) A county may determine that the public interest does not require that the entire territorial jurisdiction of the county be zoned and may designate one or more portions of that jurisdiction as a zoning area or areas. A zoning area must originally contain at least 640 acres and at least 10 separate tracts of land in separate ownership and may thereafter be expanded by the addition of any amount of territory. A zoning area may be regulated in the same manner as if the entire county were zoned, and the remainder of the county need not be regulated. (1959, c. 1006, s. 1; 1965, c. 194, s. 2; 1973, c. 822, s. 1; 1985, c. 607, s. 3; 2005-426, s. 6(b).)

§ 153A-343. Method of procedure.

(a) The board of commissioners shall, in accordance with the provisions of this Article, provide for the manner in which zoning regulations and restrictions and the boundaries of zoning districts shall be determined, established, and enforced, and from time to time amended, supplemented, or changed. The procedures adopted pursuant to this section shall provide that whenever there is a zoning map amendment, the owner of that parcel of land as shown on the county tax listing, and the owners of all parcels of land abutting that parcel of land as shown on the county tax listing, shall be mailed a notice of a public hearing on the proposed amendment by first class mail at the last addresses listed for such owners on the county tax abstracts. This notice must be deposited in the mail at least 10 but not more than 25 days prior to the date of the public hearing. Except for a county-initiated zoning map amendment, when an application is filed to request a zoning map amendment and that application is not made by the owner of the parcel of land to which the amendment would apply, the applicant shall certify to the board of commissioners that the owner of the parcel of land as shown on the county tax listing has received actual notice of the proposed amendment and a copy of the notice of public hearing. The person or persons required to provide notice shall certify to the board of commissioners that proper notice has been provided in fact, and such certificate shall be deemed conclusive in the absence of fraud.

(b) The first class mail notice required under subsection (a) of this section shall not be required if the zoning map amendment directly affects more than 50 properties, owned by a total of at least 50 different property owners, and the county elects to use the expanded published notice provided for in this subsection. In this instance, a county may elect to either make the mailed notice provided for in subsection (a) of this section or may as an alternative elect to publish notice of the hearings required by G.S. 153A-323, but provided that each of the advertisements shall not be less than one-half of a newspaper page in size. The advertisement shall only be effective for property owners who reside in the area of general circulation of the newspaper which publishes the notice. Property owners who reside outside of the newspaper circulation area, according to the address listed on the most recent property tax listing for the affected property, shall be notified according to the provisions of subsection (a) of this section.

(b1) Actual notice of the proposed amendment and a copy of the notice of public hearing required under subsection (a) of this section shall be by any manner permitted under G.S. 1A-1, Rule 4(j). If notice cannot with due diligence be achieved by personal delivery, registered or certified mail, or by a designated delivery service authorized pursuant to 26 U.S.C. § 7502(f)(2), notice may be given by publication consistent with G.S. 1A-1, Rule 4(j1). This subsection applies only to an application to request a zoning map amendment where the application is not made by the owner of the parcel of land to which the amendment would apply. This subsection does not apply to a county-initiated zoning map amendment.

(c) Repealed by Session Laws 2005-418, s. 4, effective January 1, 2006.

(d) When a zoning map amendment is proposed, the county shall prominently post a notice of the public hearing on the site proposed for rezoning or on an adjacent public street or highway right-of-way. When multiple parcels are included within a proposed zoning map amendment, a posting on each individual parcel is not required, but the county shall post sufficient notices to provide reasonable notice to interested persons. (1973, c. 822, s. 1; 1985, c. 595, s. 1; 1987, c. 807, s. 2; 1989 (Reg. Sess., 1990), c. 980, s. 2; 1993, c. 469, s. 2; 1995, c. 261, s. 1; c. 546, s. 2; 1997-456, s. 25; 2005-418, s. 4(b); 2009-178, s. 1.)

§ 153A-344. Planning board; zoning plan; certification to board of commissioners.

(a) To initially exercise the powers conferred by this Part, a county shall create or designate a planning board under the provisions of this Article or of a local act. The planning board shall prepare or shall review and comment upon a proposed zoning ordinance, including both the full text of such ordinance and maps showing proposed district boundaries. The planning board may hold public hearings in the course of preparing the ordinance. Upon completion, the planning board shall make a written recommendation regarding adoption of the ordinance to the board of commissioners. The board of commissioners shall not hold the public hearing required by G.S. 153A-323 or take action until it has received a recommendation regarding the ordinance from the planning board. Following its required public hearing, the board of commissioners may refer the ordinance back to the planning board for any further recommendations that the board may wish to make prior to final action by the board in adopting, modifying and adopting, or rejecting the ordinance.

Subsequent to initial adoption of a zoning ordinance, all proposed amendments to the zoning ordinance or zoning map shall be submitted to the planning board for review and comment. If no written report is received from the planning board within 30 days of referral of the amendment to that board, the board of county commissioners may proceed in its consideration of the amendment without the planning board report. The board of commissioners is not bound by the recommendations, if any, of the planning board.

(b) Amendments in zoning ordinances shall not be applicable or enforceable without consent of the owner with regard to buildings and uses for which either (i) building permits have been issued pursuant to G.S. 153A-357 prior to the enactment of the ordinance making the change or changes so long as the permits remain valid and unexpired pursuant to G.S. 153A-358 and unrevoked pursuant to G.S. 153A-362 or (ii) a vested right has been established pursuant to G.S. 153A-344.1 and such vested right remains valid and unexpired pursuant to G.S. 153A-344.1. (1959, c. 1006, s. 1; 1965, c. 194, s. 3; 1973, c. 822, s. 1; 1979, c. 611, s. 3; 1985, c. 540, s. 1; 1989 (Reg. Sess., 1990), c. 996, s. 5; 2005-418, s. 7(b).)

§ 153A-344.1. Vesting rights.

(a) The General Assembly finds and declares that it is necessary and desirable, as a matter of public policy, to provide for the establishment of certain vested rights in order to ensure reasonable certainty, stability, and fairness in the land-use planning process, secure the reasonable expectations of landowners, and foster cooperation between the public and private sectors in the area of land-use planning. Furthermore, the General Assembly recognizes that county approval of land-use development typically follows significant landowner investment in site evaluation, planning, development costs, consultant fees, and related expenses.

The ability of a landowner to obtain a vested right after county approval of a site specific development plan or a phased development plan will preserve the prerogatives and authority of local elected officials with respect to land-use matters. There will be ample opportunities for public participation and the public interest will be served. These provisions will strike an appropriate balance between private expectations and the public interest, while scrupulously protecting the public health, safety, and welfare.

(b) Definitions.

(1) "Landowner" means any owner of a legal or equitable interest in real property, including the heirs, devisees, successors, assigns, and personal representative of such owner. The landowner may allow a person holding a valid option to purchase to act as his agent or representative for purposes of submitting a proposed site specific development plan or a phased development plan under this section, in the manner allowed by ordinance.

(2) "County" shall have the same meaning as set forth in G.S. 153A-1(3).

(3) "Phased development plan" means a plan which has been submitted to a county by a landowner for phased development which shows the type and intensity of use for a specific parcel or parcels with a lesser degree of certainty than the plan determined by the county to be a site specific development plan.

(4) "Property" means all real property subject to zoning regulations and restrictions and zone boundaries by a county.

(5) "Site specific development plan" means a plan which has been submitted to a county by a landowner describing with reasonable certainty the type and intensity of use for a specific parcel or parcels of property. Such plan may be in the form of, but not be limited to, any of the following plans or approvals: A planned unit development plan, a subdivision plat, a preliminary or general development plan, a conditional or special use permit, a conditional or special use district zoning plan, or any other land-use approval designation as

may be utilized by a county. Unless otherwise expressly provided by the county such a plan shall include the approximate boundaries of the site; significant topographical and other natural features effecting development of the site; the approximate location on the site of the proposed buildings, structures, and other improvements; the approximate dimensions, including height, of the proposed buildings and other structures; and the approximate location of all existing and proposed infrastructure on the site, including water, sewer, roads, and pedestrian walkways. What constitutes a site specific development plan under this section that would trigger a vested right shall be finally determined by the county pursuant to an ordinance, and the document that triggers such vesting shall be so identified at the time of its approval. However, at a minimum, the ordinance to be adopted by the county shall designate a vesting point earlier than the issuance of a building permit. A variance shall not constitute a site specific development plan, and approval of a site specific development plan with the condition that a variance be obtained shall not confer a vested right unless and until the necessary variance is obtained. Neither a sketch plan nor any other document which fails to describe with reasonable certainty the type and intensity of use for a specified parcel or parcels or property may constitute a site specific development plan.

(6) "Vested right" means the right to undertake and complete the development and use of property under the terms and conditions of an approved site specific development plan or an approved phased development plan.

(c) Establishment of vested right.

A vested right shall be deemed established with respect to any property upon the valid approval, or conditional approval, of a site specific development plan or a phased development plan, following notice and public hearing by the county with jurisdiction over the property. Such vested right shall confer upon the landowner the right to undertake and complete the development and use of said property under the terms and conditions of the site specific development plan or the phased development plan including any amendments thereto. A county may approve a site specific development plan or a phased development plan upon such terms and conditions as may reasonably be necessary to protect the public health, safety, and welfare. Such conditional approval shall result in a vested right, although failure to abide by such terms and conditions will result in a forfeiture of vested rights. A county shall not require a landowner to waive his vested rights as a condition of developmental approval. A site specific development plan or a phased development plan shall be deemed approved upon the effective date of the county's action or ordinance relating thereto.

(d) Duration and termination of vested right.

(1) A right which has been vested as provided for in this section shall remain vested for a period of two years. This vesting shall not be extended by any amendments or modifications to a site specific development plan unless expressly provided by the county.

(2) Notwithstanding the provisions of subsection (d)(1), a county may provide that rights shall be vested for a period exceeding two years but not exceeding five years where warranted in light of all relevant circumstances, including, but not limited to, the size and phasing of development, the level of investment, the need for the development, economic cycles, and market conditions. These determinations shall be in the sound discretion of the county.

(3) Notwithstanding the provisions of (d)(1) and (d)(2), the county may provide by ordinance that approval by a county of a phased development plan shall vest the zoning classification or classifications so approved for a period not to exceed five years. The document that triggers such vesting shall be so identified at the time of its approval. The county still may require the landowner to submit a site specific development plan for approval by the county with respect to each phase or phases in order to obtain final approval to develop within the restrictions of the vested zoning classification or classifications. Nothing in this section shall be construed to require a county to adopt an ordinance providing for vesting of rights upon approval of a phased development plan.

(4) Following approval or conditional approval of a site specific development plan or a phased development plan, nothing in this section shall exempt such a plan from subsequent reviews and approvals by the county to ensure compliance with the terms and conditions of the original approval, provided that such reviews and approvals are not inconsistent with said original approval. Nothing in this section shall prohibit the county from revoking the original approval for failure to comply with applicable terms and conditions of the approval or the zoning ordinance.

(5) Upon issuance of a building permit, the provisions of G.S. 153A-358 and G.S. 153A-362 shall apply, except that a permit shall not expire or be revoked

because of the running of time while a vested right under this section is outstanding.

(6) A right which has been vested as provided in this section shall terminate at the end of the applicable vesting period with respect to buildings and uses for which no valid building permit applications have been filed.

(e) Subsequent changes prohibited; exceptions.

(1) A vested right, once established as provided for in this section, precludes any zoning action by a county which would change, alter, impair, prevent, diminish, or otherwise delay the development or use of the property as set forth in an approved site specific development plan or an approved phased development plan, except:

a. With the written consent of the affected landowner;

b. Upon findings, by ordinance after notice and a public hearing, that natural or man-made hazards on or in the immediate vicinity of the property, if uncorrected, would pose a serious threat to the public health, safety, and welfare if the project were to proceed as contemplated in the site specific development plan or the phased development plan;

c. To the extent that the affected landowner receives compensation for all costs, expenses, and other losses incurred by the landowner, including, but not limited to, all fees paid in consideration of financing, and all architectural, planning, marketing, legal, and other consultant's fees incurred after approval by the county, together with interest thereon at the legal rate until paid. Compensation shall not include any diminution in the value of the property which is caused by such action;

d. Upon findings, by ordinance after notice and a hearing, that the landowner or his representative intentionally supplied inaccurate information or made material misrepresentations which made a difference in the approval by the county of the site specific development plan or the phased development plan; or

e. Upon the enactment or promulgation of a State or federal law or regulation which precludes development as contemplated in the site specific development plan or the phased development plan, in which case the county may modify the affected provisions, upon a finding that the change in State or federal law has a fundamental effect on the plan, by ordinance after notice and a hearing.

(2)   The establishment of a vested right shall not preclude the application of overlay zoning which imposes additional requirements but does not affect the allowable type or intensity of use, or ordinances or regulations which are general in nature and are applicable to all property subject to land-use regulation by a county, including, but not limited to, building, fire, plumbing, electrical, and mechanical codes. Otherwise applicable new regulations shall become effective with respect to property which is subject to a site specific development plan or a phased development plan upon the expiration or termination of the vesting rights period provided for in this section.

(3)   Notwithstanding any provision of this section, the establishment of a vested right shall not preclude, change or impair the authority of a county to adopt and enforce zoning ordinance provisions governing nonconforming situations or uses.

(f)   Miscellaneous provisions.

(1)   A vested right obtained under this section is not a personal right, but shall attach to and run with the applicable property. After approval of a site specific development plan or a phased development plan, all successors to the original landowner shall be entitled to exercise such rights.

(2)   Nothing in this section shall preclude judicial determination, based on common-law principles or other statutory provisions, that a vested right exists in a particular case or that a compensable taking has occurred. Except as expressly provided in this section, nothing in this section shall be construed to alter the existing common law.

(3)   In the event a county fails to adopt an ordinance setting forth what constitutes a site specific development plan triggering a vested right, a landowner may establish a vested right with respect to property upon the approval of a zoning permit, or otherwise may seek appropriate relief from the Superior Court Division of the General Court of Justice. (1989 (Reg. Sess., 1990), c. 996, s. 6.)

§ 153A-345: Repealed by Session Laws 2013-126, s. 3(a), effective October 1, 2013, and applicable to actions taken on or after that date by any board of adjustment.

§ 153A-345.1. Board of adjustment.

(a) The provisions of G.S. 160A-388 are applicable to counties.

(b) For the purposes of this section, as used in G.S. 160A-388, the term "city council" is deemed to refer to the board of county commissioners, and the terms "city" or "municipality" are deemed to refer to the county.

(c) If a board of county commissioners does not zone the entire territorial jurisdiction of the county, each designated zoning area shall, if practicable, have at least one resident as a member of the board of adjustment; otherwise, the provisions of G.S. 153A-25 regarding qualifications for appointive office shall apply to board of adjustment appointments. (2013-126, s. 3(b).)

§ 153A-346. Conflict with other laws.

When regulations made under authority of this Part require a greater width or size of yards or courts, or require a lower height of a building or fewer number of stories, or require a greater percentage of a lot to be left unoccupied, or impose other higher standards than are required in any other statute or local ordinance or regulation, the regulations made under authority of this Part govern. When the provisions of any other statute or local ordinance or regulation require a greater width or size of yards or courts, or require a lower height of a building or a fewer number of stories, or require a greater percentage of a lot to be left unoccupied, or impose other higher standards than are required by regulations made under authority of this Part, the provisions of the other statute or local ordinance or regulation govern. (1959, c. 1006, s. 1; 1973, c. 822, s. 1.)

§ 153A-347. Part applicable to buildings constructed by the State and its subdivisions; exception.

Each provision of this Part is applicable to the erection, construction, and use of buildings by the State of North Carolina and its political subdivisions.

Notwithstanding the provisions of any general or local law or ordinance, no land owned by the State of North Carolina may be included within an overlay district or a special use or conditional use district without approval of the Council of State. (1959, c. 1006, s. 1; 1973, c. 822, s. 1; 1985, c. 607, s. 4.)

§ 153A-348. Statute of limitations.

(a) A cause of action as to the validity of any ordinance adopting or amending a zoning map or approving a special use, conditional use, or conditional zoning district rezoning request adopted under this Part or other applicable law shall accrue upon adoption of such ordinance and shall be brought within two months as provided in G.S. 1-54.1.

(b) Except as otherwise provided in subsection (a) of this section, an action challenging the validity of any zoning or unified development ordinance or any provision thereof adopted under this Part or other applicable law shall be brought within one year of the accrual of such action. Such an action accrues when the party bringing such action first has standing to challenge the ordinance. A challenge to an ordinance on the basis of an alleged defect in the adoption process shall be brought within three years after the adoption of the ordinance.

(c) Nothing in this section or in G.S. 1-54(10) or G.S. 1-54.1 shall bar a party in an action involving the enforcement of a zoning or unified development ordinance from raising as a defense to such enforcement action the invalidity of the ordinance. Nothing in this section or in G.S. 1-54(10) or G.S. 1-54.1 shall bar a party who files a timely appeal from an order, requirement, decision, or determination made by an administrative official contending that such party is in violation of a zoning or unified development ordinance from raising in the appeal the invalidity of such ordinance as a defense to such order, requirement, decision, or determination. A party in an enforcement action or appeal may not assert the invalidity of the ordinance on the basis of an alleged defect in the adoption process unless the defense is formally raised within three years of the adoption of the challenged ordinance.

(d) When a use constituting a violation of a zoning or unified development ordinance is in existence prior to adoption of the zoning or unified development ordinance creating the violation, and that use is grandfathered and subsequently terminated for any reason, a county shall bring an enforcement action within 10 years of the date of the termination of the grandfathered status, unless the violation poses an imminent hazard to health or public safety. (1981, c. 705, s. 2; 1995 (Reg. Sess., 1996), c. 746, s. 6; 2011-326, s. 22(a); 2011-384, s. 3; 2013-413, s. 5(a).)

§ 153A-349. Appeals in the nature of certiorari.

(a) Whenever appeals of quasi-judicial decisions of decision-making boards are to superior court and in the nature of certiorari as required by this Article, the provisions of G.S. 160A-393 shall be applicable to those appeals.

(b) For purposes of this section, as used in G.S. 160A-393, the term "city council" shall be deemed to refer to the "board of commissioners," and the term "city" or "municipal" shall be deemed to refer to the "county."

(c) Repealed by Session Laws 2013-126, s. 9, effective October 1, 2013, and applicable to actions taken on or after that date by any board of adjustment. (2009-421, s. 1(b); 2013-126, s. 9.)

Part 3A. Development Agreements.

§ 153A-349.1. Authorization for development agreements.

(a) The General Assembly finds:

(1) Large-scale development projects often occur in multiple phases extending over a period of years, requiring a long-term commitment of both public and private resources.

(2) Such large-scale developments often create potential community impacts and potential opportunities that are difficult or impossible to accommodate within traditional zoning processes.

(3) Because of their scale and duration, such large-scale projects often require careful integration between public capital facilities planning, financing, and construction schedules and the phasing of the private development.

(4) Because of their scale and duration, such large-scale projects involve substantial commitments of private capital by developers, which developers are usually unwilling to risk without sufficient assurances that development standards will remain stable through the extended period of the development.

(5) Because of their size and duration, such developments often permit communities and developers to experiment with different or nontraditional types of development concepts and standards, while still managing impacts on the surrounding areas.

(6) To better structure and manage development approvals for such large-scale developments and ensure their proper integration into local capital facilities programs, local governments need the flexibility in negotiating such developments.

(b) Local governments and agencies may enter into development agreements with developers, subject to the procedures and requirements of this Part. In entering into such agreements, a local government may not exercise any authority or make any commitment not authorized by general or local act and may not impose any tax or fee not authorized by otherwise applicable law.

(c) This Part is supplemental to the powers conferred upon local governments and does not preclude or supersede rights and obligations established pursuant to other law regarding building permits, site-specific development plans, phased development plans, or other provisions of law. (2005-426, s. 9(b).)

§ 153A-349.2. Definitions.

The following definitions apply in this Part:

(1) Comprehensive plan. - The comprehensive plan, land-use plan, small area plans, neighborhood plans, transportation plan, capital improvement plan, official map, and any other plans regarding land use and development that have been officially adopted by the governing board.

(2) Developer. - A person, including a governmental agency or redevelopment authority, who intends to undertake any development and who has a legal or equitable interest in the property to be developed.

(3) Development. - The planning for or carrying out of a building activity, the making of a material change in the use or appearance of any structure or property, or the dividing of land into two or more parcels. "Development", as designated in a law or development permit, includes the planning for and all other activity customarily associated with it unless otherwise specified. When appropriate to the context, "development" refers to the planning for or the act of developing or to the result of development. Reference to a specific operation is not intended to mean that the operation or activity, when part of other operations or activities, is not development. Reference to particular operations is not intended to limit the generality of this item.

(4) Development permit. - A building permit, zoning permit, subdivision approval, special or conditional use permit, variance, or any other official action of local government having the effect of permitting the development of property.

(5) Governing body. - The board of county commissioners of a county.

(6) Land development regulations. - Ordinances and regulations enacted by the appropriate governing body for the regulation of any aspect of development and includes zoning, subdivision, or any other land development ordinances.

(7) Laws. - All ordinances, resolutions, regulations, comprehensive plans, land development regulations, policies, and rules adopted by a local government affecting the development of property, and includes laws governing permitted uses of the property, density, design, and improvements.

(8) Local government. - Any county that exercises regulatory authority over and grants development permits for land development or which provides public facilities.

(9) Local planning board. - Any planning board established pursuant to G.S. 153A-321.

(10) Person. - An individual, corporation, business or land trust, estate, trust, partnership, association, two or more persons having a joint or common interest, State agency, or any legal entity.

(11) Property. - All real property subject to land-use regulation by a local government and includes any improvements or structures customarily regarded as a part of real property.

(12) Public facilities. - Major capital improvements, including, but not limited to, transportation, sanitary sewer, solid waste, drainage, potable water, educational, parks and recreational, and health systems and facilities. (2005-426, s. 9(b).)

§ 153A-349.3. Local governments authorized to enter into development agreements; approval of governing body required.

A local government may establish procedures and requirements, as provided in this Part, to consider and enter into development agreements with developers. A development agreement must be approved by the governing body of a local government by ordinance. (2005-426, s. 9(b).)

§ 153A-349.4. Developed property must contain certain number of acres; permissible durations of agreements.

(a) A local government may enter into a development agreement with a developer for the development of property as provided in this Part, provided the property contains 25 acres or more of developable property (exclusive of wetlands, mandatory buffers, unbuildable slopes, and other portions of the property which may be precluded from development at the time of application). Development agreements shall be of a term specified in the agreement, provided they may not be for a term exceeding 20 years.

(b) Notwithstanding the acreage requirements of subsection (a) of this section, a local government may enter into a development agreement with a developer for the development of property as provided in this Part for developable property of any size (exclusive of wetlands, mandatory buffers, unbuildable slopes, and other portions of the property which may be precluded from development at the time of application), if the developable property that would be subject to the development agreement is subject to an executed brownfields agreement pursuant to Part 5 of Article 9 of Chapter 130A of the

General Statutes. Development agreements shall be of a term specified in the agreement, provided they may not be for a term exceeding 20 years. (2005-426, s. 9(b); 2013-413, s. 44(a).)

§ 153A-349.5. Public hearing.

Before entering into a development agreement, a local government shall conduct a public hearing on the proposed agreement following the procedures set forth in G.S. 153A-323 regarding zoning ordinance adoption or amendment. The notice for the public hearing must specify the location of the property subject to the development agreement, the development uses proposed on the property, and must specify a place where a copy of the proposed development agreement can be obtained. In the event that the development agreement provides that the local government shall provide certain public facilities, the development agreement shall provide that the delivery date of such public facilities will be tied to successful performance by the developer in implementing the proposed development (such as meeting defined completion percentages or other performance standards). (2005-426, s. 9(b).)

§ 153A-349.6. What development agreement must provide; what it may provide; major modification requires public notice and hearing.

(a) A development agreement shall at a minimum include all of the following:

(1) A legal description of the property subject to the agreement and the names of its legal and equitable property owners.

(2) The duration of the agreement. However, the parties are not precluded from entering into subsequent development agreements that may extend the original duration period.

(3) The development uses permitted on the property, including population densities and building types, intensities, placement on the site, and design.

(4) A description of public facilities that will service the development, including who provides the facilities, the date any new public facilities, if needed,

will be constructed, and a schedule to assure public facilities are available concurrent with the impacts of the development.

(5) A description, where appropriate, of any reservation or dedication of land for public purposes and any provisions to protect environmentally sensitive property.

(6) A description of all local development permits approved or needed to be approved for the development of the property together with a statement indicating that the failure of the agreement to address a particular permit, condition, term, or restriction does not relieve the developer of the necessity of complying with the law governing their permitting requirements, conditions, terms, or restrictions.

(7) A description of any conditions, terms, restrictions, or other requirements determined to be necessary by the local government for the public health, safety, or welfare of its citizens.

(8) A description, where appropriate, of any provisions for the preservation and restoration of historic structures.

(b) A development agreement may provide that the entire development or any phase of it be commenced or completed within a specified period of time. The development agreement must provide a development schedule, including commencement dates and interim completion dates at no greater than five-year intervals; provided, however, the failure to meet a commencement or completion date shall not, in and of itself, constitute a material breach of the development agreement pursuant to G.S. 153A-349.8 but must be judged based upon the totality of the circumstances. The development agreement may include other defined performance standards to be met by the developer. The developer may request a modification in the dates as set forth in the agreement. Consideration of a proposed major modification of the agreement shall follow the same procedures as required for initial approval of a development agreement.

(c) If more than one local government is made party to an agreement, the agreement must specify which local government is responsible for the overall administration of the development agreement.

(d) The development agreement also may cover any other matter not inconsistent with this Part. (2005-426, s. 9(b).)

§ 153A-349.7. Law in effect at time of agreement governs development; exceptions.

(a) Unless the development agreement specifically provides for the application of subsequently enacted laws, the laws applicable to development of the property subject to a development agreement are those in force at the time of execution of the agreement.

(b) Except for grounds specified in G.S. 153A-344.1(e), a local government may not apply subsequently adopted ordinances or development policies to a development that is subject to a development agreement.

(c) In the event State or federal law is changed after a development agreement has been entered into and the change prevents or precludes compliance with one or more provisions of the development agreement, the local government may modify the affected provisions, upon a finding that the change in State or federal law has a fundamental effect on the development agreement, by ordinance after notice and a hearing.

(d) This section does not abrogate any rights preserved by G.S. 153A-344 or G.S. 153A-344.1, or that may vest pursuant to common law or otherwise in the absence of a development agreement. (2005-426, s. 9(b).)

§ 153A-349.8. Periodic review to assess compliance with agreement; material breach by developer; notice of breach; cure of breach or modification or termination of agreement.

(a) Procedures established pursuant to G.S. 153A-349.3 must include a provision for requiring periodic review by the zoning administrator or other appropriate officer of the local government at least every 12 months, at which time the developer must be required to demonstrate good faith compliance with the terms of the development agreement.

(b) If, as a result of a periodic review, the local government finds and determines that the developer has committed a material breach of the terms or conditions of the agreement, the local government shall serve notice in writing, within a reasonable time after the periodic review, upon the developer setting forth with reasonable particularity the nature of the breach and the evidence supporting the finding and determination, and providing the developer a reasonable time in which to cure the material breach.

(c) If the developer fails to cure the material breach within the time given, then the local government unilaterally may terminate or modify the development agreement; provided, the notice of termination or modification may be appealed to the board of adjustment in the manner provided by G.S. 160A-388(b1). (2005-426, s. 9(b); 2013-126, s. 10.)

§ 153A-349.9. Amendment or cancellation of development agreement by mutual consent of parties or successors in interest.

A development agreement may be amended or canceled by mutual consent of the parties to the agreement or by their successors in interest. (2005-426, s. 9(b).)

§ 153A-349.10. Validity and duration of agreement entered into prior to change of jurisdiction; subsequent modification or suspension.

(a) Except as otherwise provided by this Part, any development agreement entered into by a local government before the effective date of a change of jurisdiction shall be valid for the duration of the agreement, or eight years from the effective date of the change in jurisdiction, whichever is earlier. The parties to the development agreement and the local government assuming jurisdiction have the same rights and obligations with respect to each other regarding matters addressed in the development agreement as if the property had remained in the previous jurisdiction.

(b) A local government assuming jurisdiction may modify or suspend the provisions of the development agreement if the local government determines that the failure of the local government to do so would place the residents of the territory subject to the development agreement, or the residents of the local government, or both, in a condition dangerous to their health or safety, or both. (2005-426, s. 9(b).)

§ 153A-349.11. Developer to record agreement within 14 days; burdens and benefits inure to successors in interest.

Within 14 days after a local government enters into a development agreement, the developer shall record the agreement with the register of deeds in the county where the property is located. The burdens of the development agreement are binding upon, and the benefits of the agreement shall inure to, all successors in interest to the parties to the agreement. (2005-426, s. 9(b).)

§ 153A-349.12. Applicability to local government of constitutional and statutory procedures for approval of debt.

In the event that any of the obligations of the local government in the development agreement constitute debt, the local government shall comply, at the time of the obligation to incur the debt and before the debt becomes enforceable against the local government, with any applicable constitutional and statutory procedures for the approval of this debt. (2005-426, s. 9(b).)

§ 153A-349.13. Relationship of agreement to building or housing code.

A development agreement adopted pursuant to this Chapter shall not exempt the property owner or developer from compliance with the State Building Code or State or local housing codes that are not part of the local government's planning, zoning, or subdivision regulations. (2005-426, s. 9(b).)

Part 3B. Wireless Telecommunications Facilities.

§ 153A-349.50. Purpose and compliance with federal law.

(a) Purpose. - The purpose of this section is to ensure the safe and efficient integration of facilities necessary for the provision of advanced mobile broadband and wireless telecommunications services throughout the community and to ensure the ready availability of reliable wireless service to the public, government agencies, and first responders, with the intention of furthering the public safety and general welfare.

(a1)   The deployment of wireless infrastructure is critical to ensuring first responders can provide for the health and safety of all residents of North Carolina and that, consistent with section 6409 of the federal Middle Class Tax Relief and Job Creation Act of 2012, 47 U.S.C. § 1455(a), which creates a national wireless emergency communications network for use by first responders that in large measure will be dependent on facilities placed on existing wireless communications support structures, it is the policy of this State to facilitate the placement of wireless communications support structures in all areas of North Carolina. The following standards shall apply to a county's actions, as a regulatory body, in the regulation of the placement, construction, or modification of a wireless communications facility.

(b)   Compliance with the Federal Communications Act. - The placement, construction, or modification of wireless communications facilities shall be in conformity with the Federal Communications Act, 47 U.S.C. § 332 as amended, section 6409 of the federal Middle Class Tax Relief and Job Creation Act of 2012, 47 U.S.C. § 1455(a), and in accordance with the rules promulgated by the Federal Communications Commission. (2007-526, s. 2; 2013-185, s. 2.)

§ 153A-349.51. Definitions.

The following definitions apply in this Part:

(1)   Antenna. - Communications equipment that transmits, receives, or transmits and receives electromagnetic radio signals used in the provision of all types of wireless communications services.

(2a)   Base station. - A station at a specific site authorized to communicate with mobile stations, generally consisting of radio receivers, antennas, coaxial cables, power supplies, and other associated electronics.

(2)   Application. - A formal request submitted to the county to construct or modify a wireless support structure or a wireless facility.

(3)   Building permit. - An official administrative authorization issued by the county prior to beginning construction consistent with the provisions of G.S. 153A-357.

(4) Collocation. - The placement or installation of wireless facilities on existing structures, including electrical transmission towers, water towers, buildings, and other structures capable of structurally supporting the attachment of wireless facilities in compliance with applicable codes.

(4a) Eligible facilities request. - A request for modification of an existing wireless tower or base station that involves collocation of new transmission equipment or replacement of transmission equipment but does not include a substantial modification.

(5) Equipment compound. - An area surrounding or near the base of a wireless support structure within which a wireless facility is located.

(5a) Fall zone. - The area in which a wireless support structure may be expected to fall in the event of a structural failure, as measured by engineering standards.

(6) Land development regulation. - Any ordinance enacted pursuant to this Part.

(7) Search ring. - The area within which a wireless support facility or wireless facility must be located in order to meet service objectives of the wireless service provider using the wireless facility or wireless support structure.

(7a) Substantial modification. - The mounting of a proposed wireless facility on a wireless support structure that substantially changes the physical dimensions of the support structure. A mounting is presumed to be a substantial modification if it meets any one or more of the criteria listed below. The burden is on the local government to demonstrate that a mounting that does not meet the listed criteria constitutes a substantial change to the physical dimensions of the wireless support structure.

a. Increasing the existing vertical height of the structure by the greater of (i) more than ten percent (10%) or (ii) the height of one additional antenna array with separation from the nearest existing antenna not to exceed 20 feet.

b. Except where necessary to shelter the antenna from inclement weather or to connect the antenna to the tower via cable, adding an appurtenance to the body of a wireless support structure that protrudes horizontally from the edge of the wireless support structure the greater of (i) more than 20 feet or (ii) more than the width of the wireless support structure at the level of the appurtenance.

c. Increasing the square footage of the existing equipment compound by more than 2,500 square feet.

(8) Utility pole. - A structure that is designed for and used to carry lines, cables, or wires for telephone, cable television, or electricity, or to provide lighting.

(8a) Water tower. - A water storage tank, a standpipe, or an elevated tank situated on a support structure originally constructed for use as a reservoir or facility to store or deliver water.

(9) Wireless facility. - The set of equipment and network components, exclusive of the underlying wireless support structure or tower, including antennas, transmitters, receivers, base stations, power supplies, cabling, and associated equipment necessary to provide wireless data and wireless telecommunications services to a discrete geographic area.

(10) Wireless support structure. - A new or existing structure, such as a monopole, lattice tower, or guyed tower that is designed to support or capable of supporting wireless facilities. A utility pole is not a wireless support structure. (2007-526, s. 2; 2013-185, s. 2.)

§ 153A-349.51A. Local authority.

A county may plan for and regulate the siting or modification of wireless support structures and wireless facilities in accordance with land development regulations and in conformity with this Part. Except as expressly stated, nothing in this Part shall limit a county from regulating applications to construct, modify, or maintain wireless support structures, or construct, modify, maintain, or collocate wireless facilities on a wireless support structure based on consideration of land use, public safety, and zoning considerations, including aesthetics, landscaping, structural design, setbacks, and fall zones, or State and local building code requirements, consistent with the provisions of federal law provided in G.S. 153A-349.50. For purposes of this Part, public safety includes, without limitation, federal, State, and local safety regulations but does not include requirements relating to radio frequency emissions of wireless facilities. (2013-185, s. 2.)

§ 153A-349.52. Construction of new wireless support structures or substantial modifications of wireless support structures.

(a) Repealed by Session Laws 2013-185, s. 2, effective October 1, 2013, and applicable to applications received on or after that date.

(b) Any person that proposes to construct a new wireless support structure or substantially modify a wireless support structure within the planning and land-use jurisdiction of a county must do both of the following:

(1) Submit a completed application with the necessary copies and attachments to the appropriate planning authority.

(2) Comply with any local ordinances concerning land use and any applicable permitting processes.

(c) A county's review of an application for the placement or construction of a new wireless support structure or substantial modification of a wireless support structure shall only address public safety, land development, or zoning issues. In reviewing an application, the county may not require information on or evaluate an applicant's business decisions about its designed service, customer demand for its service, or quality of its service to or from a particular area or site. A county may not require information that concerns the specific need for the wireless support structure, including if the service to be provided from the wireless support structure is to add additional wireless coverage or additional wireless capacity. A county may not require proprietary, confidential, or other business information to justify the need for the new wireless support structure, including propagation maps and telecommunication traffic studies. In reviewing an application the county may review the following:

(1) Applicable public safety, land use, or zoning issues addressed in its adopted regulations, including aesthetics, landscaping, land-use based location priorities, structural design, setbacks, and fall zones.

(2) Information or materials directly related to an identified public safety, land development or zoning issue including evidence that no existing or previously approved wireless support structure can reasonably be used for the wireless facility placement instead of the construction of a new wireless support structure, that residential, historic, and designated scenic areas cannot be served from outside the area, or that the proposed height of a new wireless support structure or initial wireless facility placement or a proposed height

183

increase of a substantially modified wireless support structure, or replacement wireless support structure or collocation is necessary to provide the applicant's designed service.

(3) A county may require applicants for new wireless facilities to evaluate the reasonable feasibility of collocating new antennas and equipment on an existing wireless support structure or structures within the applicant's search ring. Collocation on an existing wireless support structure is not reasonably feasible if collocation is technically or commercially impractical or the owner of the existing wireless support structure is unwilling to enter into a contract for such use at fair market value. Counties may require information necessary to determine whether collocation on existing wireless support structures is reasonably feasible.

(d) Repealed by Session Laws 2013-185, s. 2, effective October 1, 2013, and applicable to applications received on or after that date.

(e) The county shall issue a written decision approving or denying an application under this section within a reasonable period of time consistent with the issuance of other land-use permits in the case of other applications, each as measured from the time the application is deemed complete.

(f) A county may fix and charge an application fee, consulting fee, or other fee associated with the submission, review, processing, and approval of an application to site new wireless support structures or to substantially modify wireless support structures or wireless facilities that is based on the costs of the services provided and does not exceed what is usual and customary for such services. Any charges or fees assessed by a county on account of an outside consultant shall be fixed in advance and incorporated into a permit or application fee and shall be based on the reasonable costs to be incurred by the county in connection with the regulatory review authorized under this section. The foregoing does not prohibit a county from imposing additional reasonable and cost based fees for costs incurred should an applicant amend its application. On request, the amount of the consultant charges incorporated into the permit or application fee shall be separately identified and disclosed to the applicant. The fee imposed by a county for review of the application may not be used for either of the following:

(1) Travel time or expenses, meals, or overnight accommodations incurred in the review of an application by a consultant or other third party.

(2) Reimbursements for a consultant or other third party based on a contingent fee basis or a results-based arrangement.

(g) The county may condition approval of an application for a new wireless support structure on the provision of documentation prior to the issuance of a building permit establishing the existence of one or more parties, including the owner of the wireless support structure, who intend to locate wireless facilities on the wireless support structure. A county shall not deny an initial land-use or zoning permit based on such documentation. A county may condition a permit on a requirement to construct facilities within a reasonable period of time, which shall be no less than 24 months.

(h) The county may not require the placement of wireless support structures or wireless facilities on county owned or leased property, but may develop a process to encourage the placement of wireless support structures or facilities on county owned or leased property, including an expedited approval process.

(i) This section shall not be construed to limit the provisions or requirements of any historic district or landmark regulation adopted pursuant to Part 3C of this Article. (2007-526, s. 2; 2013-185, s. 2.)

§ 153A-349.53. Collocation and eligible facilities requests of wireless support structures.

(a) Pursuant to section 6409 of the federal Middle Class Tax Relief and Job Creation Act of 2012, 47 U.S.C. § 1455(a), a county may not deny and shall approve any eligible facilities request as provided in this section. Nothing in this Part requires an application and approval for routine maintenance or limits the performance of routine maintenance on wireless support structures and facilities, including in-kind replacement of wireless facilities. Routine maintenance includes activities associated with regular and general upkeep of transmission equipment, including the replacement of existing wireless facilities with facilities of the same size. A county may require an application for collocation or an eligible facilities request.

(a1) A collocation or eligible facilities request application is deemed complete unless the county provides notice that the application is incomplete in writing to the applicant within 45 days of submission or within some other mutually agreed upon time frame. The notice shall identify the deficiencies in the application which, if cured, would make the application complete. A county may deem an application incomplete if there is insufficient evidence provided to show that the proposed collocation or eligible facilities request will comply with federal, State, and local safety requirements. A county may not deem an application incomplete for any issue not directly related to the actual content of the application and subject matter of the collocation or eligible facilities request. An application is deemed complete on resubmission if the additional materials cure the deficiencies indicated.

(a2) The county shall issue a written decision approving an eligible facilities request application within 45 days of such application being deemed complete. For a collocation application that is not an eligible facilities request, the county shall issue its written decision to approve or deny the application within 45 days of the application being deemed complete.

(a3) A county may impose a fee not to exceed one thousand dollars ($1,000) for technical consultation and the review of a collocation or eligible facilities request application. The fee must be based on the actual, direct, and reasonable administrative costs incurred for the review, processing, and approval of a collocation application. A county may engage a third-party consultant for technical consultation and the review of a collocation or eligible facilities request application. The fee imposed by a county for the review of the application may not be used for either of the following:

(1) Travel expenses incurred in a third party's review of a collocation application.

(2) Reimbursement for a consultant or other third party based on a contingent fee basis or results-based arrangement.

(b), (c) Repealed by Session Laws 2013-185, s. 2, effective October 1, 2013, and applicable to applications received on or after that date. (2007-526, s. 2; 2013-185, s. 2.)

Part 3C. Internet Access Service Grants.

§ 153A-349.60. Authorization to provide grants.

(a) A county may provide grants to unaffiliated qualified private providers of highspeed Internet access service, as that term is defined in G.S. 160A-340(4), for the purpose of expanding service in unserved areas for economic development in the county. The grants shall be awarded on a technology neutral basis, shall be open to qualified applicants, and may require matching funds by the private provider. A county shall seek and consider request for proposals from qualified private providers within the county prior to awarding a broadband grant and shall use reasonable means to ensure that potential applicants are made aware of the grant, including, at a minimum, compliance with the notice procedures set forth in G.S. 160A-340.6(c). The county shall use only unrestricted general fund revenue for the grants. For the purposes of this section, a qualified private provider is a private provider of high-speed Internet access service in the State prior to the issuance of the grant proposal.

(b) Nothing in this section authorizes a county to provide highspeed Internet broadband service. (2011-163, ss. 1, 2; 2012-86, s. 3.)

Part 4. Building Inspection.

§ 153A-350. "Building" defined.

As used in this Part, the words "building" or "buildings" include other structures. (1973, c. 822, s. 1.)

§ 153A-350.1. Tribal lands.

As used in this Part, the term:

(1) "Board of commissioners" includes the Tribal Council of such tribe.

(2) "County" or "counties" also means a federally recognized Indian Tribe, and as to such tribe includes lands held in trust for the tribe. (1999-78, s. 1.)

§ 153A-351. Inspection department; certification of electrical inspectors.

(a) A county may create an inspection department, consisting of one or more inspectors who may be given the titles of building inspector, electrical inspector, plumbing inspector, housing inspector, zoning inspector, heating and air-conditioning inspector, fire prevention inspector, deputy or assistant inspector, or any other title that is generally descriptive of the duties assigned. The department may be headed by a superintendent or director of inspections.

(a1) Every county shall perform the duties and responsibilities set forth in G.S. 153A-352 either by:

(1) Creating its own inspection department;

(2) Creating a joint inspection department in cooperation with one or more other units of local government, pursuant to G.S. 153A-353 or Part 1 of Article 20 of Chapter 160A; or,

(3) Contracting with another unit of local government for the provision of inspection services pursuant to Part 1 of Article 20 of Chapter 160A.

Such action shall be taken no later than the applicable date in the schedule below, according to the county's population as published in the 1970 United States Census:

Counties over 75,000 population - July 1, 1979

Counties between 50,001 and 75,000 - July 1, 1981

Counties between 25,001 and 50,000 - July 1, 1983

Counties 25,000 and under - July 1, 1985.

In the event that any county shall fail to provide inspection services by the date specified above or shall cease to provide such services at any time thereafter, the Commissioner of Insurance shall arrange for the provision of such services, either through personnel employed by his Department or through an arrangement with other units of government. In either event, the Commissioner shall have and may exercise within the county's jurisdiction all powers made available to the board of county commissioners with respect to building inspection under Part 4 of Article 18 of this Chapter and Part 1 of Article 20 of Chapter 160A. Whenever the Commissioner has intervened in this manner, the county may assume provision of inspection services only after giving the

Commissioner two years' written notice of its intention to do so; provided, however, that the Commissioner may waive this requirement or permit assumption at an earlier date if he finds that such earlier assumption will not unduly interfere with arrangements he has made for the provision of those services.

(b) No person may perform electrical inspections pursuant to this Part unless he has been certified as qualified by the Commissioner of Insurance. To be certified a person must pass a written examination based on the electrical regulations included in the latest edition of the State Building Code as filed with the Secretary of State. The examination shall be under the supervision of and conducted according to rules and regulations prescribed by the Chief State Electrical Inspector or Engineer of the State Department of Insurance and the Board of Examiners of Electrical Contractors. It shall be held quarterly, in Raleigh or any other place designated by the Chief State Electrical Inspector or Engineer.

The rules and regulations may provide for the certification of class I, class II, and class III inspectors, according to the results of the examination. The examination shall be based on the type and character of electrical installations being made in the territory in which the applicant wishes to serve as an electrical inspector. A class I inspector may serve anywhere in the State, but class II and class III inspectors shall be limited to service in the territory for which they have qualified.

The Commissioner of Insurance shall issue a certificate to each person who passes the examination, approving the person for service in a designated territory. To remain valid, a certificate must be renewed each January by payment of an annual renewal fee of one dollar ($1.00). The examination fee shall be five dollars ($5.00).

If the person appointed by a county as electrical inspector fails to pass the examination, the county shall continue to make appointments until an appointee has passed the examination. For the interim the Commissioner of Insurance may authorize the county to use a temporary inspector.

The provisions of this subsection shall become void and ineffective on such date as the North Carolina Code Officials Qualification Board certifies to the Secretary of State that it has placed in effect a certification system for electrical inspectors pursuant to its authority granted by Article 9C of Chapter 143 of the General Statutes. (1937, c. 57; 1941, c. 105; 1947, c. 719; 1951, c. 651; 1953,

c. 984; 1955, cc. 144, 942, 1171; 1957, cc. 415, 456, 1286, 1294; 1959, cc. 399, 940, 1031; 1961, cc. 763, 884, 1036; 1963, cc. 639, 868; 1965, cc. 243, 371, 453, 494, 846; 1967, cc. 45, 73, 113; c. 495, ss. 1, 3; 1969, cc. 675, 918; c. 1003, s. 7; c. 1010, s. 4; c. 1064, ss. 1, 4, 5; c. 1066, s. 1; 1973, c. 822, s. 1; 1977, c. 531, ss. 2, 3; 1991, c. 720, s. 77.)

§ 153A-351.1. Qualifications of inspectors.

On and after the applicable date set forth in the schedule in G.S. 153A-351, no county shall employ an inspector to enforce the State Building Code as a member of a county or joint inspection department who does not have one of the following types of certificates issued by the North Carolina Code Officials Qualification Board attesting to his qualifications to hold such position: (i) a probationary certificate, valid for one year only; (ii) a standard certificate; or (iii) a limited certificate, which shall be valid only as an authorization for him to continue in the position held on the date specified in G.S. 143-151.10(c) and which shall become invalid if he does not successfully complete in-service training prescribed by the Qualification Board within the period specified in G.S. 143-151.10(c). An inspector holding one of the above certificates can be promoted to a position requiring a higher level certificate only upon issuance by the Board of a standard certificate or probationary certificate appropriate for such new position. (1977, c. 531, s. 4.)

§ 153A-352. Duties and responsibilities.

(a)   The duties and responsibilities of an inspection department and of the inspectors in it are to enforce within the county's territorial jurisdiction State and local laws and local ordinances and regulations relating to:

(1)   The construction of buildings;

(2)   The installation of such facilities as plumbing systems, electrical systems, heating systems, refrigeration systems, and air-conditioning systems;

(3)   The maintenance of buildings in a safe, sanitary, and healthful condition;

(4)   Other matters that may be specified by the board of commissioners.

These duties and responsibilities include receiving applications for permits and issuing or denying permits, making necessary inspections, issuing or denying certificates of compliance, issuing orders to correct violations, bringing judicial actions against actual or threatened violations, keeping adequate records, and taking any other actions that may be required to adequately enforce the laws and ordinances and regulations. The board of commissioners may enact reasonable and appropriate provisions governing the enforcement of the laws and ordinances and regulations.

(b) Except as provided in G.S. 153A-364, a county may not adopt a local ordinance or resolution or any other policy that requires regular, routine inspections of buildings or structures constructed in compliance with the North Carolina Residential Code for One- and Two-Family Dwellings in addition to the specific inspections required by the North Carolina Building Code without first obtaining approval from the North Carolina Building Code Council. The North Carolina Building Code Council shall review all applications for additional inspections requested by a county and shall, in a reasonable manner, approve or disapprove the additional inspections. This subsection does not limit the authority of the county to require inspections upon unforeseen or unique circumstances that require immediate action. (1937, c. 57; 1941, c. 105; 1947, c. 719; 1951, c. 651; 1953, c. 984; 1955, cc. 144, 942, 1171; 1957, cc. 415, 456, 1286, 1294; 1959, cc. 399, 940, 1031; 1961, cc. 763, 884, 1036; 1963, cc. 639, 868; 1965, cc. 243, 371, 453, 494, 846; 1967, cc. 45, 73, 113; c. 495, ss. 1, 3; 1969, cc. 675, 918; c. 1003, s. 7; c. 1010, s. 4; c. 1064, ss. 1, 4, 5; c. 1066, s. 1; 1973, c. 822, s. 1; 2013-118, s. 1(a).)

§ 153A-353. Joint inspection department; other arrangements.

A county may enter into and carry out contracts with one or more other counties or cities under which the parties agree to create and support a joint inspection department for enforcing those State and local laws and local ordinances and regulations specified in the agreement. The governing bodies of the contracting units may make any necessary appropriations for this purpose.

In lieu of a joint inspection department, a county may designate an inspector from another county or from a city to serve as a member of the county inspection department, with the approval of the governing body of the other county or city. A county may also contract with an individual who is not a city or county employee but who holds one of the applicable certificates as provided in

G.S. 153A-351.1 or G.S. 160A-411.1 or with the employer of an individual who holds one of the applicable certificates as provided in G.S. 153A-351.1 or G.S. 160A-411.1. The inspector, if designated from another county or city under this section, while exercising the duties of the position, is a county employee. The county shall have the same potential liability, if any, for inspections conducted by an individual who is not an employee of the county as it does for an individual who is an employee of the county. The company or individual with whom the county contracts shall have errors and omissions and other insurance coverage acceptable to the county. (1937, c. 57; 1941, c. 105; 1947, c. 719; 1951, c. 651; 1959, c. 940; 1963, c. 639; 1965, c. 371; 1967, c. 495, s. 1; 1969, c. 918; c. 1010, s. 4; c. 1064, ss. 1, 5; c. 1066, s. 1; 1973, c. 822, s. 1; 1993, c. 232, s. 1; 1999-372, s. 1; 2001-278, s. 1.)

§ 153A-354. Financial support.

A county may appropriate any available funds for the support of its inspection department. It may provide for paying inspectors fixed salaries, or it may reimburse them for their services by paying over part or all of any fees collected. It may fix reasonable fees for issuing permits, for inspections, and for other services of the inspection department. (1937, c. 57; 1941, c. 105; 1947, c. 719; 1951, c. 651; 1953, c. 984; 1955, cc. 144, 942, 1171; 1957, cc. 415, 456, 1286, 1294; 1959, cc. 399, 940, 1031; 1961, cc. 763, 884, 1036; 1963, cc. 639, 868; 1965, cc. 243, 371, 453, 494, 846; 1967, cc. 45, 73, 113; c. 495, ss. 1, 3; 1969, cc. 675, 918; c. 1003, s. 7; c. 1010, s. 4; c. 1064, ss. 1, 4, 5; c. 1066, s. 1; 1973, c. 822, s. 1.)

§ 153A-355. Conflicts of interest.

Unless he or she is the owner of the building, no member of an inspection department shall be financially interested or employed by a business that is financially interested in furnishing labor, material, or appliances for the construction, alteration, or maintenance of any building within the county's territorial jurisdiction or any part or system thereof, or in making plans or specifications therefor. No member of any inspection department or other individual or an employee of a company contracting with a county to conduct inspections may engage in any work that is inconsistent with his or her duties or with the interest of the county, as determined by the county. The county must find a conflict of interest if any of the following is the case:

(1)   If the individual, company, or employee of a company contracting to perform inspections for the county has worked for the owner, developer, contractor, or project manager of the project to be inspected within the last two years.

(2)   If the individual, company, or employee of a company contracting to perform inspections for the county is closely related to the owner, developer, contractor, or project manager of the project to be inspected.

(3)   If the individual, company, or employee of a company contracting to perform inspections for the county has a financial or business interest in the project to be inspected. (1937, c. 57; 1941, c. 105; 1947, c. 719; 1951, c. 651; 1953, c. 984; 1955, cc. 144, 942, 1171; 1957, cc. 415, 456, 1286, 1294; 1959, cc. 399, 1031; 1961, cc. 763, 884, 1036; 1963, c. 868; 1965, cc. 243, 453, 494, 846; 1967, cc. 45, 73, 113; c. 495, s. 3; 1969, cc. 675, 918; c. 1003, s. 7; c. 1064, ss. 1, 4; c. 1066, s. 1; 1973, c. 822, s. 1; 1993, c. 232, s. 2; 1999-372, s. 2.)

§ 153A-356. Failure to perform duties.

If a member of an inspection department willfully fails to perform the duties required of him by law, or willfully improperly issues a permit, or gives a certificate of compliance without first making the inspections required by law, or willfully improperly gives a certificate of compliance, he is guilty of a Class 1 misdemeanor. (1969, c. 1066, s. 1; 1973, c. 822, s. 1; 1993, c. 539, s. 1064; 1994, Ex. Sess., c. 24, s. 14(c).)

§ 153A-357. Permits.

(a)   Except as provided in subsection (a2) of this section, no person may commence or proceed with any of the following without first securing from the inspection department with jurisdiction over the site of the work each permit required by the State Building Code and any other State or local law or local ordinance or regulation applicable to the work:

(1) The construction, reconstruction, alteration, repair, movement to another site, removal, or demolition of any building.

(2) The installation, extension, or general repair of any plumbing system except that in any one- or two-family dwelling unit a permit shall not be required for the connection of a water heater that is being replaced, provided that the work is performed by a person licensed under G.S. 87-21, who personally examines the work at completion and ensures that a leak test has been performed on the gas piping, and provided the energy use rate or thermal input is not greater than that of the water heater which is being replaced, there is no change in fuel, energy source, location, capacity, or routing or sizing of venting and piping, and the replacement is installed in accordance with the current edition of the State Building Code.

(3) The installation, extension, alteration, or general repair of any heating or cooling equipment system.

(4) The installation, extension, alteration, or general repair of any electrical wiring, devices, appliances, or equipment except that in any one- or two-family dwelling unit a permit shall not be required for repair or replacement of electrical lighting fixtures or devices, such as receptacles and lighting switches, or for the connection of an existing branch circuit to an electric water heater that is being replaced, provided that all of the following requirements are met:

a. With respect to electric water heaters, the replacement water heater is placed in the same location and is of the same or less capacity and electrical rating as the original.

b. With respect to electrical lighting fixtures and devices, the replacement is with a fixture or device having the same voltage and the same or less amperage.

c. The work is performed by a person licensed under G.S. 87-43.

d. The repair or replacement installation meets the current edition of the State Building Code, including the State Electrical Code.

However, a permit is not required for the installation, maintenance, or replacement of any load control device or equipment by an electric power supplier, as defined in G.S. 62-133.8, or an electrical contractor contracted by the electric power supplier, so long as the work is subject to supervision by an electrical contractor licensed under Article 4 of Chapter 87 of the General Statutes. The electric power supplier shall provide such installation, maintenance, or replacement in accordance with (i) an activity or program ordered, authorized, or approved by the North Carolina Utilities Commission pursuant to G.S. 62-133.8 or G.S. 62-133.9 or (ii) a similar program undertaken by a municipal electric service provider, whether the installation, modification, or replacement is made before or after the point of delivery of electric service to the customer. The exemption under this subdivision applies to all existing installations.

(a1) A permit shall be in writing and shall contain a provision that the work done shall comply with the State Building Code and all other applicable State and local laws and local ordinances and regulations. Nothing in this section shall require a county to review and approve residential building plans submitted to the county pursuant to Section R-110 of Volume VII of the North Carolina State Building Code; provided that the county may review and approve such residential building plans as it deems necessary. No permit may be issued unless the plans and specifications are identified by the name and address of the author thereof; and if the General Statutes of North Carolina require that plans for certain types of work be prepared only by a registered architect or registered engineer, no permit may be issued unless the plans and specifications bear the North Carolina seal of a registered architect or of a registered engineer. If a provision of the General Statutes of North Carolina or of any ordinance requires that work be done by a licensed specialty contractor of any kind, no permit for the work may be issued unless the work is to be performed by such a duly licensed contractor. No permit issued under Articles 9 or 9C of G.S. Chapter 143 shall be required for any construction, installation, repair, replacement, or alteration costing five thousand dollars ($5,000) or less in any single-family residence or farm building unless the work involves: the addition, repair or replacement of load bearing structures; the addition (excluding replacement of same size and capacity) or change in the design of plumbing; the addition, replacement or change in the design of heating, air conditioning, or electrical wiring, devices, appliances, or equipment; the use of materials not permitted by the North Carolina Uniform Residential Building Code; or the addition (excluding replacement of like grade of fire resistance) of roofing. Violation of this section constitutes a Class 1 misdemeanor.

(a2) A county shall not require more than one permit for the complete installation or replacement of any natural gas, propane gas, or electrical appliance on an existing structure when the installation or replacement is performed by a person licensed under G.S. 87-21 or G.S. 87-43. The cost of the permit for such work shall not exceed the cost of any one individual trade permit issued by that county, nor shall the county increase the costs of any fees to offset the loss of revenue caused by this provision.

(b) No permit shall be issued pursuant to subsection (a) for any land-disturbing activity, as defined in G.S. 113A-52(6), for any activity covered by G.S. 113A-57, unless an erosion and sedimentation control plan has been approved by the Sedimentation Pollution Control Commission pursuant to G.S. 113A-54(d)(4) or by a local government pursuant to G.S. 113A-61 for the site of the activity or a tract of land including the site of the activity.

(c) (1) A county may by ordinance provide that a permit may not be issued under subsection (a) of this section to a person who owes delinquent property taxes, determined under G.S. 105-360, on property owned by the person. Such ordinance may provide that a building permit may be issued to a person protesting the assessment or collection of property taxes.

(2) This subsection applies to Alexander, Alleghany, Anson, Bertie, Catawba, Chowan, Currituck, Davie, Gates, Greene, Lenoir, Lincoln, Iredell, Sampson, Stokes, Surry, Tyrrell, Wayne, and Yadkin Counties only.

(d) No permit shall be issued pursuant to subsection (a) of this section for any land-disturbing activity that is subject to, but does not comply with, the requirements of G.S. 113A-71.

(e) No permit shall be issued pursuant to subdivision (1) of subsection (a) of this section where the cost of the work is thirty thousand dollars ($30,000) or more, other than for improvements to an existing single-family residential dwelling unit as defined in G.S. 87-15.5(7) that the owner occupies as a residence, or for the addition of an accessory building or accessory structure as defined in the North Carolina Uniform Residential Building Code, the use of which is incidental to that residential dwelling unit, unless the name, physical and mailing address, telephone number, facsimile number, and electronic mail address of the lien agent designated by the owner pursuant to G.S. 44A-11.1(a) is conspicuously set forth in the permit or in an attachment thereto. The building permit may contain the lien agent's electronic mail address. The lien agent information for each permit issued pursuant to this subsection shall be maintained by the inspection department in the same manner and in the same location in which it maintains its record of building permits issued. (1969, c. 1066, s. 1; 1973, c. 822, s. 1; 1981, c. 677, s. 2; 1983, c. 377, s. 2; c. 614, s. 2; 1987 (Reg. Sess., 1988), c. 1000, s. 1; 1993, c. 539, s. 1065; 1994, Ex. Sess.,

c. 24, s. 14(c); 1993 (Reg. Sess., 1994), c. 741, s. 1; 2002-165, s. 2.19; 2005-433, s. 3; 2006-150, s. 2; 2007-58, s. 1; 2008-198, s. 8(c); 2009-117, s. 1; 2009-532, s. 2; 2010-30, s. 3; 2012-23, s. 2; 2012-158, s. 6; 2013-58, s. 2; 2013-117, s. 6; 2013-160, s. 1.)

§ 153A-358. Time limitations on validity of permits.

A permit issued pursuant to G.S. 153A-357 expires six months, or any lesser time fixed by ordinance of the county, after the date of issuance if the work authorized by the permit has not commenced. If after commencement the work is discontinued for a period of 12 months, the permit therefor immediately expires. No work authorized by a permit that has expired may thereafter be performed until a new permit has been secured. (1969, c. 1066, s. 1; 1973, c. 822, s. 1.)

§ 153A-359. Changes in work.

After a permit has been issued, no change or deviation from the terms of the application, the plans and specifications, or the permit, except if the change or deviation is clearly permissible under the State Building Code, may be made until specific written approval of the proposed change or deviation has been obtained from the inspection department. (1969, c. 1066, s. 1; 1973, c. 822, s. 1.)

§ 153A-360. Inspections of work in progress.

As the work pursuant to a permit progresses, local inspectors shall make as many inspections of the work as may be necessary to satisfy them that it is being done according to the provisions of the applicable State and local laws and local ordinances and regulations and of the terms of the permit. In exercising this power, each member of the inspection department has a right, upon presentation of proper credentials, to enter on any premises within the territorial jurisdiction of the department at any reasonable hour for the purposes of inspection or other enforcement action. If a permit has been obtained by an owner exempt from licensure under G.S. 87-1(b)(2), no inspection shall be conducted without the owner being personally present, unless the plans for the building were drawn and sealed by an architect licensed pursuant to Chapter 83A of the General Statutes. (1969, c. 1066, s. 1; 1973, c. 822, s. 1; 2011-376, s. 3.)

§ 153A-361. Stop orders.

Whenever a building or part thereof is being demolished, constructed, reconstructed, altered, or repaired in a hazardous manner, or in substantial violation of a State or local building law or local building ordinance or regulation, or in a manner that endangers life or property, the appropriate inspector may order the specific part of the work that is in violation or that presents such a hazard to be immediately stopped. The stop order shall be in writing and directed to the person doing the work, and shall state the specific work to be stopped, the specific reasons for the stoppage, and the conditions under which the work may be resumed. The owner or builder may appeal from a stop order involving alleged violation of the State Building Code or any approved local modification thereof to the North Carolina Commissioner of Insurance or his designee within five days after the day the order is issued. The owner or builder shall give to the Commissioner of Insurance or his designee written notice of appeal, with a copy to the local inspector. The Commissioner or his designee shall promptly conduct an investigation and the appellant and the inspector shall be permitted to submit relevant evidence. The Commissioner or his designee shall as expeditiously as possible provide a written statement of the decision setting forth the facts found, the decision reached, and the reasons for the decision. Pending the ruling by the Commissioner of Insurance or his designee on an appeal, no further work may take place in violation of a stop order. In the event of dissatisfaction with the decision, the person affected shall have the options of:

(1)   Appealing to the Building Code Council, or

(2)   Appealing to the Superior Court as provided in G.S.143-141.

Violation of a stop order constitutes a Class 1 misdemeanor. (1969, c. 1066, s. 1; 1973, c. 822, s. 1; 1983, c. 377, s. 4; 1989, c. 681, s. 5; 1993, c. 539, s. 1066; 1994, Ex. Sess., c. 24, s. 14(c).)

§ 153A-362. Revocation of permits.

The appropriate inspector may revoke and require the return of any permit by giving written notice to the permit holder, stating the reason for the revocation. Permits shall be revoked for any substantial departure from the approved application or plans and specifications, for refusal or failure to comply with the requirements of any applicable State or local laws or local ordinances or regulations, or for false statements or misrepresentations made in securing the permit. A permit mistakenly issued in violation of an applicable State or local law or local ordinance or regulation also may be revoked. (1969, c. 1066, s. 1; 1973, c. 822, s. 1.)

§ 153A-363. Certificates of compliance.

At the conclusion of all work done under a permit, the appropriate inspector shall make a final inspection. If he finds that the completed work complies with all applicable State and local laws and local ordinances and regulations and with the terms of the permit, he shall issue a certificate of compliance. No new building or part thereof may be occupied, no addition or enlargement of an existing building may be occupied, and no existing building that has been altered or removed may be occupied until the inspection department has issued a certificate of compliance. A temporary certificate of compliance may be issued permitting occupancy for a stated period of specified portions of the building that the inspector finds may safely be occupied before completion of the entire building. Violation of this section constitutes a Class 1 misdemeanor. (1973, c. 822, s. 1; 1993, c. 539, s. 1067; 1994, Ex. Sess., c. 24, s. 14(c).)

§ 153A-364. Periodic inspections for hazardous or unlawful conditions.

(a) The inspection department may make periodic inspections, subject to the board of commissioners' directions, for unsafe, unsanitary, or otherwise hazardous and unlawful conditions in buildings or structures within its territorial jurisdiction. Except as provided in subsection (b) of this section, the inspection department may make periodic inspections only when there is reasonable cause to believe that unsafe, unsanitary, or otherwise hazardous or unlawful conditions may exist in a residential building or structure. For purposes of this section, the term "reasonable cause" means any of the following: (i) the landlord or owner has a history of more than two verified violations of the housing ordinances or codes within a 12-month period; (ii) there has been a complaint that substandard conditions exist within the building or there has been a request that the building be inspected; (iii) the inspection department has actual knowledge of an unsafe condition within the building; or (iv) violations of the local ordinances or codes are visible from the outside of the property. In conducting inspections authorized under this section, the inspection department shall not discriminate between single-family and multifamily buildings. In exercising these powers, each member of the inspection department has a right, upon presentation of proper credentials, to enter on any premises within the territorial jurisdiction of the department at any reasonable hour for the purposes of inspection or other enforcement action. Nothing in this section shall be construed to prohibit periodic inspections in accordance with State fire prevention code or as otherwise required by State law.

(b) A county may require periodic inspections as part of a targeted effort within a geographic area that has been designated by the county commissioners. The county shall not discriminate in its selection of areas or housing types to be targeted and shall (i) provide notice to all owners and residents of properties in the affected area about the periodic inspections plan and information regarding a public hearing regarding the plan; (ii) hold a public hearing regarding the plan; and (iii) establish a plan to address the ability of low-income residential property owners to comply with minimum housing code standards.

(c) In no event may a county do any of the following: (i) adopt or enforce any ordinance that would require any owner or manager of rental property to obtain any permit or permission from the county to lease or rent residential real property, except for those rental units that have more than three verified violations of housing ordinances or codes in a 12-month period or upon the property being identified within the top 10% of properties with crime or disorder problems as set forth in a local ordinance; (ii) require that an owner or manager of residential rental property enroll or participate in any governmental program as a condition of obtaining a certificate of occupancy; or (iii) except as provided in subsection (d) of this section, levy a special fee or tax on residential rental property that is not also levied against other commercial and residential properties.

(d) A county may levy a fee for residential rental property registration under subsection (c) of this section for those rental units which have been found with more than two verified violations of housing ordinances or codes within the previous 12 months or upon the property being identified within the top 10% of properties with crime or disorder problems as set forth in a local ordinance. The fee shall be an amount that covers the cost of operating a residential registration program and shall not be used to supplant revenue in other areas. Counties using registration programs that charge registration fees for all residential rental properties as of June 1, 2011, may continue levying a fee on all residential rental properties as follows:

(1)   For properties with 20 or more residential rental units, the fee shall be no more than fifty dollars ($50.00) per year.

(2)   For properties with fewer than 20 but more than three residential rental units, the fee shall be no more than twenty-five dollars ($25.00) per year.

(3)   For properties with three or fewer residential rental units, the fee shall be no more than fifteen dollars ($15.00) per year. (1969, c. 1066, s. 1; 1973, c. 822, s. 1; 2011-281, s. 1.)

§ 153A-365. Defects in buildings to be corrected.

If a local inspector finds any defect in a building, or finds that the building has not been constructed in accordance with the applicable State and local laws and local ordinances and regulations, or finds that a building because of its condition is dangerous or contains fire-hazardous conditions, he shall notify the owner or occupant of the building of its defects, hazardous conditions, or failure to comply with law. The owner and the occupant shall each immediately remedy the defects, hazardous conditions, or violations of law in the property each owns. (1969, c. 1066, s. 1; 1973, c. 822, s. 1.)

§ 153A-366. Unsafe buildings condemned.

The inspector shall condemn as unsafe each building that appears to him to be especially dangerous to life because of its liability to fire, bad conditions of walls, overloaded floors, defective construction, decay, unsafe wiring or heating system, inadequate means of egress, or other causes; and he shall affix a notice of the dangerous character of the building to a conspicuous place on its exterior wall. (1969, c. 1066, s. 1; 1973, c. 822, s. 1.)

§ 153A-367. Removing notice from condemned building.

If a person removes a notice that has been affixed to a building by a local inspector and that states the dangerous character of the building, he is guilty of a Class 1 misdemeanor. (1969, c. 1066, s. 1; 1973, c. 822, s. 1; 1993, c. 539, s. 1068; 1994, Ex. Sess., c. 24, s. 14(c).)

§ 153A-368. Action in event of failure to take corrective action.

If the owner of a building that has been condemned as unsafe pursuant to G.S. 153A-366 fails to take prompt corrective action, the local inspector shall by certified or registered mail to his last known address or by personal service give him written notice:

(1)   That the building is in a condition that appears to constitute a fire or safety hazard or to be dangerous to life, health, or other property;

(2)   That a hearing will be held before the inspector at a designated place and time, not later than 10 days after the date of the notice, at which time the owner is entitled to be heard in person or by counsel and to present arguments and evidence pertaining to the matter; and

(3)   That following the hearing, the inspector may issue any order to repair, close, vacate, or demolish the building that appears appropriate.

If the name or whereabouts of the owner cannot after due diligence be discovered, the notice shall be considered properly and adequately served if a copy thereof is posted on the outside of the building in question at least 10 days before the day of the hearing and a notice of the hearing is published at least once not later than one week before the hearing. (1969, c. 1066, s. 1; 1973, c. 822, s. 1.)

§ 153A-369. Order to take corrective action.

If, upon a hearing held pursuant to G.S. 153A-368, the inspector finds that the building is in a condition that constitutes a fire or safety hazard or renders it dangerous to life, health, or other property, he shall issue a written order, directed to the owner of the building, requiring the owner to remedy the defective conditions by repairing, closing, vacating, or demolishing the building or taking other necessary steps, within such period, not less than 60 days, as the inspector may prescribe; provided, that where the inspector finds that there is imminent danger to life or other property, he may order that corrective action be taken in such lesser period as may be feasible. (1969, c. 1066, s. 1; 1973, c. 822, s. 1; 1979, c. 611, s. 5.)

§ 153A-370. Appeal; finality of order not appealed.

An owner who has received an order under G.S. 153A-369 may appeal from the order to the board of commissioners by giving written notice of appeal to the inspector and to the clerk within 10 days following the day the order is issued. In the absence of an appeal, the order of the inspector is final. The board of commissioners shall hear any appeal within a reasonable time and may affirm, modify and affirm, or revoke the order. (1969, c. 1066, s. 1; 1973, c. 822, s. 1.)

§ 153A-371. Failure to comply with order.

If the owner of a building fails to comply with an order issued pursuant to G.S. 153A-369 from which no appeal has been taken, or fails to comply with an order of the board of commissioners following an appeal, he is guilty of a Class 1 misdemeanor. (1969, c. 1066, s. 1; 1973, c. 822, s. 1; 1993, c. 539, s. 1069; 1994, Ex. Sess., c. 24, s. 14(c).)

§ 153A-372. Equitable enforcement.

Whenever a violation is denominated a misdemeanor under the provisions of this Part, the county, either in addition to or in lieu of other remedies, may initiate any appropriate action or proceeding to prevent, restrain, correct, or abate the violation or to prevent the occupancy of the building involved. (1969, c. 1066, s. 1; 1973, c. 822, s. 1.)

§ 153A-372.1. Ordinance authorized as to repair, closing, and demolition of nonresidential buildings or structures; order of public officer.

The provisions of G.S. 160A-439 shall apply to counties. (2007-414, s. 2.)

§ 153A-373. Records and reports.

The inspection department shall keep complete, and accurate records in convenient form of each application received, each permit issued, each inspection and reinspection made, and each defect found, each certificate of compliance granted, and all other work and activities of the department. These records shall be kept in the manner and for the periods prescribed by the North Carolina Department of Cultural Resources. The department shall submit periodic reports to the board of commissioners and to the Commissioner of Insurance as the board or the Commissioner may require. (1969, c. 1066, s. 1; 1973, c. 822, s. 1; 1983, c. 377, s. 6.)

§ 153A-374. Appeals.

Unless otherwise provided by law, any appeal from an order, decision, or determination of a member of a local inspection department pertaining to the State Building Code or any other State building law shall be taken to the Commissioner of Insurance or his designee or other official specified in G.S. 143-139, by filing a written notice with him and with the inspection department within 10 days after the day of the order, decision, or determination. Further appeals may be taken to the State Building Code Council or to the courts as provided by law. (1969, c. 1066, s. 1; 1973, c. 822, s. 1; 1989, c. 681, s. 7.)

§ 153A-375. Establishment of fire limits.

A county may by ordinance establish and define fire limits in any area within the county and not within a city. The limits may include only business and industrial areas. Within any fire limits, no frame or wooden building or addition thereto may be erected, altered, repaired, or moved (either into the fire limits or from one place to another within the limits) except upon the permit of the inspection department and approval of the Commissioner of Insurance. The board of commissioners may make additional regulations necessary for the prevention, extinguishment, or mitigation of fires within the fire limits. (1969, c. 1066, s. 1; 1973, c. 822, s. 1.)

Part 5. Community Development.

§ 153A-376. Community development programs and activities.

(a) Any county is authorized to engage in, to accept federal and State grants and loans for, and to appropriate and expend funds for community development programs and activities. In undertaking community development programs and activities, in addition to other authority granted by law, a county may engage in the following activities:

(1) Programs of assistance and financing of rehabilitation of private buildings principally for the benefit of low and moderate income persons, or for the restoration or preservation of older neighborhoods or properties, including direct repair, the making of grants or loans, the subsidization of interest payments on loans, and the guaranty of loans;

(2) Programs concerned with employment, economic development, crime prevention, child care, health, drug abuse, education, and welfare needs of persons of low and moderate income.

(b) Any board of county commissioners may exercise directly those powers granted by law to county redevelopment commissions and those powers granted by law to county housing authorities. Any board of county commissioners desiring to do so may delegate to redevelopment commission or to any housing authority the responsibility of undertaking or carrying out any specified community development activities. Any board of county commissioners and any municipal governing body may by agreement undertake or carry out for each other any specified community development activities. Any board of county commissioners may contract with any person, association, or corporation in undertaking any specified community development activities. Any county or city board of health, county board of social services, or county or city board of education, may by agreement undertake or carry out for any board of county commissioners any specified community development activities.

(c) Any board of county commissioners undertaking community development programs or activities may create one or more advisory committees to advise it and to make recommendations concerning such programs or activities.

(d) Any board of county commissioners proposing to undertake any loan guaranty or similar program for rehabilitation of private buildings is authorized to submit to its voters the question whether such program shall be undertaken, such referendum to be conducted pursuant to the general and local laws applicable to special elections in such county.

(e) No state or local taxes shall be appropriated or expended by a county pursuant to this section for any purpose not expressly authorized by G.S. 153A-149, unless the same is first submitted to a vote of the people as therein provided.

(f) All program income from Economic Development Grants from the Small Cities Community Development Block Grant Program may be retained by recipient "economically distressed counties", as defined in G.S. 143B-437.01 for the purposes of creating local economic development revolving loan funds. Such program income derived through the use by counties of Small Cities Community Development Block Grant money includes but is not limited to: (i) payment of principal and interest on loans made by the county using Community Development Block Grant Funds; (ii) proceeds from the lease or disposition of real property acquired with Community Development Block Grant Funds; and (iii) any late fees associated with loan or lease payments in (i) and (ii) above. The local economic development revolving loan fund set up by the county shall fund only those activities eligible under Title I of the federal Housing and Community Development Act of 1974, as amended (P.L. 93-383), and shall meet at least one of the three national objectives of the Housing and Community Development Act. Any expiration of G.S. 143B-437.01 or G.S. 105-129.3 shall not affect this subsection as to designations of economically distressed counties made prior to its expiration.

(g) Any county may receive and dispense funds from the Community Development Block Grant Section 108 Loan Guarantee program, Subpart M, 24 CFR 570.700 et seq., either through application to the North Carolina Department of Commerce or directly from the federal government, in accordance with State and federal laws governing these funds. Any county that receives these funds directly from the federal government may pledge current and future CDBG funds for use as loan guarantees in accordance with State and federal laws governing these funds. A county may implement the receipt, dispensing, and pledging of CDBG funds under this subsection by borrowing CDBG funds and lending all or a portion of those funds to a third party in accordance with applicable laws governing the CDBG program.

Any county that has pledged current or future CDBG funds for use as loan guarantees prior to the enactment of this subsection is authorized to have taken such action. A pledge of future CDBG funds under this subsection is not a debt or liability of the State or any political subdivision of the State or a pledge of the faith and credit of the State or any political subdivision of the State. The pledging of future CDBG funds under this subsection does not directly, indirectly, or contingently obligate the State or any political subdivision of the State to levy or to pledge any taxes. (1975, c. 435, s. 2; c. 689, s. 2; 1987 (Reg. Sess., 1988), c. 992, s. 1; 1995, c. 310, s. 2; 1995 (Reg. Sess., 1996), c. 575, s. 2; 1996, 2nd Ex. Sess., c. 13, s. 3.8; 2006-259, s. 27(a).)

§ 153A-377. Acquisition and disposition of property for redevelopment.

In addition to the powers granted by G.S. 153A-376, any county is authorized, either as a part of a community development program or independently thereof, and without the necessity of compliance with the Urban Redevelopment Law, to exercise the following powers:

(1)   To acquire, by voluntary purchase from the owner or owners, real property which is either:

a.   Blighted, deteriorated, deteriorating, undeveloped, or inappropriately developed from the standpoint of sound community development and growth;

b.   Appropriate for rehabilitation or conservation activities;

c.   Appropriate for housing construction of the economic development of the community; or

d.   Appropriate for the preservation or restoration of historic sites, the beautification of urban land, the conservation of open space, natural resources, and scenic areas, the provision of recreational opportunities, or the guidance of urban development;

(2) To clear, demolish, remove, or rehabilitate buildings and improvements on land so acquired; and

(3) To retain property so acquired for public purposes, or to dispose, through sale, lease, or otherwise, of any property so acquired to any person, firm, corporation, or governmental unit; provided, the disposition of such property shall be undertaken in accordance with the procedures of G.S. 153A-176, or the procedures of G.S. 160A-514, or any applicable local act modifying such procedures. (1977, c. 660, s. 2.)

§ 153A-378. Low-and moderate-income housing programs.

In addition to the powers granted by G.S. 153A-376 and G.S. 153A-377, any county is authorized to exercise the following powers:

(1) To engage in and to appropriate and expend funds for residential housing construction, new or rehabilitated, for sale or rental to persons and families of low and moderate income. Any board of commissioners may contract with any person, association, or corporation to implement the provisions of this subdivision.

(2) To acquire real property by voluntary purchase from the owners to be developed by the county or to be used by the county to provide affordable housing to persons of low and moderate income.

(3) Under procedures and standards established by the county, to convey property by private sale to any public or private entity that provides affordable housing to persons of low or moderate income. The county shall include as part of any such conveyance covenants or conditions that assure the property will be developed by the entity for sale or lease to persons of low or moderate income.

(4) Under procedures and standards established by the county, to convey residential property by private sale to persons of low or moderate income in accordance with G.S. 160A-267 and any terms and conditions that the board of commissioners may determine. (1999-366, s. 2.)

§§ G.S. 153A-379 through 153A-390. Reserved for future codification purposes.

Article 19.

Regional Planning Commissions.

§ 153A-391. Creation; admission of new members.

Two or more counties, cities, or counties and cities may create a regional planning commission by adopting identical concurrent resolutions to that effect in accordance with the provisions and procedures of this Article. A county or city may join an existing regional planning commission with the consent of the existing member governments.

The resolution creating a regional planning commission may be modified, amended, or repealed by the unanimous action of the member governments. (1961, c. 722, s. 3; 1973, c. 822, s. 1.)

§ 153A-392. Contents of resolution.

The resolutions creating a regional planning commission shall:

(1)   Specify the name of the commission;

(2)   Establish the number of delegates to represent each member government, fix the delegates' terms of office and the conditions, if any, for their removal, provide methods for filling vacancies, and prescribe the compensation and allowances, if any, to be paid to delegates;

(3)   Set out the method of determining the financial support that will be given to the commission by each member government;

(4)   Set out the budgetary and fiscal control procedures to be followed by the commission, which shall substantially comply with the Local Government Budget and Fiscal Control Act (Chapter 159, Subchapter III).

In addition the resolution may, but need not, contain rules and regulations for the conduct of commission business and any other matters pertaining to the organization, powers, and functioning of the commission that the member governments consider appropriate. (1961, c. 722, s. 3; 1973, c. 822, s. 1.)

§ 153A-393. Withdrawal from commission.

A member government may withdraw from a regional planning commission by giving at least two years' written notice to the other counties and cities involved. (1961, c. 722, s. 3; 1973, c. 822, s. 1.)

§ 153A-394. Organization of the commission.

Upon its creation, a regional planning commission shall meet at a time and place agreed upon by the counties and cities involved. It shall organize by electing a chairman and any other officers that the resolution specifies or that the commission considers advisable. The commission may adopt bylaws for the conduct of its business. All commission meetings shall be open to the public.

The chairman of the commission may appoint any committees authorized by the bylaws. Committee members need not be delegates to the commission. (1961, c. 722, s. 3; 1973, c. 822, s. 1.)

§ 153A-395. Powers and duties.

A regional planning commission may:

(1)   Apply for, accept, receive, and disburse funds, grants, and services made available to it by the State of North Carolina or any agency thereof, the federal government or any agency thereof, any unit of local government or any agency thereof, or any private or civic agency;

(2)   Employ personnel;

(3)   Contract with consultants;

(4)   Contract for services with the State of North Carolina, any other state, the United States, or any agency of those governments;

(5)   Study and inventory regional goals, resources, and problems;

(6) Prepare and amend regional development plans, which may include recommendations for land use within the region, recommendations concerning the need for and general location of public works of regional concern, recommendations for economic development of the region, and any other relevant matters;

(7) Cooperate with and provide assistance to federal, State, other regional, and local planning activities within the region;

(8) Encourage local efforts toward economic development;

(9) Make recommendations for review and action to its member governments and other public agencies that perform functions within the region;

(9a) For the purpose of meeting its office space and program needs, acquire real property by purchase, gift, or otherwise, and improve that property. It may pledge real property as security for an indebtedness used to finance acquisition of that property or for improvements to that property, subject to approval by the Local Government Commission as required under G.S. 159-153. It may not exercise the power of eminent domain in exercising the powers granted by this subdivision.

(10) Exercise any other power necessary to the discharge of its duties. (1961, c. 722, s. 3; 1973, c. 822, s. 1; 2006-211, s. 2.)

§ 153A-396. Fiscal affairs.

Each county and city having membership in a regional planning commission may appropriate to the commission revenues not otherwise limited as to use by law. Services of personnel, use of equipment and office space, and other services may be made available to a commission by its member governments as a part of their financial support. (1961, c. 722, s. 3; 1973, c. 822, s. 1.)

§ 153A-397. Reports.

Each regional planning commission shall prepare and distribute to its member governments and make available to the public an annual report of its activities, including a financial statement. (1961, c. 722, s. 3; 1973, c. 822, s. 1.)

§ 153A-398. Regional planning and economic development commissions.

Two or more counties, cities, or counties and cities may create a regional planning and economic development commission by adopting identical concurrent resolutions to that effect. Such a commission has the powers granted by this Article and the powers granted by Chapter 158, Article 2. If such a commission is created, it shall maintain separate books of account for appropriations and expenditures made pursuant to this Article and for appropriations and expenditures made pursuant to Chapter 158, Article 2. (1961, c. 722, s. 3; 1973, c. 822, s. 1; 2013-360, s. 15.28(e); 2013-363, s. 5.7(b).)

§§ 153A-399 through 153A-400. Reserved for future codification purposes.

Article 20.

Consolidation and Governmental Study Commissions.

§ 153A-401. Establishment; support.

(a)   Two or more counties or cities or counties and cities may by concurrent resolutions of their governing bodies establish a charter or governmental study commission as provided in this section:

(1)   Two or more counties that are contiguous or that lie within a continuous boundary may create a commission to study the consolidation of the counties or of one or more functions and services of the counties.

(2)   Two or more cities that are contiguous or that lie within a continuous boundary may create a commission to study the consolidation of the cities or of one or more functions and services of the cities.

(3) A county and one or more cities within the county may create a commission to study the consolidation of the county and the city or cities or of one or more of their functions and services.

(b) A county or city that participates in the establishment of a commission pursuant to this Article may appropriate for the support of the commission any revenues not otherwise limited as to use by law. (1973, c. 822, s. 1.)

§ 153A-402. Purposes of a commission.

A commission established pursuant to this Article may be charged with any of the following purposes:

(1) To study the powers, duties, functions, responsibilities, and organizational structures of the counties or cities that established the commission and of other units of local government and public agencies within those counties or cities;

(2) To prepare a report on its studies and findings;

(3) To prepare a plan for consolidating one or more functions and services of the governments that established the commission;

(4) To prepare drafts of any agreements or legislation necessary to effect the consolidation of one or more functions and services;

(5) To prepare a plan for consolidating into a single government some or all of the governments that established the commission;

(6) To prepare drafts of any legislation necessary to effect the plan of governmental consolidation;

(7) To call a referendum, as provided in G.S. 153A-405, on the plan of governmental consolidation. (1973, c. 822, s. 1.)

§ 153A-403. Content of concurrent resolutions.

The concurrent resolutions establishing a commission shall:

(1)   Set forth the purposes that are to be vested in the commission pursuant to G.S. 153A-402;

(2)   Determine the composition of the commission, the manner of appointment of its members, and the manner of selection of its officers;

(3)   Determine the compensation, if any, to be paid to commission members;

(4)   Provide for the organizational meeting of the commission;

(5)   Set out the method for determining the financial support that will be given to the commission by each of the governments establishing the commission;

(6)   Set forth the date by which the commission is to complete its work;

(7)   Set forth any other directions or limitations considered necessary. (1973, c. 822, s. 1.)

§ 153A-404. Powers of a commission.

A commission established pursuant to this Article may:

(1)   Adopt rules and regulations for the conduct of its business;

(2)   Apply for, accept, receive, and disburse funds, grants, and services made available to it by the State of North Carolina or any agency thereof, the federal government or any agency thereof, any unit of local government, or any private or civic agency;

(3)   Employ personnel;

(4)   Contract with consultants;

(5)   Hold hearings in the furtherance of its business;

(6) Take any other action necessary or expedient to the furtherance of its business. (1973, c. 822, s. 1.)

§ 153A-405. Referendum; General Assembly action.

(a) If authorized to do so by the concurrent resolutions that established it, a commission may call a referendum on its proposed plan of governmental consolidation. If authorized or directed in the concurrent resolutions, the ballot question may include the assumption of debt secured by a pledge of faith and credit language and may also include the assumption of the right to issue authorized but unissued faith and credit debt language as provided in subsection (b) of this section. The referendum shall be held in accordance with G.S. 163-287.

(b) The proposition submitted to the voters shall be substantially in one or more of the following forms and may include part or all of the bracketed language as appropriate and other such modifications as may be needed to reflect the issued debt secured by a pledge of faith and credit of any of the consolidating units or the portion of the authorized but unissued debt secured by a pledge of faith and credit of any of the consolidating units the right to issue which is proposed to be assumed by the consolidated city-county:

(1) "Shall the County of _____ and the County of _____ be consolidated [and the consolidated unit assume the debt of each secured by a pledge of faith and credit, [the right to issue authorized but unissued debt to be secured by a pledge of faith and credit [(including any such debt as may be authorized for said counties on the date of this referendum)] and any of said authorized but unissued debt as may be hereafter issued,] and be authorized to levy taxes in an amount sufficient to pay the principal of and the interest on said debt secured by a pledge of faith and credit]?

[ ] YES   [ ] NO"

(2) "Shall the City of _____ and the City of _____ be consolidated [and the consolidated unit assume the debt of each secured by a pledge of faith and credit, [the right to issue authorized but unissued debt to be secured by a pledge of faith and credit [(including any such debt as may be authorized for said cities on the date of this referendum)] and any of said authorized but unissued debt as may be hereafter issued,] and be authorized to levy taxes in an amount

sufficient to pay the principal of and the interest on said debt secured by a pledge of faith and credit]?

[ ] YES   [ ] NO"

(3)   "Shall the City of _____ and the County of _____ be consolidated [and the consolidated unit assume the debt of each secured by a pledge of faith and credit, [the right to issue authorized but unissued debt to be secured by a pledge of faith and credit [(including any such debt as may be authorized for said city or county on the date of this referendum)] and any of said authorized but unissued debt as may be hereafter issued,] and be authorized to levy taxes in an amount sufficient to pay the principal of and the interest on said debt secured by a pledge of faith and credit]?

[ ] YES   [ ] NO"

(c)   The proposition submitted to the voters shall be substantially in one of the following forms:

(1)   "Shall the County of _____ and the County of _____ be consolidated?

[ ] YES   [ ] NO"

(2)   "Shall the City of _____ and the City of _____ be consolidated?

[ ] YES   [ ] NO"

(3)   "Shall the City of _____ and the County of _____ be consolidated?

[ ] YES   [ ] NO"

(d)   If the proposition is to consolidate two or more counties or to consolidate two or more cities, to be approved it must receive the votes of a majority of those voting in each of the counties or cities, as the case may be. If the proposition is to consolidate one or more cities with a county, to be approved it must receive the votes of a majority of those voting in the referendum. In addition, no governmental consolidation may become effective until enacted into law by the General Assembly.

(e)   Subsection (b) of this section applies to any county that has (i) a population over 120,000 according to the most recent federal decennial census and (ii) an area of less than 200 square miles. Subsection (c) of this section applies to all other counties. If any subsection or provision of this section is declared unconstitutional or invalid by the courts, it does not affect the validity of the section as a whole or any part other than the part so declared to be unconstitutional or invalid, provided that if the classifications in subsections (b) and (c) of this section are held unconstitutional or invalid then subsection (c) of this section is repealed and subsection (b) of this section shall be applicable uniformly to all counties. (1973, c. 822, s. 1; 1995, c. 461, s. 5; 1995 (Reg. Sess., 1996), c. 742, s. 38; 2013-381, s. 10.24.)

Article 21.

§§ 153A-406 through 153A-420. Reserved for future codification purposes.

Article 22.

Regional Solid Waste Management Authorities.

§ 153A-421. Definitions; applicability; creation of authorities.

(a)   Unless a different meaning is required by the context, terms relating to the management of solid waste used in this Article have the same meaning as in G.S. 130A-2 and in G.S. 130A-290. As used in this Article, the term "solid waste" means nonhazardous solid waste, that is, solid waste as defined in G.S. 130A-290 but not including hazardous waste. In addition to the meaning set out in G.S. 130A-290, the term "unit of local government" means the Eastern Band of the Cherokee Indians in North Carolina.

(b)   This Article shall not be construed to authorize any authority created pursuant to this Article to regulate or manage hazardous waste. An authority created under this Article may manage sludges, other than a sludge that is a hazardous waste, under rules of the Commission for Public Health and criteria established by the Department of Environment and Natural Resources for the management of sludge.

(c)   Any two or more units of local government may create a regional solid waste management authority by adopting substantially identical resolutions to that effect in accordance with the provisions of this Article. The resolutions creating a regional solid waste management authority and any amendments thereto are referred to in this Article as the "charter" of the regional solid waste management authority. Units of local government which participate in the creation of a regional solid waste management authority are referred to in this Article as "members".

(d)   As used in G.S. 153A-427(a)(24), the term "transferred" means placed at or delivered to any (i) place normally and customarily used by the authority for the collection of solid waste, (ii) other place agreed upon by the generator or owner of recyclable materials and the authority, or (iii) facility owned, operated, or designated by the authority. (1989 (Reg. Sess., 1990), c. 888, s. 1; 1991, c. 580, s. 2; 1991 (Reg. Sess., 1992), c. 932, s. 4; c. 948, s. 1; 1997-443, s. 11A.123; 2007-182, s. 2.)

§ 153A-422. Purposes of an authority.

The purpose of a regional solid waste management authority is to provide environmentally sound, cost effective management of solid waste, including storage, collection, transporting, separation, processing, recycling, and disposal of solid waste in order to protect the public health, safety, and welfare; enhance the environment for the people of this State; and recover resources and energy which have the potential for further use and to encourage, implement and promote the purposes set forth in Part 2A of Article 9 of Chapter 130A of the General Statutes. (1989 (Reg. Sess., 1990), c. 888, s. 1.)

§ 153A-423. Membership; board; delegates.

(a)   Each unit of local government initially adopting a resolution under G.S. 153A-421 shall become a member of the regional solid waste management authority. Thereafter, any unit of local government may join the authority by ratifying its charter and by being admitted by a unanimous vote of the existing members. All of the rights and privileges of membership in a regional solid waste management authority shall be exercised on behalf of the member units of local government by a board composed of delegates to the authority who shall be appointed by and shall serve at the pleasure of the governing boards of their respective units of local government. A vacancy on the board shall be filled by appointment by the governing board of the unit of local government having the original appointment.

(b) Any delegate appointed by a member unit of local government to an authority created pursuant to this Article who is a county commissioner or city or town alderman or commissioner serves on the board of the authority in an ex officio capacity and such service shall not constitute the holding of an office for the purpose of determining dual office holding under Section 9 of Article VI of the Constitution of North Carolina or of Article 1 of Chapter 128 of the General Statutes. (1989 (Reg. Sess., 1990), c. 888, s. 1.)

§ 153A-424. Contents of charter.

(a) The charter of a regional solid waste management authority shall:

(1) Specify the name of the authority;

(2) Establish the powers, duties and functions that the authority may exercise and perform;

(3) Establish the number of delegates to represent the member units of local government and prescribe the compensation and allowances, if any, to be paid to delegates;

(4) Set out the method of determining the financial support that will be given to the authority by each member unit of local government; and

(5) Establish a method for amending the charter, and for dissolving the authority and liquidating its assets and liabilities.

(b) The charter of a regional solid waste management authority may, but need not, contain rules for the conduct of authority business and any other matter pertaining to the organization, powers, and functioning of the authority that the member units of local government deem appropriate. (1989 (Reg. Sess., 1990), c. 888, s. 1.)

§ 153A-425. Organization of authorities.

The governing board of a regional solid waste management authority shall hold an initial organizational meeting at such time and place as is agreed upon by its member units of local government and shall elect a chairman and any other officers that the charter may specify or the delegates may deem advisable. The authority shall then adopt bylaws for the conduct of its business. All meetings of regional solid waste management authorities shall be subject to the provisions of Article 33C of Chapter 143 of the General Statutes. (1989 (Reg. Sess., 1990), c. 888, s. 1.)

§ 153A-426. Withdrawal from an authority.

If the authority has no outstanding indebtedness, any member may withdraw from a regional solid waste management authority effective at the end of the current fiscal year by giving at least six months notice in writing to each of the other members. Withdrawal of a member shall not dissolve the authority if at least two members remain. (1989 (Reg. Sess., 1990), c. 888, s. 1.)

§ 153A-427. Powers of an authority.

(a) The charter may confer on the regional solid waste management authority any or all of the following powers:

(1) To apply for, accept, receive, and disburse funds and grants made available to it by the State or any agency thereof, the United States of America or any agency thereof, any unit of local government whether or not a member of the authority, any private or civic agency, and any persons, firms, or corporations;

(2) To employ personnel;

(3) To contract with consultants;

(4) To contract with the United States of America or any agency or instrumentality thereof, the State or any agency, instrumentality, political subdivision, or municipality thereof, or any private corporation, partnership, association, or individual, providing for the acquisition, construction,

improvement, enlargement, operation or maintenance of any solid waste management facility, or providing for any solid waste management services;

(5) To adopt bylaws for the regulation of its affairs and the conduct of its business and to prescribe rules and policies in connection with the performance of its functions and duties, not inconsistent with this Article;

(6) To adopt an official seal and alter the same;

(7) To establish and maintain suitable administrative buildings or offices at such place or places as it may determine by purchase, construction, lease, or other arrangements either by the authority alone or through appropriate cost-sharing arrangements with any unit of local government or other person;

(8) To sue and be sued in its own name, and to plead and be impleaded;

(9) To receive, administer, and comply with the conditions and requirements respecting any gift, grant, or donation of any property or money;

(10) To acquire by purchase, lease, gift, or otherwise, or to obtain options for the acquisition of any property, real or personal, improved or unimproved, including an interest in land less than the fee thereof;

(11) To sell, lease, exchange, transfer, or otherwise dispose of, or to grant options for any such purposes with respect to any real or personal property or interest therein;

(12) To pledge, assign, mortgage, or otherwise grant a security interest in any real or personal property or interest therein, including the right and power to pledge, assign, or otherwise grant a security interest in any money, rents, charges, or other revenues and any proceeds derived by an authority from any and all sources;

(13) To issue revenue bonds of the authority and enter into other financial arrangements including those permitted by this Chapter and Chapters 159, 159I, and 160A of the General Statutes to finance solid waste management activities, including but not limited to systems and facilities for waste reduction, materials recovery, recycling, resource recovery, landfilling, ash management, and disposal and for related support facilities, to refund any revenue bonds or notes issued by the authority, whether or not in advance of their maturity or

earliest redemption date, or to provide funds for other corporate purposes of the authority;

(14) With the approval of any unit of local government, to use officers, employees, agents, and facilities of the unit of local government for such purposes and upon such terms as may be mutually agreeable;

(15) To develop and make data, plans, information, surveys, and studies of solid waste management facilities within the territorial jurisdiction of the members of the authority, to prepare and make recommendations in regard thereto;

(16) To study, plan, design, construct, operate, acquire, lease, and improve systems and facilities, including systems and facilities for waste reduction, materials recovery, recycling, resource recovery, landfilling, ash management, household hazardous waste management, transportation, disposal, and public education regarding solid waste management, in order to provide environmentally sound, cost-effective management of solid waste including storage, collection, transporting, separation, processing, recycling, and disposal of solid waste in order to protect the public health, safety, and welfare; to enhance the environment for the people of this State; recover resources and energy which have the potential for further use, and to promote and implement the purposes set forth in Part 2A of Article 9 of Chapter 130A of the General Statutes;

(17) To locate solid waste facilities, including ancillary support facilities, as the authority may see fit;

(18) To assume any responsibility for disposal and management of solid waste imposed by law on any member unit of local government;

(19) To operate such facilities together with any person, firm, corporation, the State, any entity of the State, or any unit of local government as appropriate and otherwise permitted by its charter and the laws of this State;

(20) To set and collect such fees and charges as is reasonable to offset operating costs, debt service, and capital reserve requirements of the authority;

(21) To apply to the appropriate agencies of the State, the United States of America or any state thereof, and to any other appropriate agency for such permits, licenses, certificates, or approvals as may be necessary, and to

construct, maintain, and operate projects in accordance with such permits, licenses, certificates, or approvals in the same manner as any other person or operating unit of any other person;

(22)   To employ engineers, architects, attorneys, real estate counselors, appraisers, financial advisors, and such other consultants and employees as may be required in the judgment of the authority, to fix and pay their compensation from funds available to the authority therefor, to select and retain, subject to approval of the Local Government Commission, the financial consultants, underwriters, and bond attorneys to be associated with the issuance of any revenue bonds, and to pay for services rendered by financial consultants, underwriters, or bond attorneys from funds available to the authority including the proceeds of any revenue bond issue with regard to which the services were performed;

(23)   To acquire property located within the territorial jurisdiction of any member unit of local government by eminent domain pursuant to authority granted to counties;

(24)   To require that any and all (i) solid waste generated within the authority's service area and (ii) recyclable materials generated within the authority's service area and transferred to the authority be separated and delivered to specific locations and facilities provided that if a private landfill shall be substantially affected by such requirement then the regional solid waste management authority shall be required to give the operator of the affected landfill at least two years written notice prior to the effective date of the requirement; and

(25)   To do all things necessary, convenient, or desirable to carry out the purposes and to exercise the powers granted to an authority under its charter.

(b)   The acquisition and disposal of real and personal property by an authority created under this Article shall be governed by those provisions of the General Statutes which govern the acquisition and disposal of real and personal property by counties, except that Article 8 of Chapter 143 of the General Statutes and Part 3 of Article 8 of Chapter 153A of the General Statutes do not apply. No authority created pursuant to this Article shall exercise any power of eminent domain with respect to any property located outside the territorial jurisdiction of the members of such authority.

(c)   Each authority's plan shall take into consideration facilities and other resources for management of solid waste which may be available through private enterprise. This Article shall be construed to encourage the involvement and participation of private enterprise in solid waste management. An authority created pursuant to this Article shall establish goals for the procurement of goods and services from minority and historically underutilized businesses. (1989 (Reg. Sess., 1990), c. 888, s. 1; 1991, c. 580, s. 1; 2007-131, ss. 1, 2.)

§ 153A-428. Fiscal accountability; support from other governments.

(a) A regional solid waste management authority is a public authority subject to the provisions of Chapter 159 of the General Statutes.

(b) The establishment and operation of an authority as herein authorized are governmental functions and constitute a public purpose, and the State and any unit of local government may appropriate funds to support the establishment and operation of an authority.

(c) The State and any unit of local government may also dedicate, sell, convey, donate, or lease any of their interests in any property to an authority. (1989 (Reg. Sess., 1990), c. 888, s. 1.)

§ 153A-429. Long-term contract permitted by and with an authority.

(a) To the extent authorized by its charter, an authority may enter into long-term and continuing contracts, not to exceed a term of 60 years, with member or other units of local government for the acquisition, construction, improvement, enlargement, operation, or maintenance of any solid waste management facility or for solid waste management services with respect to solid waste generated within their geographic boundaries or brought into their geographic boundaries.

(b) Contracts entered into by an authority may include, but are not limited to, provisions for:

(1) Payment by the members of the authority and other units of local government of a fee or other charge by the authority to accept and dispose of solid waste;

(2) Periodic adjustments to the fee or other charges to be paid by each member of the authority and such other units of local government;

(3) Warranties from the members of the authority and such other units of local government with respect to the quantity of the solid waste which will be delivered to the authority and warranties relating to the content or quality of the solid waste; and

(4) Legal and equitable title to the solid waste passing to the authority upon delivery of the solid waste to the authority. (1989 (Reg. Sess., 1990), c. 888, s. 1.)

§ 153A-430. Compliance with other law.

(a) Repealed by Session Laws 1989 (Regular Session, 1990), c. 1004, s. 47, effective July 20, 1990.

(b) An authority created pursuant to this Article shall comply with all applicable federal and State laws, regulations, and rules, including specifically those enacted or adopted for the management of solid waste or for the protection of the environment or public health.

(c) Except as provided by subsection (d) of this section, a unit of local government that is exempt from compliance with State laws or rules enacted or adopted for the management of solid waste or for the protection of the environment shall, by becoming a member of a regional solid waste management authority created under this Article and as a condition of such membership, agree to comply with and to be bound by all applicable federal and State laws, regulations, and rules enacted or adopted for the management of solid waste and for the protection of the environment with respect to all solid waste management activities of the authority within the territorial jurisdiction of the unit of local government and with respect to all solid waste management activities performed by the unit of local government in connection with membership in the authority.

(d) A unit of local government that is exempt from compliance with State laws or rules enacted or adopted for the management of solid waste shall obtain all permits that may be necessary for the conduct of solid waste management activities within the territorial jurisdiction of the unit of local government as provided by federal law and regulations. Responsibility for the enforcement of laws, regulations, and rules enacted or adopted for the management of solid waste within the territorial jurisdiction of a unit of local government that is exempt from compliance with State laws or rules enacted or adopted for the management of solid waste shall be as provided by federal law and regulations. (1989 (Reg. Sess., 1990), c. 888, s. 1; c. 1004, s. 47; c. 1075, s. 5; 1991 (Reg. Sess., 1992), c. 948, s. 2.)

§ 153A-431. Issuance of revenue bonds and notes.

The State and Local Government Revenue Bond Act, Article 5 of Chapter 159 of the General Statutes, governs the issuance of revenue bonds by an authority. Article 9 of Chapter 159 of the General Statutes governs the issuance of notes in anticipation of the sale of revenue bonds. (1989 (Reg. Sess., 1990), c. 888, s. 1.)

§ 153A-432. Advances.

Any member or other units of local government may make advances from any monies that may be available for such purpose, in connection with the creation of an authority and to provide for the preliminary expenses of an authority. Any such advances may be repaid to such member or other units of local government from the proceeds of the revenue bonds or anticipation notes issued by such authority or from funds otherwise available to the authority. (1989 (Reg. Sess., 1990), c. 888, s. 1.)

§§ 153A-433 through 153A-434: Reserved for future codification purposes.

Article 23.

Miscellaneous Provisions.

§ 153A-435. Liability insurance; damage suits against a county involving governmental functions.

(a) A county may contract to insure itself and any of its officers, agents, or employees against liability for wrongful death or negligent or intentional damage to person or property or against absolute liability for damage to person or property caused by an act or omission of the county or of any of its officers, agents, or employees when acting within the scope of their authority and the course of their employment. The board of commissioners shall determine what liabilities and what officers, agents, and employees shall be covered by any insurance purchased pursuant to this subsection.

Purchase of insurance pursuant to this subsection waives the county's governmental immunity, to the extent of insurance coverage, for any act or omission occurring in the exercise of a governmental function. Participation in a local government risk pool pursuant to Article 23 of General Statute Chapter 58 shall be deemed to be the purchase of insurance for the purposes of this section. By entering into an insurance contract with the county, an insurer waives any defense based upon the governmental immunity of the county.

If a county uses a funded reserve instead of purchasing insurance against liability for wrongful death, negligence, or intentional damage to personal property, or absolute liability for damage to person or property caused by an act or omission of the county or any of its officers, agents, or employees acting within the scope of their authority and the course of their employment, the county board of commissioners may adopt a resolution that deems the creation of a funded reserve to be the same as the purchase of insurance under this section. Adoption of such a resolution waives the county's governmental immunity only to the extent specified in the board's resolution, but in no event greater than funds available in the funded reserve for the payment of claims.

(b) If a county has waived its governmental immunity pursuant to subsection (a) of this section, any person, or if he dies, his personal representative, sustaining damages as a result of an act or omission of the county or any of its officers, agents, or employees, occurring in the exercise of a governmental function, may sue the county for recovery of damages. To the extent of the coverage of insurance purchased pursuant to subsection (a) of this section, governmental immunity may not be a defense to the action. Otherwise, however, the county has all defenses available to private litigants in any action brought pursuant to this section without restriction, limitation, or other effect, whether the defense arises from common law or by virtue of a statute.

Despite the purchase of insurance as authorized by subsection (a) of this section, the liability of a county for acts or omissions occurring in the exercise of governmental functions does not attach unless the plaintiff waives the right to have all issues of law or fact relating to insurance in the action determined by a jury. The judge shall hear and determine these issues without resort to a jury, and the jury shall be absent during any motion, argument, testimony, or announcement of findings of fact or conclusions of law relating to these issues unless the defendant requests a jury trial on them. (1955, c. 911, s. 1; 1973, c. 822, s. 1; 1985 (Reg. Sess., 1986), c. 1027, s. 27; 2003-175, s. 2.)

§ 153A-436. Photographic reproduction of county records.

(a) A county may provide for the reproduction, by photocopy, photograph, microphotograph, or any other method of reproduction that gives legible and permanent copies, of instruments, documents, and other papers filed with the register of deeds and of any other county records. The county shall keep each reproduction of an instrument, document, paper, or other record in a fire-resistant file, vault, or similar container. If a duplicate reproduction is made to provide a security-copy, the county shall keep the duplicate in a fire-resistant file, vault, or similar container separate from that housing the principal reproduction.

If a county has provided for reproducing records, any custodian of public records of the county may cause to be reproduced any of the records under, or coming under, his custody.

(b) If a county has provided for reproducing some or all county records, the custodian of any instrument, document, paper, or other record may permit it to be removed from its regular repository for up to 24 hours in order to be reproduced. An instrument, document, paper or other record may be removed from the county in order to be reproduced. The board of commissioners may permit an instrument, document, paper, or other record to be removed for longer than 24 hours if a longer period is necessary to complete the process of reproduction.

(c) The original of any instrument, document, or other paper received by the register of deeds and reproduced pursuant to this Article shall be filed, maintained, and disposed of in accordance with G.S. 161-17 and G.S. 121-5. The original of any other county record that is reproduced pursuant to this Article may be kept by the county or disposed of pursuant to G.S. 121-5.

(d) If an instrument, document, or other paper received by the register of deeds is reproduced pursuant to this Article, the recording of the reproduction is a sufficient recording for all purposes.

(e) A reproduction, made pursuant to this Article, of an instrument, document, paper, or other record is as admissible in evidence in any judicial or administrative proceeding as the original itself, whether the original is extant or not. An enlargement or other facsimile of the reproduction is also admissible in evidence if the original reproduction is extant and available for inspection under the direction of the court or administrative agency.

(f) The provisions of this section shall apply to records stored on any form of permanent, computer-readable media, such as a CD-ROM, if the medium is not subject to erasure or alteration. Nonerasable, computer-readable storage media may be used for preservation duplicates, as defined in G.S. 132-8.2, or for the preservation of permanently valuable records as provided in G.S. 121-5(d). (1945, c. 286, ss. 1-7; c. 944; 1951, c. 19, ss. 1-6; 1953, c. 675, ss. 23, 24; 1957, c. 330, s. 3; 1973, c. 822, s. 1; 1999-131, s. 4; 1999-456, s. 47(d); 2011-326, s. 13(d).)

§ 153A-437. Assistance to historical organizations.

(a) A county or city may appropriate revenues not otherwise limited as to use by law to a local historical or preservation society, museum, or other similar organization. Before such an appropriation may be made, the recipient organization shall adopt and present to the county or city a resolution requesting the funds and describing the intended use of the funds. The funds may be used for preserving historic sites, buildings, structures, areas, or objects; for recording and publishing materials relating to the history of the area; for establishing or maintaining historical museums or projects; for paying salaries of personnel employed in such museums or projects; for the costs of acquiring, recording, and maintaining materials and equipment; and for any other purposes that are approved by the county or city and that contribute to the preservation of historic sites, buildings, structures, areas, or objects, or historic materials. The ordinance making the appropriation shall state specifically what the appropriation is to be used for, and the governing board of the county or city shall require that the recipient account for the appropriation at the close of the fiscal year.

(b) A county or city, a board of education, or the board of trustees of a public library may make available space in a building under its control to a local historical society, historical museum, or other historical organization.

(c) This section is supplemental to and does not supersede any other law. (1955, c. 371, ss. 1-4; 1957, c. 398; 1973, c. 822, s. 1.)

§ 153A-438. Beach erosion control and flood and hurricane protection works.

A county may appropriate revenues not otherwise limited as to use by law to finance the acquisition, construction, reconstruction, extension, maintenance, improvement, or enlargement of groins, jetties, dikes, moles, walls, sand dunes, vegetation, or other types of works or improvements that are designed for controlling beach erosion, for protection from hurricane floods, or for preserving or restoring facilities and natural features that afford protection to the beaches and other land areas of the county and to the life and property of the county. (1965, c. 307, s. 1; 1971, c. 1159, s. 3; 1973, c. 822, s. 1.)

§ 153A-439. Support of extension activities; personnel rules for extension employees.

(a) A county may support the work of the North Carolina Cooperative Extension Service and for these purposes may appropriate revenues not otherwise limited as to use by law.

(b) The policies adopted by the Board of Trustees of North Carolina State University for the employees of the North Carolina Cooperative Extension Service shall govern the employment of employees exempted from certain provisions of Chapter 126 of the General Statutes pursuant to G.S. 126-5(c1)(9a). The policies adopted by the University of North Carolina Board of Governors and the employing constituent institution shall govern the employment of employees of the North Carolina Cooperative Extension Service exempted from certain provisions of Chapter 126 of the General Statutes pursuant to G.S. 126-5(c1)(8). (1911, c. 1; C.S., s. 1297; 1957, c. 1004, s. 5; 1973, c. 822, s. 1; 2007-195, s. 3.)

§ 153A-440. Promotion of soil and water conservation work.

A county may cooperate with and support the work of the Federal Soil Conservation Service and the State and local soil and water conservation agencies and districts and for these purposes may appropriate revenues not otherwise limited as to use by law. (1959, c. 1213; 1961, cc. 266, 290, 301, 579, 581, 582, 584, 656, 693, 705, 809, 1126; 1963, cc. 290, 701; 1965, cc. 531, 702; 1967, c. 319; 1969, c. 64, s. 1; c. 174, s. 1; c. 1003, s. 1; 1973, c. 822, s. 1.)

§ 153A-440.1. Watershed improvement programs; drainage and water resources development projects.

(a) A county may establish and maintain a county watershed improvement program pursuant to G.S. 139-41 or 139-41.1 and for these purposes may appropriate funds not otherwise limited as to use by law. A county watershed improvement program or project may also be financed pursuant to G.S. 153A-301, G.S. 153A-185 or by any other financing method available to counties for this purpose.

(b) A county may establish and maintain drainage projects and water resources development projects (as those projects are defined by G.S. 153A-301) and for these purposes may appropriate funds not otherwise limited as to use by law. A county drainage project or water resources development project may also be financed pursuant to G.S. 153A-301, G.S. 153A-185, or by any other financing method available to counties for this purpose. (1981, c. 251, s. 2; 1983, c. 321, ss. 5, 6.)

§ 153A-441. County surveyor.

A county may appoint a person registered as a land surveyor pursuant to Chapter 89 as county surveyor. (Const., art. 7, s. 1; Rev., s. 4296; C. S., s. 1383; 1959, c. 1237, s. 1; 1973, c. 822, s. 1.)

§ 153A-442. Animal shelters.

A county may establish, equip, operate, and maintain an animal shelter or may contribute to the support of an animal shelter, and for these purposes may appropriate funds not otherwise limited as to use by law. The animal shelters shall meet the same standards as animal shelters regulated by the Department of Agriculture pursuant to its authority under Chapter 19A of the General Statutes. (1973, c. 822, s. 1; 2004-199, s. 39(a).)

§ 153A-443. Redesignation of site of "courthouse door," etc.

If a county determines that the traditional location of the "courthouse," the "courthouse door," the "courthouse bulletin board" or the "courthouse steps" has become inappropriate or inconvenient for the doing of any act or the posting of any notice required by law to be done or posted at such a site, the county may by ordinance designate some appropriate or more convenient location for the site. The board of commissioners shall cause such an ordinance to be published at least once within 30 days after the day it is adopted and shall cause a copy of it to be posted for 60 days at the traditional location. (1973, c. 822, s. 1.)

§ 153A-444. Parks and recreation.

A county may establish parks and provide recreational programs pursuant to Chapter 160A, Article 18. (1973, c. 822, s. 1.)

§ 153A-445. Miscellaneous powers found in Chapter 160A.

(a)   A county may take action under the following provisions of Chapter 160A:

(1)   Chapter 160A, Article 20, Part 1. - Joint Exercise of Powers.

(2)   Chapter 160A, Article 20, Part 2. - Regional Councils of Governments.

(3)   G.S. 160A-487. - Financial support for rescue squads.

(4)   G.S. 160A-488. - Art galleries and museums.

(5)   G.S. 160A-492. - Human relations programs.

(6)   G.S. 160A-497. - Senior citizens programs.

(7)   G.S. 160A-489. - Auditoriums, coliseums, and convention and civic centers.

(8)   G.S. 160A-498. - Railroad corridor preservation.

(b)   This section is for reference only, and the failure of any section of Chapter 160A to appear in this section does not affect the applicability of that section to counties. (1973, c. 822, s. 1; 1975, c. 19, s. 61; 1979, 2nd Sess., c. 1094, s. 3; 1981, c. 692, s. 3; 1989, c. 600, s. 6.)

§ 153A-446. County may offer reward for information as to persons damaging county property.

The board of county commissioners is authorized to offer and pay rewards in an amount not exceeding five hundred dollars ($500.00) for information leading to the arrest and conviction of any person who willfully defaces, damages or destroys, or commits acts of vandalism or larceny of any county property. The amount necessary to pay said rewards shall be an item in the current expense budget of the county. (1975, c. 258.)

§ 153A-447. Certain counties may appropriate funds to Western North Carolina Development Association, Inc.

(a)   The board of county commissioners of the counties hereafter named are authorized to appropriate funds to the Western North Carolina Development Association, Inc., for the public good and welfare of said counties. The amount to be expended by each county shall be determined in the discretion of the board of commissioners.

(b)   This section shall apply to the counties of Avery, Buncombe, Burke, Cherokee, Clay, Graham, Haywood, Henderson, Jackson, McDowell, Macon,

Madison, Mitchell, Polk, Rutherford, Swain, Transylvania, and Yancey. (1979, c. 674, ss. 1, 2.)

§ 153A-448. Mountain ridge protection.

Counties may enact and enforce mountain ridge protection ordinances pursuant to Article 14 of Chapter 113A of the General Statutes, and in such enactment and enforcement shall comply with all applicable provisions of Article 14 unless the county has removed itself from the coverage of Article 14 through the procedure provided by law. (1983, c. 676, s. 2.)

§ 153A-449. Contracts with private entities; contractors must use E-Verify.

(a) Authority. - A county may contract with and appropriate money to any person, association, or corporation, in order to carry out any public purpose that the county is authorized by law to engage in. A county may not require a private contractor under this section to abide by any restriction that the county could not impose on all employers in the county, such as paying minimum wage or providing paid sick leave to its employees, as a condition of bidding on a contract.

(b) Contractors Must Use E-Verify. - No county may enter into a contract unless the contractor and the contractor's subcontractors comply with the requirements of Article 2 of Chapter 64 of the General Statutes. (1985, c. 271, s. 2; 2013-413, s. 5(c); 2013-418, s. 2(a).)

§ 153A-450. Contracts for construction of satellite campuses of community colleges.

(a) Boards of county commissioners may enter into contracts for the construction of satellite campuses of community colleges, to be located in their counties.

(b) The board of county commissioners of the county in which a satellite campus of a community college is to be constructed shall submit the plans for the satellite facility's construction to the board of trustees of the community college that will be operating the facility for its approval prior to entering into any contract for the construction of the satellite facility.

(c) A satellite facility may be used only as a satellite facility of the community college that operates it and for no other purpose except as approved by the board of trustees of the community college that has been assigned the county where the satellite facility is located as a service delivery area either by an act of the General Assembly or by the State Board of Community Colleges. (1985, c. 757, s. 148(b), (d), (e); 1987, c. 564, ss. 11, 12.)

§ 153A-451. Reimbursement agreements.

(a) A county may enter into reimbursement agreements with private developers and property owners for the design and construction of municipal infrastructure that is included on the county's Capital Improvement Plan and serves the developer or property owner. For the purpose of this act, municipal infrastructure includes, without limitation, water mains, sanitary sewer lines, lift stations, stormwater lines, streets, curb and gutter, sidewalks, traffic control devices, and other associated facilities.

(b) A county shall enact ordinances setting forth procedures and terms under which such agreements may be approved.

(c) A county may provide for such reimbursements to be paid from any lawful source.

(d) Reimbursement agreements authorized by this section shall not be subject to Article 8 of Chapter 143 of the General Statutes, except as provided by this subsection. A developer or property owner who is party to a reimbursement agreement authorized under this section shall solicit bids in accordance with Article 8 of Chapter 143 of the General Statutes when awarding contracts for work that would have required competitive bidding if the contract had been awarded by the county. (2005-426, s. 8(b).)

§ 153A-452. Restriction of certain forestry activities prohibited.

(a) The following definitions apply to this section:

(1) Development. - Any activity, including timber harvesting, that is associated with the conversion of forestland to nonforest use.

(2) Forest management plan. - A document that defines a landowner's forest management objectives and describes specific measures to be taken to achieve those objectives. A forest management plan shall include silvicultural practices that both ensure optimal forest productivity and environmental protection of land by either commercially growing timber through the establishment of forest stands or by ensuring the proper regeneration of forest stands to commercial levels of production after the harvest of timber.

(3) Forestland. - Land that is devoted to growing trees for the production of timber, wood, and other forest products.

(4) Forestry. - The professional practice embracing the science, business, and art of creating, conserving, and managing forests and forestland for the sustained use and enjoyment of their resources, materials, or other forest products.

(5) Forestry activity. - Any activity associated with the growing, managing, harvesting, and related transportation, reforestation, or protection of trees and timber, provided that such activities comply with existing State rules and regulations pertaining to forestry.

(b) A county shall not adopt or enforce any ordinance, rule, regulation, or resolution that regulates either:

(1) Forestry activity on forestland that is taxed on the basis of its present-use value as forestland under Article 12 of Chapter 105 of the General Statutes.

(2) Forestry activity that is conducted in accordance with a forest management plan.

(c) This section shall not be construed to limit, expand, or otherwise alter the authority of a county to:

(1) Regulate activity associated with development. A county may deny a building permit or refuse to approve a site or subdivision plan for either a period of up to:

a. Three years after the completion of a timber harvest if the harvest results in the removal of all or substantially all of the trees that were protected under county regulations governing development from the tract of land for which the permit or approval is sought.

b. Five years after the completion of a timber harvest if the harvest results in the removal of all or substantially all of the trees that were protected under county regulations governing development from the tract of land for which the permit or approval is sought and the harvest was a willful violation of the county regulations.

(2) Regulate trees pursuant to any local act of the General Assembly.

(3) Adopt ordinances that are necessary to comply with any federal or State law, regulation, or rule.

(4) Exercise its planning or zoning authority under Article 18 of this Chapter. (2005-447, s. 1.)

§ 153A-453. Quarterly reports by Mental Health, Developmental Disabilities, and Substance Abuse Services area authority or county program.

Quarterly reports by the area director and finance officer of Mental Health, Developmental Disabilities, and Substance Abuse Services area authorities or county programs shall be submitted to the county finance officer as provided under G.S. 122C-117(c). (2006-142, s. 3(b).)

§ 153A-454. Stormwater control.

(a) A county may adopt and enforce a stormwater control ordinance to protect water quality and control water quantity. A county may adopt a stormwater management ordinance pursuant to this Chapter, other applicable laws, or any combination of these powers.

(b) A federal, State, or local government project shall comply with the requirements of a county stormwater control ordinance unless the federal, State, or local government agency has a National Pollutant Discharge Elimination

System (NPDES) stormwater permit that applies to the project. A county may take enforcement action to compel a State or local government agency to comply with a stormwater control ordinance that implements the National Pollutant Discharge Elimination System (NPDES) stormwater permit issued to the county. To the extent permitted by federal law, including Chapter 26 of Title 33 of the United States Code, a county may take enforcement action to compel a federal government agency to comply with a stormwater control ordinance.

(c)   A county may implement illicit discharge detection and elimination controls, construction site stormwater runoff controls, and post-construction runoff controls through an ordinance or other regulatory mechanism to the extent allowable under State law.

(d)   A county that holds a National Pollutant Discharge Elimination System (NPDES) permit issued pursuant to G.S. 143-214.7 may adopt an ordinance to establish the stormwater control program necessary for the county to comply with the permit. A county may adopt an ordinance that bans illicit discharges. A county may adopt an ordinance that requires (i) deed restrictions and protective covenants to ensure that each project, including the stormwater management system, will be maintained so as to protect water quality and control water quantity and (ii) financial arrangements to ensure that adequate funds are available for the maintenance and replacement costs of the project. (2006-246, s. 17(a).)

§ 153A-455. Program to finance energy improvements.

(a)   Purpose. - The General Assembly finds it is in the best interest of the citizens of North Carolina to promote and encourage renewable energy and energy efficiency within the State in order to conserve energy, promote economic competitiveness, and expand employment in the State. The General Assembly also finds that a county has an integral role in furthering this purpose by promoting and encouraging renewable energy and energy efficiency within the county's territorial jurisdiction. In furtherance of this purpose, a county may establish a program to finance the purchase and installation of distributed generation renewable energy sources or energy efficiency improvements that are permanently affixed to residential, commercial, or other real property.

(b)   Financing Assistance. - A county may establish a revolving loan fund and a loan loss reserve fund for the purpose of financing or assisting in the financing of the purchase and installation of distributed generation renewable energy sources or energy efficiency improvements that are permanently fixed to residential, commercial, or other real property. A county may establish other local government energy efficiency and distributed generation renewable energy source finance programs funded through federal grants. A county may use State and federal grants and loans and its general revenue for this financing. The annual interest rate charged for the use of funds from the revolving fund may not exceed eight percent (8%) per annum, excluding other fees for loan application review and origination. The term of any loan originated under this section may not be greater than 20 years.

(c)   Definition. - As used in this Article, "renewable energy source" has the same meaning as "renewable energy resource" in G.S. 62-133.8. (2009-522, s. 2; 2010-167, s. 4(a).)

§ 153A-456. Limitation on the use of public funds.

A county shall not use public funds to endorse or oppose a referendum, election or a particular candidate for elective office. (2010-114, s. 1.5(a).)

§ 153A-457. Reserved for future codification purposes.

§ 153A-458. Reserved for future codification purposes.

§ 153A-459. Reserved for future codification purposes.

§ 153A-460. Reserved for future codification purposes.

§ 153A-461. Reserved for future codification purposes.

§ 153A-462. Reserved for future codification purposes.

§ 153A-463. Reserved for future codification purposes.

§ 153A-464. Reserved for future codification purposes.

§ 153A-465. Reserved for future codification purposes.

§ 153A-466. Reserved for future codification purposes.

§ 153A-467. Reserved for future codification purposes.

§ 153A-468. Reserved for future codification purposes.

§ 153A-469. Reserved for future codification purposes.

§ 153A-470. Reserved for future codification purposes.

Article 24.

Unified Government.

§ 153A-471. Unified government.

(a) Except as provided in this section, the powers, duties, functions, rights, privileges, and immunities of a city are vested with any county that has either:

(1) No portion of an incorporated municipality located within its boundaries; or

(2) One incorporated municipality located within the county, but the land area of that municipality is located primarily in another county and consists of less than 100 acres within the county exercising powers under this Article.

(b) All of the following shall apply to any county exercising the powers, duties, functions, rights, privileges, and immunities of a city under this Article:

(1) It may not exercise any such powers, duties, functions, rights, privileges, and immunities outside the boundaries of the county.

(2) Article 4A of Chapter 160A of the General Statutes (Extension of Corporate Limits) does not apply.

(3) Article 5 of Chapter 160A of the General Statutes (Form of Government) does not apply.

(4) Article 7 of Chapter 160A of the General Statutes (Administrative Offices) does not apply.

(5) Article 13 of Chapter 160A of the General Statutes (Law Enforcement) does not apply.

(6) G.S. 153A-340(b) (Zoning of Bona Fide Farms) shall apply to all areas within the county boundaries.

(7) The provisions of Chapter 163 of the General Statutes relating to municipal elections do not apply except to the extent they applied to the county absent this Article.

(8) If the county is subject to this Article under subdivision (a)(2) of this section, it may not exercise any such powers, duties, functions, rights, privileges, and immunities within the corporate limits of the municipality located partly within the county.

(c) The board of commissioners may by ordinance provide that this Article does not confer the power, duty, function, right, privilege, or immunity of a city upon the county as to a specific power, duty, function, right, privilege, or immunity, and as to such specified power, duty, function, right, privilege, or immunity it shall not be considered as a city.

(d) If the board of commissioners exercises any power, duty, function, right, privilege, or immunity authorized under both Chapter 153A and Chapter 160A of the General Statutes, and those statutes conflict, the board of commissioners shall state in their minutes under which Chapter the power, duty, function, right, privilege, or immunity is being exercised. (2005-35, s. 1; 2005-433, s. 10(a).)

§ 153A-472. Definitions.

For the purposes of this Article, any statutory reference to:

(1) A city shall be construed as a reference to a county.

(2) A city council or governing board shall be construed as a reference to the board of commissioners.

(3) The mayor shall be construed as a reference to the chair of the board of commissioners.

(4) Any other city official shall be construed as a reference to the equivalent county official. (2005-35, s. 1.)

§ 153A-472.1. Property tax levy.

If a county is subject to this Article under G.S. 153A-471(a)(2), it may not levy property taxes on the entire county for any function authorized by this Article but not otherwise authorized by law for counties. Instead, the county may establish a county service district under Part 1 of Article 16 of this Chapter, to consist of the entire area of the county not in an incorporated municipality. (2005-433, s. 10(a).)

§ 153A-473. Applicability.

This Article only applies to a county if approved by the qualified voters of the county in a referendum called by the board of commissioners in accordance with G.S. 163-287. The referendum shall be conducted by the county board of elections in accordance with the provisions of law generally applicable to special elections. The ballot question shall be determined by the board of commissioners after consultation with the county attorney as to form. (2005-35, s. 1.)

Chapter 153B.

Mountain Resources Planning Act.

§§ 153B-1 through 153B-4: Repealed by Session Laws 2013-413, s. 43. For effective date, see editor's note.

Chapter 153C.

Uwharrie Regional Resources Act.

§§ 153C-1 through 153C-4: Repealed by Session Laws 2013-360, s. 15.1A, effective July 1, 2013.

Chapter 154.

County Surveyor.

§§ 154-1 through 154-2. Repealed by Session Laws 1973, c. 822, s. 5.

§ 154-3. Repealed by Session Laws 1969, c. 1003, s. 8.

Chapter 155.

County Treasurer.

§§ 155-1 through 155-8. Repealed by Session Laws 1971, c. 780, s. 34.

§ 155-9. Repealed by Session Laws 1953, c. 973, s. 3.

§§ 155-10 through 155-14. Repealed by Session Laws 1971, c. 780, s. 34.

§ 155-15. Repealed by Session Laws 1953, c. 973, s. 3.

§§ 155-16 through 155-18. Repealed by Session Laws 1971, c. 780.

Chapter 156.

Drainage.

SUBCHAPTER I. DRAINAGE BY INDIVIDUAL OWNERS.

Article 1.

Jurisdiction in Clerk of Superior Court.

Part 1. Petition by Individual Owner.

§ 156-1. Supplemental proceeding.

The proceedings initiated under this Chapter may be, to the extent practicable, supplemented by the procedures of Chapter 40A. (Code, s. 1324; Rev., s. 4028; C.S., s. 5260; 1981, c. 919, s. 23.)

§ 156-2. Petition filed; commissioners appointed.

Any person owning pocosin, swamp, or flatlands, or owning lowlands subject to inundation, which cannot be conveniently drained or embanked so as to drain off or dam out the water from such lands, except by cutting a canal or ditch, or erecting a dam through or upon the lands of other persons, may by petition apply to the superior court of the county in which the lands sought to be drained or embanked or some part of such lands lie, setting forth the particular circumstances of the case, the situation of the land to be drained or embanked, to what outlet and through whose lands he desires to drain, or on what lands he would erect his dam, and who are the proprietors of such lands; whereupon a summons shall be served on each of the proprietors, and, on the hearing of the petition the court shall appoint three persons as commissioners, who shall be duly sworn to do justice between the parties. (1795, c. 436, P.R.; 1852, c. 57, ss. 1, 2; R.C., c. 40, s. 1; Code, s. 1297; Rev., s. 3983; C.S., s. 5261.)

§ 156-3. Duty of commissioners.

The commissioners, or a majority of them, on a day of which each proprietor of land aforesaid is to be notified at least five days, shall meet on the premises and view the lands to be drained or embanked, and the lands through or on which the drain is to pass or the embankment to be erected, and shall determine and report whether the lands of the petitioner can be conveniently drained or embanked except through or on the lands of the defendants or some of them; and if they are of opinion that the same cannot be conveniently done except through or on such lands, they shall decide and determine the route of the canal, ditch, or embankment, the width thereof, and the depth or height, as the case may be, and the manner in which the same shall be cut or thrown up, considering all the circumstances of the case, and providing as far as possible for the effectual drainage or embankment of the water from the petitioner's land, and also securing the defendant's lands from inundation, and every other injury to which the same may be probably subjected by such canal, ditch, or embankment; and they shall assess, for each of the defendants, such damage as in their judgment will fully indemnify him for the use of his land in the mode proposed; but in assessing such damages, benefits shall be deducted. (1795, c. 436, P.R.; 1852, c. 57, ss. 1, 2; R.C., c. 40, s. 2; Code, s. 1298; Rev., s. 3984; C.S., s. 5262.)

§ 156-4. Report and confirmation; easement acquired; exceptions.

The commissioners shall report in writing, under their hands, the whole matter to the court, which shall confirm the same, unless good cause be shown to the contrary; and on payment of the damages and cost of the proceedings the court shall order and decree that the petitioner may cut the canal or ditch, or raise the embankment in the manner reported and determined by the commissioners; and thereupon the petitioner shall be seized in fee simple of the easement aforesaid: Provided, that, without the consent of the proprietor, such canal, ditch, or embankment shall not be cut or raised through or on his yard or curtilage, nor be allowed when the same shall injure any mill, by cutting off or stopping the water flowing thereto; nor shall such dam be allowed so as to create a nuisance by stagnant water, or cut off the flow of useful springs or necessary streams of water, or stop any ditches of such proprietor when there is no freshet. (1795, c. 436, s. 2, P.R.; 1835, c. 7; 1852, c. 57, ss. 1, 2; R.C., c. 40, s. 3; Code, s. 1299; Rev., s. 3985; C.S., s. 5263.)

§ 156-5. Width of right-of-way for repairs.

The commissioners, when they may deem it necessary, shall designate the width of the land to be left on each side of the canal, ditch, or dam, to be used for the protection and reparation thereof, which land shall be altogether under the control and dominion of the owner of the canal, ditch, or dam, except as aforesaid: Provided, that in no case shall a greater width of land on both sides, inclusive of a dam, be taken than five times the base of such dam. (R.C., c. 40, s. 6; Code, s. 1302; Rev., s. 3985a; C.S., s. 5264.)

§ 156-6. Right of owner to fence; entry for repairs.

Any proprietor, through or on whose land such canal or ditch may be cut or embankment raised, may put a fence or make paths across the same, provided the usefulness thereof be not impaired; and the owner of the canal, ditch, or dam, his heirs and assigns, shall at all times have free access to the same for the purpose of making and repairing them; doing thereby no unnecessary damage to the lands of the proprietors. (1795, c. 436, s. 2, P.R.; 1835, c. 7; 1852, c. 57, ss. 1, 2; R.C., c. 40, s. 4; Code, s. 1300; Rev., s. 3986; C.S., s. 5265.)

§ 156-7. Earth for construction of dam; removal of dam.

The earth necessary for the erection of a dam may be taken from either side of it, or wherever else the commissioners may designate and allow. And such dam may be removed by the proprietor of the land, his heirs or assigns, to any other part of his lands, and he may adjoin any dam of his own thereto, if allowed by the court on a petition and such proceedings therein as are provided in this Chapter, as far as the same may apply to his case: Provided always, that the usefulness of the dam will not be thereby impaired or endangered. (R.C., c. 40, s. 5; Code, s. 1301; Rev., s. 3987; C.S., s. 5266.)

§ 156-8. Earth from canal removed or leveled.

The earth excavated from the canal or ditch shall be removed away or leveled as nearly as may be with the surface of the adjacent land, unless the commissioners shall otherwise specially allow. (R.C., c. 40, s. 7; Code, s. 1303; Rev., s. 3988; C.S., s. 5267.)

§ 156-9. No drain opened within 30 feet.

The proprietor of any swamp or flatlands through which a canal or ditch passes shall not have a right to open or cut any drain within 30 feet thereof but by the consent of the owner. Such proprietor, however, and other persons may cut into such canal or ditch in the manner hereinafter provided. (R.C., c. 40, s. 8; Code, s. 1304; Rev., s. 3989; C.S., s. 5268.)

§ 156-10. Right to drain into canal.

Any person desirous of draining into the canal or ditch of another person as an outlet may do so in the manner hereinbefore provided, and in addition to the persons directed to be made parties, all others shall be parties through whose lands, canals, or ditches the water to be drained may pass till it shall have reached the furthest artificial outlet. And the privilege of cutting into such canal or ditch may be granted under the same rules and upon the same conditions and restrictions as are provided in respect to cutting the first canal or ditch: Provided, that no canal or ditch shall be allowed to be cut into another if thereby the safety or utility of the latter shall be impaired or endangered: Provided, further, that if such impairing and danger can be avoided by imposing on the petitioner duties or labor in the enlarging or deepening of such canal or ditch, or otherwise, the same may be done; but no absolute decree for cutting such second canal or ditch shall pass till the duties or work so imposed shall be performed and the effect thereof is seen, so as to enable the commissioners to determine the matter whether such second canal or ditch ought to be allowed or not: Provided, that any party to the proceeding may appeal from the judgment of the court rendered under this section to the superior court of the county, where a trial and determination of all issues raised in the pleadings shall be had as in other cases before a judge and jury. (R.C., c. 40, s. 9; Code, s. 1305; 1887, c. 222; Rev., s. 3990; C.S., s. 5269; 1973, c. 108, s. 94.)

§ 156-11. Expense of repairs apportioned.

Besides the damages which the commissioners may assess against the petitioner for the privilege of cutting into such canal or ditch, they shall assess and apportion the labor which the petitioner and defendants shall severally contribute towards repairing the canal or ditch into or through which the petitioner drains the water from his lands, and report the same to court; which, when confirmed, shall stand as a judgment of the court against each of the parties, his executors and administrators, heirs and assigns. (R.C., c. 40, s. 10; Code, s. 1306; Rev., s. 3991; C.S., s. 5270.)

§ 156-12. Notice of making repairs.

Whenever the canals or ditches for the reparation of which more than one person shall be bound under the provisions of G.S. 156-11 shall need to be repaired, any of the persons so bound may notify the others thereof, and of the time he proposes to repair the same; and thereupon each of the persons shall jointly work on the same and contribute his proportion of labor till the same be repaired or the work cease by consent. (R.C., c. 40, s. 11; Code, s. 1307; Rev., s. 3992; C.S., s. 5271.)

§ 156-13. Judgment against owner in default; lien.

In case the person so notified shall make default, any of the others may perform his share of labor and recover against him the value thereof, on a notice to be issued for such default, in which shall be stated on oath made before the clerk the value of such labor, and unless good cause to the contrary be shown on the return of the notice, the court shall render judgment for the same with interest and costs; which judgment shall be a lien upon the lands from the date of the performance of the work. (R.C., c. 40, s. 12; Code, s. 1308; 1899, c. 396; Rev., s. 3993; C.S., s. 5272.)

§ 156-14. Subsequent owners bound.

All persons to whom may descend, or who may otherwise own or occupy lands drained by any canal or ditch, for the privilege of cutting which any labor for repairing is assessed, shall contribute the same, and shall be bound therefor to all intents and purposes, and in the same manner and by the same judgment as the original party himself would be if he occupied the land. (R.C., c. 40, s. 13; Code, s. 1309; Rev., s. 3994; C.S., s. 5273.)

§ 156-15. Amount of contribution for repair ascertained.

Whenever there shall be a dam, canal, or ditch, in the repairing and keeping up of which two or more persons shall be interested and receive actual benefit therefrom, and the duties and proportion of labor which each one ought to do and perform therefor shall not be fixed by agreement or by the mode already in this Subchapter provided for assessing and apportioning such labor, any of the parties may have the same assessed and apportioned by applying to a magistrate, who shall give all parties at least three days' notice, and shall summon two disinterested freeholders who, together with the magistrate, shall meet on the premises and assess the damages sustained by the applicant, whereupon the magistrate shall enter judgment in favor of the applicant for damages or for work done on such ditch or lands. (R.C., c. 40, s. 14; Code, s. 1310; 1889, c. 101; Rev., s. 3995; C.S., s. 5274; 1973, c. 108, s. 95.)

§ 156-16. Petition by servient owner against dominant owner.

Any person owning lands lying upon any creek, swamp, or other stream not navigable, which are subject to inundation and which cannot be conveniently drained or embanked on account of the volume of water flowing over the same from lands lying above, and by draining the same the lands above will be benefited and better drained, such person may by petition apply to the superior court of the county in which the lands sought to be drained or embanked, or some part of such lands, lie, setting forth the particular circumstances of the case, the valuation of the lands to be drained or embanked, and what other lands above would be benefited, and who are the proprietors of such lands; whereupon a summons shall be served upon each of the proprietors, who are not petitioners, requiring them to appear before the court at a time to be named in the summons, which shall not be less than 10 days from the service thereof, and upon such day the petition shall be heard and the court shall appoint three persons as commissioners, who shall, before entering upon the discharge of their duties, be sworn to do justice between the parties. (1889, c. 253; Rev., s. 4016; C.S., s. 5275.)

§ 156-17. Commissioners to examine lands and make report.

The commissioners, or a majority of them, on a day of which each proprietor is to be notified at least five days, shall meet on the premises and view the land to be drained and the lands affected thereby, and shall determine and report whether the lands of the petitioner or petitioners ought to be drained exclusively by him or them, and if they are of the opinion that the same ought not to be drained exclusively at the expense of the petitioner or petitioners, they shall decide and determine the route of the canal, ditch, or embankment, the width thereof, and the depth and height, as the case may be, and the manner in which the same shall be cut or thrown up, considering all the circumstances of the case, and providing as far as possible for the effectual drainage of the petitioner's land, and the protection and benefit of the defendant's lands; and they shall apportion the labor to be done or assess the amount to be paid by each of the owners of the lands affected by such canal, ditch, or embankment, towards the construction and keeping the same in repair, and report the same to the court, which, when confirmed, shall stand as a judgment of the court against each of the parties, his executors, administrators, heirs and assigns. (1889, c. 253, s. 2; Rev., s. 4017; C.S., s. 5276.)

§ 156-18. Cost of repairs enforced by judgment.

Whenever any such ditch, canal, or embankment shall need repairs or cleaning out, and any of the parties interested therein refuse to perform the labor apportioned to them, or refuse to contribute the amount assessed against them, the same shall be enforced in the manner hereinbefore provided for the joint repair of canals and ditches. (1889, c. 253, s. 3; Rev., s. 4018; C.S., s. 5277.)

§ 156-19. Obstructing canal or ditch dug under agreement.

Where two or more persons have dug a canal or ditch along any natural drain or waterway under parol agreement, or otherwise, wherein all the parties shall have contributed to the digging thereof, if any servient or lower owner shall fill up or obstruct said canal or ditch without the consent of the higher owners and without providing other drainage for the higher lands, he shall be guilty of a Class 3 misdemeanor. (1899, c. 255; Rev., s. 3375; C.S., s. 5278; 1993, c. 539, s. 1070; 1994, Ex. Sess., c. 24, s. 14(c).)

§ 156-20. Right of dominant owner to repair.

In the absence of any agreement for maintaining the efficiency of such ditch or canal, or should the servient owner neglect or refuse to clean out or aid in cleaning out the same through his lands, it shall be lawful for the dominant or higher owner, after giving three days' notice to the servient owner, to enter along such canal and not more than 12 feet therefrom and clean out or remove obstructions or accumulated debris therefrom at his own personal expense or without cost to the servient owner. (1899, c. 255, s. 2; Rev., s. 4025; C.S., s. 5279.)

§ 156-21. Canal maintained for seven years presumed a necessity; drainage assessments declared liens.

After a canal has been dug along any natural depression or waterway and maintained for seven years, it shall be prima facie evidence of its necessity, and upon application to the clerk of the superior court of any landowner who is interested in maintaining the same, it shall be the duty of the clerk of the superior court to appoint and cause to be summoned three disinterested and discreet freeholders, who, after being duly sworn, shall go upon the lands drained or intended to be drained by such canal, and after carefully examining the same and hearing such testimony as may be introduced touching the question of cost of canal, the amount paid, and the advantages and disadvantages to be shared by each of the parties to the action, shall make their report in writing to the clerk of the superior court stating the facts and apportioning the cost of maintaining such canal among the parties to the action, and the cost of the action shall be divided in the same ratio; and their report when approved shall be properly registered by the clerk and the said report or reports shall, when filed in the office of the clerk of the superior court, be a lien upon each tract of land embraced in said report or reports to the extent of the proportionate part of the costs stipulated in said report or reports as a charge against same, and shall have the effect and force of a judgment thereon, and such judgments shall be subject to execution and collection as in cases of other judgments. (1899, c. 255, s. 3; Rev., s. 4026; 1917, c. 248, s. 1; C.S., s. 5280; 1931, c. 227, s. 1.)

§ 156-22. Supplemental assessments to make up deficiency; vacancy appointments of assessment jurors.

The freeholders, commissioners or jurors, appointed in any application or proceeding filed or instituted under G.S. 156-21 or any other section of Article 1 of this Chapter, are authorized and empowered during the establishment of and providing for the construction, maintenance and payment therefor, of such ditch, canal or drain, to make other and further assessments for the costs of establishment, construction and expense, when it shall be determined by the clerk of the court that the provisions in the former report for the payment thereof are insufficient, and that such supplementary reports shall be made on the same basis of an equitable and just proportion, as made in the former report, which report or reports shall be filed with the clerk of the superior court and have the same force and effect as the former or original report.

In case of death, resignation, removal or for any other cause there becomes a vacancy as to the freeholders, commissioners or jurors, appointed to carry out the provisions of the sections contained in this Chapter, the clerk of the superior court is authorized to fill such vacancy by the appointment of some disinterested freeholder in the county, and the said person so appointed to fill such vacancy shall qualify before the clerk of the superior court before entering upon his duties. (1931, c. 227, s. 2.)

§ 156-23. Easement of drainage surrendered.

If any persons, or those claiming through or under them, who have cut any ditch or canal into which any other person has been permitted to drain land under any proceeding authorized in this Subchapter, shall desire to surrender their easement or right in such ditch or canal and be discharged from any judgment rendered and existing under such proceedings, such persons may on motion have such proceeding reinstated for hearing and file a petition therein setting forth such fact or any other grounds for relief thereunder, and upon proof satisfactory to the court that such petitioners have cut another ditch or canal which drains their lands formerly drained by the first ditch or canal, and have abandoned the use of it for any purpose of drainage, the court shall adjudge the easement or right of the petitioners surrendered and determined, and from that time the petitioners and their land shall forever be discharged and released from the judgment heretofore rendered in such former proceedings: Provided, however, that all parties then having an easement or right in such ditch or canal shall be served with notice of such petition 20 days before the hearing thereof. (1887, c. 222, s. 3; Rev., s. 4027; C.S., s. 5281.)

§ 156-24. Obstructing drain cut by consent.

If any person shall stop or in any way obstruct the passage of the water in any ditch or canal having been cut through lands of any person by consent of the owner of said land, before giving the interested parties a reasonable time to comply with the mode of proceedings provided for the drainage of lowlands, he shall be guilty of a Class 3 misdemeanor. (1891, c. 434; Rev., s. 3376; C.S., s. 5282; 1993, c. 539, s. 1071; 1994, Ex. Sess., c. 24, s. 14(c).)

§ 156-25. Protection of canals, ditches, and natural drains.

If any person shall fell any tree in any ditch, canal, or natural drainway of any farm, unless he shall remove the same and put such ditch, canal, or natural drainway in as good condition as it was before such tree was so felled; or if any person shall stop up or fill in such ditch, canal, or drainway and thereby obstruct the free passage of water along the said ditch, canal, or drainway, unless the said person shall first secure the written consent of the landowner, and those damaged by such obstruction in said ditch, canal, or drainway, or unless such person so filling in and stopping up such ditch, canal, or drainway shall, upon the demand of the person so damaged, clean out and put the said ditch, canal, or drainway in as good condition as the same was before such filling in and stopping up of the said ditch, canal, or drainway happened, he shall be guilty of a Class 3 misdemeanor. (1901, c. 478; Rev., s. 3382; C.S., s. 5283; 1993, c. 539, s. 1072; 1994, Ex. Sess., c. 24, s. 14(c).)

Part 2. Petition under Agreement for Construction.

§ 156-26. Procedure upon agreement.

(a) Agreement; Names Filed. - Whenever a majority of the landowners or the persons owning three fifths of all the lands in any well-defined swamp or lowlands shall, by a written agreement, agree to give a part of the land situated in such swamp or lowlands as compensation to any person, firm, or corporation who may propose to cut or dig any main drainway through such swamp or lowlands, or shall, by written agreement, contract with any person, firm or corporation to cut or dig any main drainway through such swamp or lowlands, then the person, firm, or corporation so proposing to cut or dig such main drainway shall file with the clerk of the superior court of the county, or, if there be two or more counties, with the clerk of the superior court of either county in or through which the proposed canal or drainway is to pass, the names of the landowners, with the approximate number of acres owned by each to be affected by the proposed drainway who have entered into the written agreement with the person, firm, or corporation, together with a brief outline of the proposed improvement, and in addition thereto shall file with the clerk the names and addresses, as far as can be ascertained, of the landowners, with the number of acres owned by each of them to be affected by the proposed drainway, who have not made any agreement with the person, firm, or corporation proposing to do the improvement.

(b) Notice. - Upon the filing of such names, it shall be the duty of the clerk to forthwith issue a notice which shall be served by the sheriff to all landowners who have not made any agreement to appear before him at a certain date, which date shall be not less than 10 and not more than 20 days from the service of such notice, or, in lieu of the personal service hereinabove required, it shall be sufficient for the clerk to publish in a newspaper published in the county once a week for four weeks a notice to all landowners who have not made any agreement to appear before him at a certain date, which date shall be not less than 30 days and not more than 40 days from the first publication of notice, at which time and place the landowners shall state their objections to the proposed improvement, and in addition thereto make an estimate of the amount of damage that might be done to the land owned by each of them on account of the proposed drainway.

(c) Hearing; Viewers. - Upon the hearing it shall be the duty of the clerk of the superior court to forthwith appoint three disinterested persons, none of whom shall own land to be affected by such drainway, if requested by the person, firm, or corporation proposing to do the improvement, whose duty it shall be to familiarize themselves with the proposed improvement, view the premises of the landowners, estimating damages, and make an estimate themselves of the amount of damages that might accrue to the lands of each landowner filing objections on account of the proposed improvement, and report the same to the clerk of the superior court within 15 days from the date of their appointment.

(d) Report; Bond. - Immediately upon the filing of the reports the clerk of the superior court shall forthwith notify the person, firm, or corporation proposing to dig the drainway or canal of the estimated damages contained in the reports, and the person, firm, or corporation shall execute and deliver a bond in a surety company authorized to do business in the State of North Carolina in twice the sum total of the estimated amount of damages, which bond shall be payable to the clerk of the superior court and conditioned upon the payment to the landowners of the amount of damages that may be assessed in the manner hereinafter provided.

(e) Construction Authorized. - Upon the execution and delivery to the clerk of the said bond, the person, firm, or corporation so proposing to cut or dig such main drainway shall be and they are hereby authorized to proceed with the cutting or digging of the drainway through any lands in its proposed course, whether the owners of the land may have consented thereto or not, and the person, firm, or corporation so proposing to cut or dig the drainway shall have the proper and necessary right-of-way for that purpose and for all things incident thereto through any lands or timbers situated in such swamp or lowlands. (1917, c. 273, s. 1; C.S., s. 5284; 1969, c. 1046.)

§ 156-27. Recovery for benefits; payment of damages.

After the drainway herein provided for shall be completed the person, firm, or corporation cutting or digging the same shall be entitled to recover of the landowners owning that part of the land with reference to which no contract for compensating those cutting or digging the drainway may have been made, an amount equal to the benefits to accrue to such lands by reason of the drainway, and shall be required by the clerk of the superior court to pay to any landowner the amount of damages in excess of benefits which may be done to the land to be determined in the manner hereinafter provided: Provided, that the recovery from any owner of the land shall be limited to the benefits to accrue to that land owned by such person, and situated in such swamp or lowlands or adjacent thereto; and provided further, that the amount to be so recovered as herein provided for until fully paid shall be and constitute a lien upon such land, the lien to be in force regardless of who may own the land at the time the amount to be recovered as compensation for digging or cutting the drainway shall be determined. (1917, c. 273, s. 2; C.S., s. 5285.)

§ 156-28. Notice to landowners; assessments made by viewers.

After the completion of the main drainway, upon the application of the person, firm, or corporation, or their heirs or assigns, digging or cutting the same, the clerk of the superior court of the county in which any land through which the drainway may pass is situated shall issue a notice to be served by the sheriff upon any person who may have failed to agree with the person, firm, or corporation digging or cutting such drainway, upon a compensation to be paid by the landowner for the digging or cutting of such drainway, notifying the landowner that on a certain day, which shall be named in the notice and not less than 20 days from the date of the issuing of the notice, the clerk of the superior court will appoint three competent and disinterested persons, one of whom may be a surveyor, and none of whom shall own land to be affected by the drainway, to view the land so drained and for which no compensation for the drainage may have been agreed upon as aforesaid, and report to the clerk of the superior court what amount shall be paid therefor by the various landowners who may have failed to arrange for and agree upon the compensation for the drainage as aforesaid, and the amount of damages in cases where the damages have exceeded the benefits, which shall be paid to the landowners by the person, firm, or corporation cutting or digging such canal or drainway. In making the appointment of the viewers the clerk of the superior court shall hear any objections which may be advanced by those interested to any of the persons the clerk may consider to be appointed as viewers, but the clerk shall name those whom he considers best qualified. (1917, c. 273, s. 3; C.S., s. 5286.)

§ 156-29. Report filed; appeal and jury trial.

A report signed by two of the persons appointed as viewers shall be entered by the clerk as the report of the viewers. Any landowner affected by the report, and the person, firm, or corporation digging or cutting the drainway, has the right of appeal and the right to have any issue arising upon the report tried by a jury, provided exceptions shall be filed to the report within 20 days after the filing of the report with the clerk, in which exceptions so filed may be a demand for a jury trial. If a jury trial is demanded, the clerk shall transfer the proceedings to the civil-issue docket, and it shall be heard as other civil actions. If no jury trial is demanded, the clerk shall hear the parties upon the exceptions filed, and appeal may be had as in special proceedings except as modified by this section, but no jury trial may be had unless demanded as provided in this section. (1917, c. 273, s. 4; C.S., s. 5287; 1999-216, s. 17.)

§ 156-30. Confirmation of report.

Unless an appeal is taken, the clerk of superior court shall confirm the report of the viewers. If exceptions are filed and no jury trial is demanded, the clerk shall hear the exceptions and enter judgment as in other special proceedings. If the report is confirmed by the clerk because no exceptions or demand for a jury trial is filed, the judgment of confirmation is the judgment of the court. Any judgment entered against the person, firm, or corporation cutting or digging the drainway is a judgment against the person, firm, or corporation and against the surety on the bond required by G.S. 156-26. (1917, c. 273, s. 5; C.S., s. 5288; 1999-216, s. 18.)

§ 156-31. Payment in installments.

The amount to be recovered from any person as compensation for digging or cutting the drainway after the amount shall be definitely determined as herein provided for, shall be payable in five equal annual installments, the first payable one year from the filing of the report of the viewers with the clerk of the superior court, and one payment on the same day of each year thereafter until the full amount be paid. The amount to be recovered from the person, firm, or corporation cutting or digging the drainway, on account of any damages in excess of benefits to the lands of any landowner, shall be payable in one installment which shall be due and payable one year from the filing of the report of the viewers with the clerk of the superior court. (1917, c. 273, s. 6; C. S., s. 5289.)

Article 2.

Jurisdiction in County Commissioners.

§ 156-32. Petition filed; board appointed; refusal to serve misdemeanor.

Upon the petition of three citizens in any county to the county commissioners, petitioning for the draining of any creek, swamp, or branch, either upon the plea of health or to promote and advance the agricultural interest of the farmers who may own lands lying on such creek, swamp, or branch petitioned to be drained, the county commissioners shall within 10 days after the filing of such petition order the county surveyor to summon three disinterested freeholders, good and lawful men of intelligence and discretion, who shall constitute a board, and the county surveyor shall be the chairman of such board; and the chairman shall give all persons who may be interested in having such creek, swamp, or branch drained three days' notice of the time and place of the meeting of the board: Provided, the petitioners shall deposit with the county treasurer the sum of twenty-five dollars ($25.00) for the payment of current expenses not otherwise provided for in this Article. Any person duly summoned by the county surveyor to act as a commissioner for the drainage of any such creek, swamp, or branch, who shall refuse to serve, shall be guilty of a Class 3 misdemeanor. (1887, c. 267; Rev., ss. 3379, 4011; C.S., s. 5290; 1993, c. 539, s. 1073; 1994, Ex. Sess., c. 24, s. 14(c).)

§ 156-33. Duty of board; refusal to comply with their requirements misdemeanor.

The board provided for in G.S. 156-32 shall meet at the call of the chairman and shall proceed to inspect and examine the lands as described in the petition to be drained, and the board shall have power to summon witnesses, administer oaths, and take testimony, and if the board decides that the lands specified in the petition shall be drained, either upon the plea of health or for the benefit of the farms lying on or contiguous to such watercourse, then the board shall select a place at which the ditch shall be begun. They shall also decide the depth and width of the ditch to be dug, and shall proceed to survey, locate, lay off, and mark the course of the ditch, and the board shall assign to the landowners the amount of the labor to be performed and the amount of money to be paid for the purpose of defraying the necessary expenses by each landowner in proportion to the amount of lands drained or pro rata benefits received by the drainage of such lands, and the board shall specify the time in which the work so assigned shall be completed: Provided, no one shall be required to commence on the work assigned to him until the person next below him shall have completed his work in accordance with the specifications of the board. If any person shall refuse to comply with any of the requirements of the board he shall be guilty of a Class 1 misdemeanor. (1887, c. 267, ss. 2, 7; Rev., ss. 3377, 4012; C.S., s. 5291; 1993, c. 539, s. 1074; 1994, Ex. Sess., c. 24, s. 14(c).)

§ 156-34. Report filed.

The board shall make a written report to the county commissioners showing all the acts and decisions of the board as to the length, depth, and width of the ditch, the names of all the owners of the lands that will be drained, and the amount of work to be performed and the amount of money to be paid by each person benefited by such drainage. But in case the board determines that the lands described in the petition shall not be drained, then the expenses of the board shall be paid out of the funds deposited with the county treasurer by the petitioners. (1887, c. 267, s. 3; Rev., s. 4013; C.S., s. 5292.)

§ 156-35. Owners to keep ditch open.

All persons whose lands shall be drained under the provisions of this Article shall keep the ditch on their lands clear of all rafts of logs, brush, or any trash that will obstruct the flow of water through the ditch. (1887, c. 267, s. 4; Rev., s. 4014; C.S., s. 5293.)

§ 156-36. Compensation of board.

The compensation of the board shall be as follows: The county surveyor shall receive three dollars ($3.00) per day and the other members shall receive one dollar and fifty cents ($1.50) per day while engaged in the duties imposed in this Chapter. (1887, c. 267, s. 5; Rev., s. 4015; C.S., s. 5294.)

SUBCHAPTER II. DRAINAGE BY CORPORATION.

Article 3.

Manner of Organization.

§ 156-37. Petition filed in superior court.

Any proprietor in fee of swamplands, which cannot be drained except by cutting a canal through the lands of another or other proprietor in fee, situated at a lower level and which would also be materially benefited by the cutting of such canal, who desires that such canal be cut on the terms on which it is hereinafter allowed, may apply by petition, setting forth the facts, to the superior court of the county in which any of the lands through which the canal will pass may lie. (1868-9, c. 164, s. 2; Code, s. 1311; Rev., s. 3996; C.S., s. 5295.)

§ 156-38. Commissioners appointed; report required.

On the establishment by the petitioner of his allegations, the court shall appoint three persons as commissioners who, having been duly sworn, shall examine the premises and inquire and report:

(1)   Whether the lands of the petitioner can be conveniently drained otherwise than through those of some other person.

(2)   Through the lands of what other persons a canal to drain the lands of the petitioner would properly pass, considering the interests of all concerned.

(3)   A description of the several pieces of lands through which the canal would pass, and the present values of such portions of the pieces of lands as would be benefited by it, and the reasons for arriving at the conclusion as to the benefit.

(4)   The route and plan of the canal, including its breadth, depth, and slope, as nearly as they can be calculated, with all other particulars necessary for calculating its cost.

(5)   The probable cost of the canal and of a road on its bank, and of such other work, if any, as may be necessary for its profitable use.

(6)   The proportion of the benefit (after a deduction of all damages) which each proprietor would receive by the proposed canal and a road on its bank if deemed necessary and in which each ought, in equity and justice, to pay toward their construction and permanent support.

(7)   With their report they shall return a map explaining, as accurately as may be, the various matters required to be stated in their report. (1868-9, c. 164, s. 3; Code, s. 1312; Rev., s. 3997; C.S., s. 5296.)

§ 156-39. Surveyor employed.

The commissioner may employ a surveyor to prepare the map required to accompany their report. (1868-9, c. 164, s. 4; Code, s. 1313; Rev., s. 3998; C.S., s. 5297.)

§ 156-40. Confirmation of report.

If it appear that the lands on the lower level will be increased in value twenty-five percent (25%) or upwards by the proposed improvement, within one year after the completion thereof, and that the cost of making such improvement will not exceed three fourths of the present estimated value of the land to be benefited, and that the proprietors of at least one half in value of the land to be affected consent to the improvement, the court may confirm such report, either in full or with such modifications therein as shall be just and equitable. (1868-9, c. 164, s. 5; Code, s. 1314; Rev., s. 3999; C.S., s. 5298.)

§ 156-41. Proprietors become a corporation.

Upon a final adjudication, confirming the report, the proprietors of the several pieces of land adjudged to be benefited by the improvement shall be declared a corporation, of which the capital stock shall be double the estimated cost of the improvements, and in which the several owners of the land adjudged to be benefited shall be corporators, holding shares of stock in the proportions in which they are adjudged liable for the expense of making and keeping up the improvement. (1868-9, c. 164, s. 6; Code, s. 1315; Rev., s. 4000; C.S., s. 5299.)

§ 156-42. Organization; corporate name, officers and powers.

The clerk of the court of the county in which the proceeding is pending or any corporator, who is a petitioner, may call a meeting of the corporators, at which meeting the corporators shall choose a name for the corporation, unless the commissioners selected the name, elect a president, vice-president, secretary and treasurer, but said officers shall be chosen or elected from the corporators who are petitioners in the proceeding; and they shall also choose or elect a board of directors and they shall be chosen or elected from the corporators who are petitioners in the proceeding. The corporators shall also make all bylaws and regulations, not contrary to law, which may be necessary and proper for effecting the purpose of the corporation, but said duty may be delegated to the board of directors. They shall fix the number of shares of stock, and assign to each proprietor or corporator his proper number, but this duty and right may be delegated to and done by the board of directors. The board of directors shall have such powers as are generally given to directors under the corporation law of the State; and they shall assess the sums or amount which shall be paid by each proprietor or corporator in conformity with and in compliance with the report of the commissioners on which the corporation is based. When said assessments against said proprietors or corporators and their lands affected are duly certified to the clerk of the superior court of the county in which such proceeding was instituted, the same shall be passed upon by the clerk of court and when approved by the clerk, said assessments shall become judgments against the several proprietors, corporators and owners so assessed, and the same shall be liens on the lands of the owners or corporators against whom said assessments were made and judgments entered, subject only to taxes, but said judgments shall be judgments in rem only. The board of directors will also have power, if they deem it proper, to fix and prescribe the time, mode and manner of payment; and do such other things as are necessary for the construction, enlargement and keeping up or maintaining said canal and improvement. In every meeting of the corporators or stockholders, each proprietor or corporator shall have one vote for each share of stock owned by him. (1868-9, c. 164, s. 7; Code, s. 1316; Rev., s. 4001; C.S., s. 5300; 1939, c. 180, s. 1.)

§ 156-43. Incorporation of canal already constructed; commissioners; reports.

Whenever the proprietors of any canal already cut shall desire to become incorporated, any number of the proprietors, not less than one third in number, may file their petition before the clerk of the superior court of the county in which the canal is located, or in either county, where the canal may be located in more than one county, setting forth the names of the proprietors, the length and size of the canal, the names of the owners of land draining in such canal, and the quantity of land tributary thereto. And upon filing the petition, summons shall issue to all parties having an easement in the canal, returnable as in other special proceedings; upon the return thereof, or upon a day fixed by the clerk for hearing same, all owners of the canal may become corporators therein, and upon failure of any to avail themselves of that right, they shall not be entitled to become corporators, except under such bylaws and regulations as such corporation shall make and declare. But those who fail to avail themselves of the benefit of this Subchapter shall not be deprived of their easement in the canal, but shall enjoy the same upon payment to the corporation of the assessment made upon them pro rata with the corporators; such assessment shall be made on the land tributary to the canal and apportioned pro rata to each owner thereof; it shall be made by the corporation on 10 days' notice to each owner of the land, under such rules and regulations as the bylaws may prescribe; but any person dissatisfied therewith shall have the right to appeal to a jury at the regular term of the superior court of the county, and the amount of damages assessed shall be a first lien on the land of the owner against whom judgment shall be rendered.

Upon the return date of the summons or on the hearing by the clerk as provided in this section, the clerk of the court may appoint three persons as commissioners, who having been duly sworn shall examine the premises and inquire and report:

(1)   The route and plan of the canal, including the breadth, depth and slope as nearly as they can be calculated, with all other particulars necessary for calculating the cost of enlarging and improving said canal.

(2)   The probable cost of the improvement and enlargement of said canal.

(3)   The proportion which each proprietor or corporator ought in equity and justice to pay toward the enlargement, improvement and permanent support and upkeep of said canal.

(4)   With their report they shall return a map explaining as accurately as may be, the various matters required and necessary in aid or explanation of their report.

(5)   The said report shall be heard and determined as other reports in special proceedings, and if approved by the clerk, such proprietors shall become a body corporate or a corporation.

(6)   A meeting of the corporators may be called by the clerk of court or by any corporator or proprietor who is a petitioner in the proceeding, and at such meeting a president, vice-president, secretary and treasurer shall be elected from the proprietors or corporators who are petitioners; and also a board of

directors shall be elected from the proprietors or corporators who are petitioners in the proceeding.

(7) The board of directors shall assess the sum or amount which shall be paid by each proprietor or corporator in conformity and compliance with the report of the commissioners on which the corporation was based. When said assessments against said proprietors or corporators and their lands affected are duly certified to the clerk of the superior court of the county in which said proceeding was pending and instituted, the same shall be passed upon by the clerk of court, and when approved by the clerk, said assessments shall become judgments against the several proprietors or corporators so assessed, and the same shall be liens on the lands of the owners or corporators against whom said assessments were made and judgments entered, subject only to taxes, but said judgments shall be judgments in rem only. The board of directors will also, if they deem it proper, fix and prescribe the time, manner and mode of payment. (1889, c. 380; 1901, c. 670; Rev., s. 4008; C.S., s. 5301; 1939, c. 180, s. 2.)

Article 4.

Rights and Liabilities in the Corporation.

§ 156-44. Shares of stock annexed to land.

The ownership of the shares of stock is indissolubly annexed to the ownership of the pieces of land adjudged to be benefited by the improvement; and such shares, or a part thereof proportionate to the area of such land that may descend or be conveyed for any longer time than three years, shall, upon such descent or conveyance, descend and pass with the land, even although such shares be not mentioned in the deed of conveyance, and although their transfer be forbidden by such deed so that every owner of such land in possession, except a tenant for a term of years, not exceeding three, and every owner in reversion or remainder after a term not exceeding three years, shall, during his ownership, be entitled to all the rights and privileges and be subject to all the obligations and burdens of a corporator. Every attempted sale of shares otherwise than as annexed to the land shall be void. (1868-9, c. 164, s. 8; Code, s. 1317; Rev., s. 4002; C.S., s. 5302.)

§ 156-45. Shareholders to pay assessments.

Every corporator shall be bound to obey the lawful bylaws of the company, and pay all dues lawfully assessed on him: Provided, he shall in no case pay more than his proportion of the expenses as fixed by this Subchapter; and such dues may be collected in the corporate name in any court having jurisdiction; and every assessment duly docketed in the county where the land to be affected lies shall be a lien on the lands of the debtor which are connected with the corporation from the date of such docketing. (1868-9, c. 164, s. 9; Code, s. 1318; Rev., s. 4003; C.S., s. 5303.)

§ 156-46. Payment of dues entitles to use of canal.

Every corporator paying his dues legally assessed without regard to the number of his shares, shall be entitled to the full and free use of the canal for drainage and navigation, and of the road for passage and transportation. Bylaws may be made to regulate these rights, but not so as to produce an inequality. (1868-9, c. 164, s. 10; Code, s. 1319; Rev., s. 4004; C.S., s. 5304.)

§ 156-47. Rights of infant owners protected.

If any proprietor whose lands are adjudged to be benefited by a canal shall be an infant, no process shall be issued against him during his minority, or within 12 months thereafter, to enforce payments of any assessment, and he may, at any time within such 12 months, apply to have any order, judgment, or decree made against him set aside as to him. If the infant or his guardian shall, during his minority, and the 12 months next thereafter, pay the dues assessed on him, he shall have all the rights and privileges of corporator, to be exercised through his guardian. If the infant shall fail to pay, he shall not have any such rights, but if no action to set aside the judgment of the court creating the corporation shall have been brought by him as aforesaid, or upon the decision of such action against him, he shall be entitled to receive his proper share of stock and to possess all the rights and be bound by all the liabilities of a corporator, including a liability for assessments made during his minority, but not for interest on such, nor for any penalty for their prior nonpayment. (1868-9, c. 164, s. 11; Code, s. 1320; Rev., s. 4005; C.S., s. 5305.)

§ 156-48. Compensation for damage to lands.

If any proprietor of lands shall be damaged by any improvement proposed, the commissioners shall so report, and he shall be entitled to be compensated as may be just by the proprietor whose lands are benefited in proportion to the benefit to them respectively; but in estimating such damages the benefit shall be deducted, and such proprietor shall be entitled to all the rights and privileges of a corporator as respects the use of the improvement, but shall not be entitled to a vote, or be bound for the assessment. (1868-9, c. 164, s. 12; Code, s. 1321; Rev., s. 4006; C.S., s. 5306.)

§ 156-49. Dissolution of corporation.

If, from any cause, the canal or other improvement shall become or shall prove to be valueless, any corporator may apply as is provided in other cases of special proceedings, and the court may dissolve the corporation created in connection with it. (1868-9, c. 164, s. 13; Code, s. 1322; Rev., s. 4007; C.S., s. 5307.)

§ 156-50. Laborer's lien for work on canal.

Whenever work or repair shall be done on such canal and any of the parties owning lands liable to be assessed for such work or repairs shall fail or refuse to pay the amount assessed upon their land, then and in that event the laborers performing such work shall have a lien upon such land to the extent of the amount assessed against the same by the corporation, and such lien may be enforced in the same manner as provided by the laws of this State for the enforcement of laborers' lien. (1899, c. 600, s. 2; Rev., s. 4009; C.S., s. 5308.)

§ 156-51. Penalty for nonpayment of assessments.

Whenever any person whose lands have been adjudged liable to contribute to the maintenance or repair of such canal shall fail or refuse to pay the amount assessed against his land for such maintenance or repair for 30 days after such payment has been demanded by the company, then the company may give such person notice in writing of its intention to cut off his right of drainage into the canal, and if such person shall still neglect and refuse to pay such assessment for 30 days after such notice, then the company may proceed to so obstruct and dam up the ditches of such delinquent as will effectually prevent his draining in the canal. (1899, c. 600, s. 3; Rev., s. 4010; C.S., s. 5309.)

§ 156-52. Corporation authorized to issue bonds.

The corporations organized under this Subchapter are authorized to issue bonds to such an amount and in such denomination as they may elect, payable at such times as may be provided, and to sell the same at not less than par, the proceeds of the sale of such bonds to be used for the payment of the costs of survey and construction and maintenance of the canal. The bonds shall constitute a lien upon the lands drained or improved by the canal as described in the reports of the commissioners. (1908, c. 75, s. 1; C.S., s. 5310.)

§ 156-53. Payment of bonds enforced.

Upon default of the payment of the interest or principal of such bonds, the holders of the bonds of the corporations organized under this Subchapter shall have a right to enforce the lien created by G.S. 156-52 by civil actions in the superior courts of the State. (1908, c. 75, s. 2; C.S., s. 5311.)

SUBCHAPTER III. DRAINAGE DISTRICTS.

Article 5.

Establishment of Districts.

§ 156-54. Jurisdiction to establish districts.

The clerk of the superior court of any county in the State of North Carolina shall have jurisdiction, power and authority to establish levee or drainage districts either wholly or partly located in his county, and which shall constitute a political subdivision of the State, and to locate and establish levees, drains or canals, and cause to be constructed, straightened, widened or deepened, any ditch, drain or watercourse, and to build levees or embankments and erect tidal gates and pumping plants for the purpose of draining and reclaiming wet, swamp or overflowed land; and it is hereby declared that the drainage of swamplands and the drainage of surface water from agricultural lands and the reclamation of tidal marshes shall be considered a public use and benefit and conducive to the public health, convenience and welfare, and that the districts heretofore and hereafter created under the law shall be and constitute political subdivisions of the State, with authority to provide by law to levy taxes and assessments for the construction and maintenance of said public works. (1909, c. 442, s. 1; C.S., s. 5312; 1921, c. 7.)

§ 156-55. Venue; special proceedings.

When the lands proposed to be drained and created into a drainage district are located in two or more counties, the clerk of the superior court of either county has the jurisdiction conferred by this Subchapter. Venue is in that county in which the petition is first filed. The law and the rules regulating special proceedings apply in the proceeding, except as modified by this Subchapter. The proceedings may be ex parte or adversary. (1909, c. 42, ss. 2, 38; C.S., s. 5313; 1999-216, s. 19.)

§ 156-56. Petition filed.

A petition signed by a majority of the resident landowners in a proposed drainage district or by the owners of three fifths of all the land which will be affected or assessed for the expense of the proposed improvements may be filed in the office of the clerk of the superior court of any county in which a part of the lands is located, setting forth that any specific body or district of land in the county and adjoining counties, described in such a way as to convey an intelligent idea as to the location of such land, is subject to overflow or too wet for cultivation, and the public benefit or utility or the public health, convenience or welfare will be promoted by draining, ditching, or leveeing the same or by changing or improving the natural watercourses, and setting forth therein, as far as practicable, the starting point, route, and terminus and lateral branches, if necessary, of the proposed improvement.

The petition will also show whether or not the proposed drainage is for the reclamation of lands not then fit for cultivation or for the improvement of land already under cultivation. It shall also state that, if a reclamation district is proposed to be established, such lands so reclaimed will be of such value as to justify the reclamation. (1909, c. 442, s. 2; C.S., s. 5314; 1921, c. 76; Pub. Loc. 1923, c. 88, s. 2; 1925, c. 85; 1927, c. 98.)

§ 156-57. Bond filed and summons issued.

Upon filing with the petition a bond for the amount of fifty dollars ($50.00) per mile for each mile of the ditch or proposed improvement, signed by two or more sureties or by some lawful and authorized surety company, to be approved by the clerk of superior court, conditioned for the payment of all costs and expenses incurred in the proceeding in case the court does not grant the prayer of the petition, the clerk, shall at any time thereafter, issue summons to be served on all the defendant landowners, who have not joined in the petition and whose lands are included in the proposed drainage district. The summons may be served by publication as to any defendant who cannot be personally served as provided by law.

The attorney for the petitioners shall certify to the clerk of the superior court, prior to the hearing on the final report of the board of viewers, that due diligence has been used to determine the names of all landowners within the area of the proposed drainage district; and, that summons has been issued for such landowners, so determined, and served either by personal service or by publication for all known and unknown landowners, insofar as could be determined by due diligence. (1909, c. 442, s. 2; C.S., s. 5315; 1967, c. 621.)

§ 156-58. Publication in case of unknown owners.

If, at the time of the filing of the petition, or at any time subsequent thereto, it shall be made to appear to the court by affidavit or otherwise that the names of the owners of the whole or any share of any tracts of land are unknown, and cannot after due diligence be ascertained by the petitioners, the court shall order a notice in the nature of a summons to be given to all such persons by a publication of the petition, or of the substance thereof, and describing generally the tracts of land as to which the owners are unknown, with the order of the court thereon, in some newspaper published in the county wherein the land is located, or in some other county if no newspaper shall be published in the first-named county, which newspaper shall be designated in the order of the court, and a copy of such publication shall be also posted in at least three conspicuous places within the boundaries of the proposed district, and at the courthouse door of the county. Such publication in a newspaper and by posting shall be made for a period of four weeks. After the time of publication shall have expired, if no person claiming and asserting title to the tracts of land and entitled to notice shall appear, the court in its discretion may appoint some disinterested person to represent the unknown owners of such lands, and thereupon the court shall assume jurisdiction of the tracts of land and shall adjudicate as to such lands to the same extent as if the true owners were present and represented, and shall proceed against the land itself. If at any time during the pendency of the drainage proceeding the true owners of the lands shall appear in person, they may be made parties defendant of their own motion and without the necessity of personal service, and shall thereafter be considered as parties to the proceeding; but they shall have no right to except to or appeal from any order or judgment theretofore rendered, as to which the time for filing exceptions on notice shall have expired. (1911, c. 67, s. 1; C.S., s. 5316; 1953, c. 675, s. 25.)

§ 156-59. Board of viewers appointed by clerk.

The clerk shall, on the filing of petition and bond, appoint a disinterested and competent civil and drainage engineer and two resident freeholders of the county or counties in which the lands are located as a board of viewers to examine the lands described in the petition and make a preliminary report thereon. The drainage engineer shall be appointed upon the recommendation of the Department of Environment and Natural Resources; and no member of the board of viewers so appointed shall own any land within the boundaries of the proposed district. In the selection of the two members of the board of viewers, other than the engineer, the clerk before making the appointment shall make careful inquiry into the character and qualifications of the proposed members, to the end that the members so appointed shall possess the necessary character, capacity, fitness, and impartiality for the discharge of their important duties. (1909, c. 442, s. 2; 1917, c. 152, s. 1; C.S., s. 5317; 1961, c. 614, s. 4; c. 1198; 1973, c. 1262, s. 23; 1977, c. 771, s. 4; 1989, c. 727, s. 218(157); 1997-443, s. 11A.123.)

§ 156-60. Attorney for petitioners.

The petitioners shall select some learned attorney or attorneys to represent them, who shall prosecute the drainage proceeding and advise with the petitioners and board of viewers, and shall agree upon the compensation for his professional services up to the time when the district shall be established and the board of drainage commissioners elected, or as nearly so as the same may be approximated. If the petitioners are unable to agree upon the selection of an attorney or attorneys, the selection may be made by the clerk of the court. The foregoing provision shall not interfere with the right of any individual petitioner in the selection of an attorney to represent his individual interests if he shall deem the same desirable or necessary. (1917, c. 152, s. 1; C.S., s. 5318.)

§ 156-61. Estimate of expense and manner of payment; advancement of funds and repayment from assessments.

The clerk may make an estimate of the aggregate sum of money which shall appear to be necessary to pay all the expenses incident to the performance of the duties by the board of viewers, including the compensation of the drainage engineer and his necessary assistants, and also including the sum for the compensation of the attorney for the district, and such court costs as may probably accrue, which estimates shall embrace the period of services up to and including the establishment of the drainage district and the selection and appointment of the board of drainage commissioners. The clerk shall then estimate the number of acres of land owned or represented by the petitioners, as nearly so as may be practicable without actual survey, and shall assess each acre so represented a level rate per acre, to the end that such assessment will realize the sum of money which he has estimated as necessary to pay all necessary costs of the drainage proceeding up to the time of the appointment of the drainage commissioners, as above provided. The assessment above provided for which has been or may hereafter be levied shall constitute a first and paramount lien, second only to State and county taxes, upon the lands so assessed, and shall be collected in the same manner and by the same officers as county taxes are collected. The board of viewers, including the drainage engineer, shall not be required to enter upon the further discharge of their duties until the amount so estimated and assessed shall be paid in cash to the clerk of the court, which shall be retained by him as a court fund, and for which he shall be liable in his official capacity, and he shall be authorized to disburse the same in the prosecution of the drainage proceeding. Unless all the assessments shall be paid within a time to be fixed by the court, which may be extended from time to time, no further proceedings shall be had, and the proceeding shall be dismissed at the cost of the petitioners. If the entire sum so estimated and assessed shall not be paid to the clerk within the time limited, the amounts so paid shall be refunded to the petitioners pro rata after paying the necessary costs accrued. Nothing herein contained shall prevent one or more of the petitioners from subscribing and paying any sum in addition to their assessment in order to make up any deficiency arising from the delinquency of one or more of the petitioners. When the sum of money so estimated shall be paid, the board of viewers shall proceed with the discharge of their duties, and in all other respects the proceeding shall be prosecuted according to the law. After the district shall have been established and the board of drainage commissioners appointed, it shall be the duty of the board of drainage commissioners to refund to each of the petitioners the amount so paid by them as above provided, out of the first moneys which shall come into the hands of the board from the sale of bonds or otherwise, and the same shall be included in ascertaining the total cost of improvement.

In lieu of the procedures set forth in the preceding paragraph, the board of county commissioners may advance funds, or any part thereof, for the purposes set forth in the preceding paragraph. Such advances shall be made to a county official designated by the commissioners, and shall be disbursed upon such terms as the county commissioners may direct. If the district shall be organized, the funds advanced shall be repaid from assessments thereafter levied. (1917, c. 152, s. 1; C.S., s. 5319; 1941, c. 342; 1961, c. 614, s. 6; c. 662.)

§ 156-62. Examination of lands and preliminary report.

The board of viewers shall proceed to examine the land described in the petition, and other land if necessary to locate properly such improvement or improvements as are petitioned for, along the route described in the petition, or any other route answering the same purpose if found more practicable or feasible, and may make surveys such as may be necessary to determine the boundaries and elevation of the several parts of the district, and shall make and return to the clerk of the superior court within 30 days, unless the time shall be extended by the court, a written report, which shall set forth:

(1)   Whether the proposed drainage is practicable or not.

(2)   Whether it will benefit the public health or any public highway or be conducive to the general welfare of the community.

(3) Whether the improvement proposed will benefit the lands sought to be benefited.

(4) Whether or not all the lands that are benefited are included in the proposed drainage district.

(5) Whether or not the district proposed to be formed is to be a reclamation district or an improvement district. A reclamation district is defined to be a district organized principally for reclaiming lands not already under cultivation. An improvement district is defined to be a district organized principally for the improvement of lands then under cultivation. The board of viewers shall further report, if the district is a reclamation district within the above definition, whether or not the proposed drainage would be justified by the additional value for agricultural purposes given to land so drained.

They shall also file with this report a map of the proposed drainage district, showing the location of the ditch or ditches or other improvement to be constructed and the lands that will be affected thereby, and such other information as they may have collected that will tend to show the correctness of their findings. (1909, c. 442, s. 3; C.S., s. 5320; 1927, c. 98, s. 2.)

§ 156-63. First hearing of preliminary report.

The clerk of the superior court shall consider this report. If the viewers report that the drainage is not practicable or that it will not benefit the public health or any public highway or be conducive to the general welfare of the community, and the court shall approve such findings, the petition shall be dismissed at the cost of the petitioners, and such petition shall likewise be dismissed at the cost of the petitioners if it is sought to set up a reclamation district and the viewers report that the cost of reclaiming the land would be so great as not to justify the expense of draining it. Such petition or proceeding may again be instituted by the same or additional landowners at any time after six months, upon proper allegations that conditions have changed or that material facts were omitted or overlooked. If the viewers report that the drainage is practicable and that it will benefit the public health or any public highway or be conducive to the general welfare of the community, and the court shall so find, then the court shall fix a day when the report will be further heard and considered. (1909, c. 442, s. 4; C.S., s. 5321; 1927, c. 98, s. 3.)

§ 156-64. Notice of further hearing.

If the petition is entertained by the court, notice shall be given by publication once a week for at least two consecutive weeks in some newspaper of general circulation within the county or counties, if one shall be published in such counties, and also by posting a written or printed notice at the door of the courthouse and at five conspicuous places within the drainage district, that on the date set, naming the day, the court will consider and pass upon the report of the viewers. At least 15 days shall intervene between the date of the publication and the posting of the notices and the date set for the hearing. (1909, c. 442, s. 5; C.S., s. 5322; 1963, c. 767, s. 1.)

§ 156-65. Further hearing, and district established.

At the date appointed for the hearing the court shall hear and determine any objections that may be offered to the report of the viewers. If it appear that there is any land within the proposed levee or drainage district that will not be affected by the leveeing or drainage thereof, such lands shall be excluded and the names of the owners withdrawn from such proceeding; and if it shall be shown that there is any land not within the proposed district that will be affected by the construction of the proposed levee or drain, the boundary of the district shall be so changed as to include such land, and such additional landowners shall be made parties plaintiff or defendant, respectively, and summons shall issue accordingly, as hereinbefore provided. After such change in the boundary is made, the sufficiency of the petition shall be verified, to determine whether or not it conforms to the requirements hereinbefore provided. The efficiency of the drainage or levees may also be determined, and if it appears that the location of any levee or drain can be changed so as to make it more effective, or that other branches or spurs should be constructed, or that any branch or spur projected may be eliminated or other changes made that will tend to increase the benefits of the proposed work, such modification and changes shall be made by the board. The engineer and the other two viewers may attend this meeting and give any information or evidence that may be sought to verify and substantiate their report. If necessary, the petition, as amended, shall be referred by the court to the engineer and two viewers for further report. The above facts having been determined to the satisfaction of the court, and the boundaries of the proposed district so determined, it shall declare the establishment of the drainage or levee district, which shall be designated by a name or number, for the object and purpose as herein set forth.

If any lands shall be excluded from the district because of the court having found that such lands will not be affected or benefited, and the names of the owners of such lands have been withdrawn from such proceeding, but such lands are so situated as necessarily to be located within the outer boundaries of the district, such fact shall not prevent the establishment of the district, and such lands shall not be assessed for any drainage tax; but this shall not prevent the district from acquiring a right-of-way across such lands for constructing a canal or ditch or for any other necessary purpose authorized by law.

The court shall further determine, if it is sought to establish a reclamation district, whether or not the increased value of the particular land should be so great as to justify the cost and expenses of its reclaiming. (1909, c. 442, s. 6; 1911, c. 67, s. 2; C.S., s. 5323; 1927, c. 98, s. 4.)

§ 156-66. Right of appeal.

Any person owning lands within the drainage or levee district which he thinks will not be benefited by the improvement and should not be included in the district may appeal from the decision of the court to the superior court of such county, in termtime, by filing an appeal, accompanied by a bond conditioned for the payment of the costs if the appeal should be decided against him, for such sum as the court may require, not exceeding two hundred dollars ($200.00), signed by two or more solvent sureties or in some approved surety company to be approved by the court. (1909, c. 442, s. 8; C.S., s. 5324.)

§ 156-67. Condemnation of land.

If it shall be necessary to acquire a right-of-way or an outlet over and through lands not affected by the drainage, and the same cannot be acquired by purchase, then and in such event the power of eminent domain is hereby conferred, and the same may be condemned. The owners of the land proposed to be condemned may be made parties defendant in the manner of an ancillary proceeding, and the procedure shall be, to the extent practicable, supplemented by the provisions of Chapter 40A Eminent Domain and such damages as may be awarded as compensation shall be paid by the board of drainage commissioners out of the first funds which shall be available from the proceeds of sale of bonds or otherwise. (1909, c. 442, s. 7; C.S., s. 5325; 1981, c. 919, s. 24.)

§ 156-68. Complete survey ordered.

After the district is established the court shall refer the report of the engineer and viewers back to them to make a complete survey, plans, and specifications for the drains or levees or other improvements, and fix a time when the engineer and viewers shall complete and file their report, not exceeding 60 days. (1909, c. 442, s. 9; C.S., s. 5326.)

§ 156-69. Nature of the survey; conservation and replacement of fish and wildlife habitat; structures to control and store water.

The engineer and viewers shall have power to employ such assistants as may be necessary to make a complete survey of the drainage district, and shall enter upon the ground and make a survey of the main drain or drains and all its laterals. The line of each ditch, drain, or levee shall be plainly and substantially marked on the ground. The course and distance of each ditch shall be carefully noted and sufficient notes made, so that it may be accurately plotted and mapped. A line of levels shall be run for the entire work and sufficient data secured from which accurate profiles and plans may be made. Frequent bench marks shall be established among the line, on permanent objects, and their elevation recorded in the field books. If it is deemed expedient by the engineer and viewers, other levels may be run to determine the fall from one part of the district to another. If an old watercourse ditch, or channel is being widened, deepened, or straightened, it shall be accurately cross-sectioned so as to compute the number of cubic yards saved by the use of such old channel. A drainage map of the district shall then be completed, showing the location of the ditch or ditches and other improvements and the boundary, as closely as may be determined by the records, of the lands owned by each individual landowner within the district. The location of any railroads or public highways and the boundary of any incorporated towns or villages within the district shall be shown on the map. There shall also be prepared to accompany this map a profile of each levee, drain, or watercourse, showing the surface of the ground, the bottom or grade of the proposed improvement, and the number of cubic yards of excavation or fill in each mile or fraction thereof, and the total yards in the proposed improvement and the estimated cost thereof, and plans and specifications, and the cost of any other work required to be done.

The board of viewers shall consider the effect of the proposed improvements upon the habitat of fish and wildlife, and the laws and regulations of the Commission for Public Health. Their report shall include their recommendations and the estimated cost thereof, as to the conservation and replacement of fish and wildlife habitat, if they shall determine such shall be damaged or displaced by the proposed improvement. The board, to determine their recommendations, may consult governmental agencies, wildlife associations, individuals, or such other sources as they may deem desirable, to assist them in their considerations of and recommendations relating to, the conservation and replacement of fish and wildlife habitat.

The board of viewers shall consider the need for and feasibility of, the construction of structures which will do one or more of the following:

(1)   Control the flow of water,

(2)   Impound or store water and,

(3)   Provide areas for conservation and replacement of fish and wildlife habitat.

If structures are recommended for any one or more of said purposes, their report shall include:

(1)   Specifications therefor.

(2)   Location thereof together with the description of the area of land needed for the purpose of said structure, i.e., water storage or impoundment, or fish and wildlife habitat.

(3)   Estimate of cost thereof.

The report of the board of viewers shall set forth, in regard to the foregoing, the following information:

(1)   The areas of land needed for construction and maintenance of:

a.   The canals and drainage system.

b. Structures to:

1. To control the water,

2. Impound or store water and,

3. To conserve and replace fish and wildlife habitat.

(2) Upon whose land such areas are located.

(3) The area of land necessary to be acquired from each landowner.

The map accompanying the report shall have shown thereon, the location of the areas of land needed for the construction and maintenance of the following:

(1) The canal and drainage system.

(2) Structures to:

a. Control the flow of water,

b. Impound or store the water,

c. Conserve and replace fish and wildlife habitat.

The board of viewers may, in its discretion, agree with the Soil Conservation Service of the Department of Agriculture or any agency of the government of the United States or of the State of North Carolina whereby such agency will furnish all or a part of the service necessary to obtain the information set forth in the preceding paragraph and in G.S. 156-68.

The board of viewers may accept such information as furnished by such agencies and include such information in their final report to the clerk.

The board of viewers and engineers of the district may use control or semicontrol, mosaic aerial photographs or other sources and stereoscopic or other methods, generally used and deemed acceptable by civil and drainage engineers for the purpose of obtaining the information required in this section and in lieu of a detailed ground survey. In the event a detailed ground survey is not made, only those ground markings need be made as the board of viewers deem necessary. The location of the proposed canals must be shown on the ground prior to actual construction. (1909, c. 442, s. 10; C.S., s. 5327; 1959, c. 597, s. 1; 1961, c. 614, ss. 5, 9; 1965, c. 1143, s. 1; 1973, c. 476, s. 128; 2007-182, s. 2.)

§ 156-70. Assessment of damages.

It shall be the further duty of the engineer and viewers to assess the damages claimed by anyone that are justly right and due to him for land taken or for inconvenience imposed because of the construction of the improvement, or for any other legal damages sustained. Such damages shall be considered separate and apart from any benefit the land would receive because of the proposed work, and shall be paid by the board of drainage commissioners when funds shall come into their hands. (1909, c. 442, s. 11; 1915, c. 238; 1917, c. 152, s. 16; C.S., s. 5328.)

§ 156-70.1. When title deemed acquired for purpose of easements or rights-of-way; notice to landowner; claim for compensation; appeal.

The district shall be deemed to have acquired title for the purpose of easements or rights-of-way to those areas of land identified in the final report of the board of viewers and as shown on the map accompanying said report, at the time said final report is confirmed by the clerk of the superior court.

The board of viewers shall cause notice as to the area or areas of land involved, to be given to each landowner so affected, which notice shall be in writing and mailed to the last known address of the landowner at least seven days prior to the hearing on the final report as provided by G.S. 156-73.

If the landowner desires compensation for the land areas so acquired by the district, claim for the value of the same shall be submitted to the board of viewers on or before the time of the adjudication upon the final report as provided for by G.S. 156-74.

If the board of viewers shall approve the claim, the amount so approved shall be added to the total cost of the district as estimated in said final report and this shall be done by amendment to the final report submitted to the clerk of the superior court on or before the adjudication provided for in G.S. 156-74.

If the board of viewers shall not approve said claim, the clerk of the superior court shall consider the claim and determine what in his opinion is a fair value and the amount so determined shall be shown in the said final report as amended and confirmed by said adjudication. The landowner or the drainage district may appeal from the decision of the clerk of the superior court, to the superior court, upon the question of the value of the land taken and such value shall be determined by a jury. The procedure for the appeal shall be in accordance with the provision of G.S. 156-75. (1959, c. 597, s. 2; c. 1085; 1965, c. 1143, s. 2.)

§ 156-71. Classification of lands and benefits.

It shall be the further duty of the engineer and viewers to personally examine the land in the district and classify it with reference to the benefit it will receive from the construction of the levee, ditch, drain, or watercourse or other improvement. In the case of drainage, the degree of wetness on the land, its proximity to the ditch or a natural outlet, and the fertility of the soil shall be considered in determining the amount of benefit it will receive by the construction of the ditch. The land benefited shall be separated in five classes. The land receiving the highest benefit shall be marked "Class A"; that receiving the next highest benefit, "Class B"; that receiving the next highest benefit, "Class C"; that receiving the next highest benefit, "Class D," and that receiving the smallest benefit, "Class E." The holdings of any one landowner need not be all in one class, but the number of acres in each class shall be ascertained, though its boundary need not be marked on the ground or shown on the map. The total number of acres owned by one person in each class and the total number of acres benefited shall be determined. The total number of acres of each class in the entire district shall be obtained and presented in tabulated form. The scale of assessment upon the several classes of land returned by the engineer and viewers shall be in the ratio of five, four, three, two, and one; that is to say, as often as five mills per acre is assessed against the land in "Class A," four mills per acre shall be assessed against the land in "Class B," three mills per acre in "Class C," two mills per acre in "Class D," and one mill per acre in "Class E." This shall form the basis of the assessment of benefits to the lands for drainage purposes. In any district lands may be included which are not benefited for the agriculture or crop production, or slightly so, but which will receive benefit by improvement in health conditions, and as to such lands the engineer and viewers may assess each tract of land without regard to the ratio and at such a sum per acre as will fairly represent the benefit of such lands. Villages or towns or parts thereof and small parcels of land located outside thereof and used primarily for residence or other specific purposes, and which require drainage, may also be included in any drainage district which by reason of their improved conditions and the limited area in each parcel under individual ownership, it is impracticable to fairly assess the benefits to each separated parcel of land by the ratio herein provided, and as to such parcels of land the engineer and viewers may assess each parcel of land without regard to the ratio and at a higher rate per acre respectively by reason of the greater benefits. If the streets or other property owned by any incorporated town or village are likewise benefited by such drainage works, the corporation may be assessed in proportion to such benefits, which assessment shall constitute a liability against the corporation and may be enforced as provided by law.

The board of viewers may determine that some areas of the district will receive more benefits than other areas and if such is determined, the varying benefits shall be reflected in the manner of classification of benefits to each area and the tracts of land therein. (1909, c. 442, s. 12; C.S., s. 5329; 1923, c. 217, s. 1; 1961, c. 614, s. 7.)

§ 156-72. Extension of time for report.

In case the work is delayed by high water, sickness, or any other good cause, and the report is not completed at the time fixed by the court, the engineer and viewers shall appear before the court and state in writing the cause of such failure and ask for sufficient time in which to complete the work, and the court shall set another date by which the report shall be completed and filed. (1909, c. 442, s. 14; C.S., s. 5330.)

§ 156-73. Final report filed; notice of hearing.

When the final report is completed and filed it shall be examined by the court, and if it is found to be in due form and in accordance with the law it shall be accepted, and if not in due form it may be referred back to the engineer and viewers, with instructions to secure further information, to be reported at a subsequent date to be fixed by the court. When the report is fully completed and accepted by the court a date not less than 20 days thereafter shall be fixed by the court for the final hearing upon the report, and notice thereof shall be given by publication in a newspaper of general circulation in the county and by posting a written or printed notice on the door of the courthouse and at five conspicuous places throughout the district, such publication to be made once a week for at least three consecutive weeks before the final hearing. During this time a copy of the report shall be on file in the office of the clerk of the superior court, and shall be open to the inspection of any landowner or other persons interested within the district. (1909, c. 442, s. 15; C.S., s. 5331; 1959, c. 807, ss. 1, 2; 1963, c. 767, s. 2.)

§ 156-74. Adjudication upon final report.

At the date set for hearing any landowner may appear in person or by counsel and file his objection in writing to the report of the viewers; and it shall be the duty of the court to carefully review the report of the viewers and the objections filed thereto, and make such changes as are necessary to render substantial and equal justice to all the landowners in the district. If, in the opinion of the court, the cost of construction, together with the amount of damages assessed, is not greater than the benefits that will accrue to the land affected, the court shall confirm the report of the viewers. If, however, the court finds that the cost of construction, together with the damages assessed, is greater than the resulting benefit that will accrue to the lands affected, the court shall dismiss the proceedings at the cost of the petitioners, and the sureties upon the bond so filed by them shall be liable for such costs. Provided, that the Department of Environment and Natural Resources may remit and release to the petitioners the costs expended by the board on account of the engineer and his assistants. The court may from time to time collect from the petitioners such amounts as may be necessary to pay costs accruing, other than costs of the engineer and his assistants, such amounts to be repaid from the special tax hereby authorized.

The court shall, at the time of consideration of said report, determine whether:

(1) The petitioners constitute a majority of the resident landowners, whose lands are adjudged to be benefited by the proposed construction work as shown in the final report of the board of viewers and finally approved by the court; or

(2) The petitioners own three fifths of the land area which is adjudged to be benefited by the proposed construction work as shown in the final report of the board of viewers and finally approved by the court.

If the petitioners do not constitute either a majority of the resident landowners or own three fifths of the land as set out in subdivisions (1) or (2) above, then the proceedings shall be dismissed. (1909, c. 442, s. 16; 1915, c. 238, s. 2; 1917, c. 152, s. 16; C.S., s. 5332; 1925, c. 122, s. 4; 1959, c. 1312, s. 1; 1961, c. 1198; 1973, c. 1262, s. 23; 1977, c. 771, s. 4; 1989, c. 727, s. 218(158); 1997-443, s. 11A.123.)

§ 156-75. Appeal from final hearing.

Any landowner, party petitioner, or the drainage district may, within 10 days after the entry of an order or judgment by the clerk upon the report of the board of viewers, appeal to the superior court in session time or in chambers. The procedures for taking appeal are as provided in Article 27A of Chapter 1 of the General Statutes, except as provided otherwise by this Subchapter. In an appeal to the superior court taken under this section or any other section or provision of the drainage laws of the State, general or local, the appeal has precedence in consideration and trial by the court. If other issues also have precedence in the superior court under existing law, the court, in its discretion, determines the order in which they are heard. (1909, c. 442, s. 17; 1911, c. 67, s. 3; C.S., s. 5333; 1923, c. 217, s. 2; 1969, c. 192, s. 1; 1973, c. 108, s. 96; 1999-216, s. 20.)

§ 156-76. Compensation of board of viewers.

The compensation of the engineer, including his necessary assistants, rodmen, and laborers, and also the compensation of the viewers, shall be fixed by the clerk. In fixing such compensation, particularly of the drainage engineer, the clerk shall confer fully with the Department of Environment and Natural Resources and with the petitioners. The compensation to be paid the two members of the board of viewers, other than the engineer, shall be in such amount per day as may be fixed by the clerk of the superior court for the time actually employed in the discharge of their duties, and in addition any actual and necessary expenses of travel and subsistence while in the actual discharge of their duties, an itemized report of which shall be submitted and verified. (1909, c. 442, s. 36; 1917, c. 152, ss. 1, 2; C.S., s. 5334; 1925, c. 122, s. 4; 1959, c. 288; 1961, c. 1198; 1973, c. 1262, s. 23; 1977, c. 771, s. 4; 1989, c. 727, s. 218(159); 1997-443, s. 11A.123.)

§ 156-77. Account of expenses filed.

The engineer and viewers shall keep an accurate account and report to the court the name and number of days each person was employed on the survey and the kind of work he was doing, and any expenses that may have been incurred in going to and from the work, and the cost of any supplies or material that may have been used in making the survey. (1909, c. 442, s. 13; C.S., s. 5335.)

§ 156-78. Drainage record.

The clerk of the superior court shall provide a suitable book, to be known as the "Drainage Record," in which he shall transcribe every petition, motion, order, report, judgment, or finding of the board in every drainage transaction that may come before it, in such a manner as to make a complete and continuous record of the case. Copies of all the maps and profiles are to be furnished by the engineer and marked by the clerk "official copies," which shall be kept on file by him in his office, and one other copy shall be pasted or otherwise attached to his record book. (1909, c. 442, s. 18; C.S., s. 5336.)

§ 156-78.1. Municipalities.

(a) Any municipality may participate in drainage district works or projects upon mutually agreeable terms relating to such matters as the construction, financing, maintenance and operation thereof.

(b) Any municipality may contribute funds toward the construction, maintenance and operation of drainage district works or projects, to the extent that such works or projects:

(1) Provide a source of municipal water supply for the municipality, or protect an existing source of such supply, enhance its quality or increase its

dependable capacity or quantity, or implement or facilitate the disposal of sewage of the municipality; or

(2) Protect against or alleviate the effects of floodwater or sediment damages affecting, or provide drainage benefits for property owned by the municipality or its inhabitants.

(c) Municipal expenditures for the aforesaid purposes are declared to be for necessary expenses. Municipalities may enter continuing contracts, some portion or all of which may be performed in an ensuing year, agreeing to make periodic payments in ensuing fiscal years to drainage districts in consideration of benefits set forth in subsection (b)(2) of this section, but no such contract may be entered into unless sufficient funds have been appropriated to meet any amount to be paid under the contract in the fiscal year in which the contract is made. The municipal governing body shall, in the budget ordinance of each ensuing fiscal year during which any such contract is in effect, appropriate sufficient funds to meet the amount to be paid under the contract in such ensuing fiscal year. The statement required by G.S. 160-411.1 to be printed, written or typewritten on all contracts, agreements, or requisitions requiring the payment of moneys shall be placed on such a continuing contract only if sufficient funds have been appropriated to meet the amount to be paid under the contract in the fiscal year in which the contract is made.

(d) The provisions of this section are permissive. If a municipality does not participate in accordance with the provisions of this section, then the other provisions of Subchapter III shall apply and be followed. (1961, c. 614, s. 10.)

Article 6.

Drainage Commissioners.

§ 156-79. Appointment and organization under original act.

After the drainage district has been declared established, as aforesaid, and the survey and plan therefor approved, the court shall appoint three persons, in the manner set forth in G.S. 156-81, who shall be designated as the board of drainage commissioners. Any vacancy thereafter occurring shall be filled by the clerk or clerks of the superior court in the manner set forth in G.S. 156-81. Such three drainage commissioners, when so appointed, shall be immediately created a body corporate under the name and style of "The Board of Drainage Commissioners of _____ District," with the right to hold property and convey the same, to sue and be sued, and shall possess such other powers as usually pertain to corporations. They shall organize by electing from among their number a chairman and a vice-chairman. They shall also elect a secretary, either within or without their body. Such board of drainage commissioners shall adopt a seal, which they may alter at pleasure. The board of drainage commissioners shall have and possess such powers as are herein granted. (1909, c. 442, s. 19; 1917, c. 152, s. 17; C.S., s. 5337; 1947, c. 273; 1963, c. 767, s. 3; 1989 (Reg. Sess., 1990), c. 959, s. 2.)

§ 156-80. Name of districts.

The name of such drainage district shall constitute a part of its corporate name; for illustration, the board of drainage commissioners of Mecklenburg Drainage District, No. 1. In the naming of a drainage district the clerk of the court, notwithstanding the name given in the petition, shall so change the name as to make it conform to the county within which the district, or the main portion of the district, is located, and such district shall also be designated by number, the number to indicate the number of districts petitioned for in the county. For illustration, the first district organized in Mecklenburg County would be Mecklenburg County Drainage District, No. 1; the name of the second would be Mecklenburg County Drainage District, No. 2; the fifth one organized would be Mecklenburg County Drainage District, No. 5: Provided, that so much of this section as provides for numbering the districts in each county shall not apply to districts in which bonds have been issued and sold prior to the fifth day of March, 1917. (1909, c. 442, s. 19; 1917, c. 152, s. 17; C.S., s. 5338.)

§ 156-81. Appointment and organization under amended act.

(a) Method of Appointment. - The manner of appointment shall be as follows:

(1) If the drainage district shall lie solely within one county, the clerk of superior court for such county shall appoint such commissioners.

(2) If the said district shall lie in more than one county, then such commissioners shall be appointed by unanimous action of the clerks of court for the counties wherein any part of such district lies.

(b) Organization. - Immediately after the appointment of the board of drainage commissioners, the clerk of the court of the county wherein such drainage proceeding is pending shall notify each of the commissioners in writing to appear at a certain time and place within the district and organize. The clerk or clerks of court, as the case may be, shall appoint one of the three members as chairman of the board of drainage commissioners, and in doing so he or they shall consider carefully and impartially the respective qualifications of each of the members for the position.

(c) Term of Office. - The term of service of the members of the board of drainage commissioners so appointed shall begin upon their appointment. Where all three commissioners are appointed at once, one commissioner shall serve for one year, one for two years, and the other for three years, the term to be computed from the first day of October following their organization. The members so serving for one, two, and three years, respectively, shall be unanimously designated by the clerk or clerks of the court. Thereafter each member shall be appointed for three years. The clerk of the court for the county wherein the proceeding is pending shall record in the drainage record the date of appointment, the members appointed, and the beginning and expiration of their term of office.

(d) Vacancies Filled. - If a vacancy shall occur in the office of any commissioner by death, resignation, or otherwise, the remaining two members are to discharge the necessary duties of the board until the vacancy shall be filled; and if the vacancy shall be in the office of chairman or secretary, the two remaining members may elect a secretary, and the clerk or clerks, as the case may be, shall appoint one of the two remaining members to act as chairman to hold until the vacancy in the board shall be filled. The clerk of the county wherein the proceeding is pending shall keep a similar record of any appointment to fill vacancies. The person appointed to fill the vacancy shall be appointed in the manner set forth in subsection (a) of this section and shall serve until the expiration of the term of his predecessor. The secretary of the board of drainage commissioners shall promptly notify the appropriate clerk or clerks of the superior court of any vacancy in the board.

(e) Failure to Appoint. - If for any reason the clerk or clerks of the court shall fail to provide for the appointment of drainage commissioners prior to the expiration of a term, the incumbents shall continue to hold their office as commissioners until their successors are appointed and qualified. The term of office of boards of drainage commissioners heretofore elected and appointed shall expire immediately upon the appointment of new commissioners pursuant to subsection (a) of this section.

(f) Meetings. - The board shall meet once each month at a stated time and place during the progress of drainage construction, and more often if necessary. After the drainage work is completed, or at any time, the chairman shall have the power to call special meetings of the board at a certain time and place. The chairman shall also call a meeting at any time upon the written request of the owners of a majority in area of the land in the district.

(g) Compensation. - The chairman of the board of drainage commissioners shall receive compensation and allowances as fixed by the clerk of the superior court. In fixing such compensation and allowances, the clerk shall give due consideration to the duties and responsibilities imposed upon the chairman of the board. The other members of the board shall receive a per diem not to exceed twenty-five dollars ($25.00) a day, while engaged in attendance upon meetings of the board, or in the discharge of duties imposed by the board. The secretary of the board shall receive such compensation and expense allowances as may be determined by the board.

The chairman and members of the board of drainage commissioners shall also receive their actual travel and subsistence expenses while engaged in attendance upon meetings of the board, or in the discharge of duties imposed by the board. The compensation and expense allowances as herein set out shall be paid from the assessments made annually for the purpose of maintaining the canals of the drainage district, or from any other funds of the district.

(h) Application of Section. - The provisions of this section shall apply to all drainage districts now or hereafter existing in this State, without regard to the date of organization.

(i) Repealed by Session Laws 1989 (Regular Session, 1990), c. 959, s. 3. (1917, c. 152, s. 5; 1919, cc. 109, 217; C.S., s. 5339; 1947, c. 935; 1949, c. 956, ss. 1-3; 1957, c. 912, s. 1; 1975, c. 494; 1989 (Reg. Sess., 1990), c. 959, s. 3.)

§ 156-81.1. Treasurer.

The appointing authority as determined by G.S. 156-81 shall appoint a treasurer for the drainage district for a term not to exceed 12 months. The treasurer so appointed may be a member of the board of commissioners of the district or some other person deemed competent, and shall furnish bond as may be required by the said clerk of the superior court. The treasurer shall continue in office until a successor has been appointed and qualified.

All references in Subchapter III of Chapter 156 of the General Statutes of North Carolina, to "treasurer" or "county treasurer" or "county auditor" are hereby amended to refer exclusively to the treasurer appointed as hereinbefore provided. (1963, c. 767, s. 4; 1989 (Reg. Sess., 1990), c. 959, s. 6.)

§ 156-82. Validation of election of members of drainage commission.

All irregularities caused by failure of any officer whose duty it was to provide for the election of a member or members of board of drainage commissioners of any drainage district, or the failure of any candidate to make a deposit as may be required by law, shall not invalidate such election where the following facts appear affirmatively:

(1)   That said election was held at the time and place prescribed by law.

(2)   That a ballot box was provided for the ballots cast for drainage commissioner.

(3)   That the ballots were canvassed and the results declared by the judge of the general election.

(4)   That the candidate receiving the greatest number of votes was declared elected.

(5)   That no candidate for election as a member of board of drainage commissioners made any deposit as prescribed by law.

(6)   That the candidate receiving the majority votes at said election has already qualified and is acting as such drainage commissioner.

This section shall not apply to any election contested before March 9, 1921. (1921, c. 210; C.S., s. 5339(a).)

§ 156-82.1. Duties and powers of the board of drainage commissioners.

(a) The board of drainage commissioners shall proceed with the levying of assessments, issuance of bonds and construction of canals, water retardant structures and other improvements and acquisition of equipment as approved by the court in the adjudication upon the final report of the board of viewers, either in the creation of the district or in subsequent proceedings authorized by Article 7B.

(b) The commissioners shall maintain the canals, water retardant structures, and all other improvements and equipment of the district.

(c) The commissioners, with the approval of the clerk of the superior court, may use surplus funds in such manner as they deem best for (i) the maintenance of the improvements, (ii) construction or enlargement of canals and water retardant structures, or other improvements or equipment, (iii) replacement or acquisition of equipment or structures, and (iv) for payment of any or all operating expenses including salaries, fees and costs of court.

The term "surplus funds" is defined to mean any funds remaining after the payment of those items set forth specifically in the certificate of assessment, as well as funds provided in said certificate for maintenance and contingencies, and also, shall include maintenance and any other funds which the said commissioners may have on hand and which are not necessary for the payment of the bonds and interest thereon which have been issued by the said district.

(d) The board of commissioners may agree, or contract, with any agency of the government of the United States or of North Carolina for such engineering or other services as may be provided by such agency.

(e) The board of commissioners may, in its discretion, release areas taken for rights-of-way if it determines, after the construction of the canals, that such are not needed for the purpose of the district. The release must be approved by the clerk of the superior court and such release shall be filed in the proceedings by virtue of which the district was created.

(f) The board of drainage commissioners shall have all the duties and powers as set forth and imposed upon them by the various sections of this Subchapter and all others which are necessary to promote the purposes of the district.

(g) The board of commissioners may authorize the use of stored or impounded water for recreational purposes. They may acquire title, by gift or purchase, but not by condemnation, of land to be used in conjunction with the stored and impounded water, for the development of recreational facilities.

The said commissioners are not authorized to use funds obtained from assessments upon the lands within the drainage district, for the purposes of the acquisition and development of recreational facilities. They are authorized to issue revenue bonds or notes, for the acquisition of land and construction and development of recreational facilities. The funds received from the use of the said recreational facilities, may be pledged for the payment of said revenue bonds and notes.

The terms and conditions of the issuance and payment of the said revenue bonds or notes, must be approved by the clerk of the superior court who has jurisdiction of the said drainage district.

The commissioners are authorized to enter into a contract with persons, association of persons or municipal or private corporations, for the operation of recreational facilities, owned by the drainage district. The contract may be entered into by negotiation or by award to the highest bidder at a public rental to be advertised as directed by the clerk of the superior court. The terms of the contract must be approved by the clerk of the superior court who has jurisdiction of the said drainage district.

(h) The commissioners may enter into a contract with a municipality or other nonprofit organizations, for the joint use of a facility for the impoundment or storage of water. The contract must be approved by the clerk of the superior court who has jurisdiction of the drainage district.

(i) All improvements constructed and acquired under the provisions of this Subchapter shall be under the control and supervision of the board of drainage commissioners. It shall be their duty to keep all improvements in good repair. (1961, c. 614, s. 2; 1965, c. 1143, s. 3.)

§ 156-82.2. Appointment of drainage commissioners.

Notwithstanding any other provision of law (including, where applicable, any special acts or local modification of general law), the General Assembly hereby appoints all sitting drainage district commissioners and drainage commission treasurers, as of the date of ratification of this section, as commissioners, officers, and treasurers of their respective districts. Said commissioners, officers, and treasurers shall continue in office until such time as appointments shall be made as provided in G.S. 156-81 and G.S. 156-81.1, which appointments shall be made by the clerk or clerks of the superior court not later than January 1, 1991. (1989 (Reg. Sess., 1990), c. 959, s. 1.)

§ 156-82.3. Validation of previous actions.

(a)   All expenditures heretofore incurred, and all actions heretofore taken, by a drainage district for purposes authorized by this Chapter are hereby validated notwithstanding any defect in the selection of any or all of its commissioners or any other defect.

(b)   The provisions of this section are expressly made applicable to any and all bonds and other financial obligations of any such district. No action based on the alleged invalidity of the assessments heretofore made or of any such bonds or other obligations of a district shall lie after January 1, 1991, to enjoin or contest the enforceability of any such assessment, bond, or other obligation. (1989 (Reg. Sess., 1990), c. 959, s. 5.)

Article 7.

Construction of Improvement.

§ 156-83. Superintendent of construction.

The board of drainage commissioners shall appoint a competent drainage engineer of good repute as superintendent of construction. Such superintendent of construction shall furnish a copy of his monthly and final estimates to the Department of Environment and Natural Resources, in addition to other copies herein provided which shall be filed and preserved. In the event of the death, resignation, or removal of the superintendent of construction, his successor shall be appointed in the same manner.

The board of drainage commissioners may, in its discretion, agree with the Soil Conservation Service of the Department of Agriculture or any agency of the government of the United States or of North Carolina whereby such agency may furnish the service required of the superintendent of construction. If this is done by the board, any reference in this Chapter to the superintendent of construction and/or his duties shall include or be exercised by the said agency subject to the approval of the board of commissioners. (1909, c. 442, s. 20; C.S., s. 5340; 1923, c. 217, s. 3; 1925, c. 122, s. 5; 1959, c. 597, s. 3; 1961, c. 1198; 1963, c. 767, s. 5; 1973, c. 1262, s. 23; 1977, c. 771, s. 4; 1989, c. 727, s. 218(160); 1997-261, s. 109; 1997-443, s. 11A.123.)

§ 156-84. Letting contracts.

The board of drainage commissioners shall cause notice to be given of the letting of the contract. The notice shall be posted at the courthouse door in the county wherein the district was organized. Notice shall be posted no less than 15 days prior to the opening of the bids and shall be published at least once a week for two consecutive weeks immediately prior to the opening of the bids, in some newspaper published in the county wherein such improvement is located, if such there be, and such additional publication elsewhere as they may deem expedient, of the time and place of letting the work of construction of such improvement, and in such notice they shall specify the approximate amount of work to be done and the time fixed for the completion thereof; and on the date appointed for the letting they, together with the superintendent of construction, shall convene and let to the lowest responsible bidder, either as a whole or in sections, as they may deem most advantageous for the district, the proposed work. No bid shall be entertained that exceeds the estimated cost, except for good and satisfactory reasons it shall be shown that the original estimate was erroneous. They shall have the right to reject all bids and advertise again the work, if in their judgment the interest of the district will be subserved by doing so. The successful bidder shall be required to enter into a contract with the board of drainage commissioners and to execute a bond for the faithful performance of such contract, with sufficient sureties, in favor of the board of drainage commissioners for the use and benefit of the levee or drainage district, in an amount equal to no less than 25 nor more than one hundred per centum (100%) of the estimated cost of the work awarded to him. In canvassing bids and letting the contract, the superintendent of construction shall act only in an advisory capacity to the board of drainage commissioners. The contract shall be based on the plans and specifications submitted by the viewers in their final report as confirmed by the court, the original of which shall remain on file in the office of the clerk of the superior court and shall be open to the inspection of all prospective bidders. All bids shall be sealed and shall not be opened except under the authority of the board of drainage commissioners and on the day theretofore appointed for opening the bids. The drainage commissioners shall have power to correct errors and modify the details of the report of the engineer and viewers if, in their judgment, they can increase the efficiency of the drainage plan and afford better drainage to the lands in the district without increasing the estimated cost submitted by the engineer and viewers and confirmed by the court. (1909, c. 442, s. 21; 1911, c. 67, s. 4; C.S., s. 5341; 1959, c. 806; 1963, c. 767, s. 6.)

§ 156-85. Monthly estimates for work and payments thereon; final payment.

The superintendent in charge of construction shall make monthly estimates of the amount of work done, and furnish one copy to the contractor and file the other with the secretary of the board of drainage commissioners; and the commissioners shall, within five days after the filing of such estimate, meet and direct the secretary to draw a warrant in favor of such contractor for ninety per centum (90%) of the work done, according to the specifications and contracts; and upon the presentation of such warrant, properly signed by the chairman and secretary, to the treasurer of the drainage fund, he shall pay the amount due thereon. When the work is fully completed and accepted by the superintendent he shall make an estimate for the whole amount due, including the amounts withheld on the previous monthly estimates, which shall be paid from the drainage fund as before provided. (1909, c. 442, s. 22; C.S., s. 5342.)

§ 156-86. Failure of contractors; reletting.

If any contractor to whom such work has been let shall fail to perform the same according to the terms specified in his contract, action may be had in behalf of the board of drainage commissioners against such contractor and his bond in the superior court for damages sustained by the levee or drainage district, and recovery made against such contractor and his sureties. In such an event the work shall be advertised and relet in the same manner as the original letting. (1909, c. 442, s. 23; 1911, c. 67, s. 5; C.S., s. 5343.)

§ 156-87. Right to enter upon lands; removal of timber.

In the construction of the work the contractor shall have the right to enter upon the lands necessary for this purpose and the right to remove private or public bridges or fences and to cross private lands in going to or from the work. In case the right-of-way of the improvement is through timber the owner thereof shall have the right to remove it, if he so desires, before the work of construction begins, and in case it is not removed by the landowner it shall become the property of the contractor and may be removed by him. (1909, c. 442, s. 24; C.S., s. 5344.)

§ 156-88. Drainage across public or private ways.

Where any public ditch, drain or watercourse established under the provisions of this Subchapter crosses or, in the opinion of the board of viewers, should cross a public highway under the supervision of the Department of Transportation the actual cost of constructing the same across the highway shall be paid for from the funds of the drainage district, and it shall be the duty of the Department of Transportation, upon notice from the court, to show cause why it should not be required to repair or remove any old bridge and/or build any new bridge to provide the minimum drainage space determined by the court; whereupon the court shall hear all evidence pertaining thereto and shall determine whether the Department of Transportation shall be required to do such work, and whether at its own expense or whether the cost thereof should be prorated between the Department of Transportation and the drainage district. Either party shall have the right of appeal from the clerk to the superior court and thence to the appellate division, and should the court be of the opinion that the cost should be prorated then the percentage apportioned to each shall be determined by a jury.

Whenever the Department of Transportation is required to repair or remove any old bridge and/or build any new bridge as hereinbefore provided, the same may be done in such manner and according to such specifications as it deems best, and no assessment shall be charged the Department of Transportation for any benefits to the highway affected by the drain under the same, and such bridge shall thereafter be maintained by and at the expense of the Department of Transportation.

Where any public ditch, drain, or watercourse established under the provisions of this Subchapter crosses a public highway or road, not under the supervision of the Department of Transportation, the actual cost of constructing the same across the highway or removing old bridges or building new ones shall be paid for from the funds of the drainage district. Whenever any highway within the levee or drainage district shall be beneficially affected by the construction of any improvement or improvements in such district it shall be the duty of the viewers appointed to classify the land, to give in their report the amount of benefit to such highway, and notice shall be given by the clerk of the superior court to the commissioners of the county where the road is located, of the amount of such assessment, and the county commissioners shall have the right to appear before the court and file objections, the same as any landowner. When it shall become necessary for the drainage commissioners to repair any bridge or construct a new bridge across a public highway or road not under the supervision of the Department of Transportation, by reason of enlarging any watercourse, or of excavating any canal intersecting such highway, such bridge shall thereafter be maintained by and at the expense of the official board or authority which by law is required to maintain such highway so intersected.

Where any public canal established under the provisions of the general drainage law shall intersect any private road or cartway the actual cost of constructing a bridge across such canal at such intersection shall be paid for from the funds of the drainage district and constructed under the supervision of the board of drainage commissioners, but the bridge shall thereafter be maintained by and at the expense of the owners of the land exercising the use and control of the private roads; provided, if the private road shall be converted into a public highway the maintenance of the bridge shall devolve upon the Department of Transportation or such other authority as by law shall be required to maintain public highways and bridges. (1909, c. 442, s. 25; 1911, c. 67, s. 6; 1917, c. 152, s. 6; C.S., s. 5345; 1947, c. 1022; 1953, c. 675, s. 26; 1957, c. 65, s. 11; 1969, c. 44, s. 78; 1973, c. 507, s. 5; 1977, c. 464, s. 34.)

§ 156-89. Drainage across railroads; procedure.

Whenever the engineer and the viewers in charge shall make a survey for the purpose of locating a public levee or drainage district or changing a natural watercourse, and the same would cross the right-of-way of any railroad company, it shall be the duty of the owner in charge of the work to notify the railroad company, by serving written notice upon the agent of such company or its lessee or receiver, that they will meet the company at the place where the proposed ditch, drain, or watercourse crosses the right-of-way of such company, the notice fixing the time of such meeting, which shall not be less than 10 days after the service of the same, for the purpose of conferring with the railroad company with relation to the place where and the manner in which such improvement shall cross such right-of-way. When the time fixed for such conference shall arrive, unless for good cause more time is agreed upon, it shall be the duty of the viewers in charge and the railroad company to agree, if possible, upon the place where and the manner and method in which such improvement shall cross such right-of-way. If the viewers in charge and the railroad company cannot agree, or if the railroad company shall fail, neglect, or refuse to confer with the viewers, they shall determine the place and manner of crossing the right-of-way of the railroad company, and shall specify the number and size of openings required, and the damages, if any, to the railroad company, and so specify in their report. The fact that the railroad company is required by the construction of the improvement to build a new bridge or culvert or to enlarge or strengthen an old one shall not be considered as damages to the railroad company. The engineer and viewers shall also assess the benefits that will accrue to the right-of-way, roadbed, and other property of the company by affording better drainage or a better outlet for drainage, but no benefits shall be assessed because of the increase in business that may come to the road because of the construction of the improvement. The benefits shall be assessed as a fixed sum, determined solely by the physical benefit that its property will receive by the construction of the improvement, and it shall be reported by the viewers as a special assessment, due personally from the railroad company as a special assessment; it may be collected in the manner of an ordinary debt in any court having jurisdiction. (1909, c. 442, s. 26; C.S., s. 5346.)

§ 156-90. Notice to railroad.

The clerk of the superior court shall have notice served upon the railroad company of the time and place of the meeting to hear and determine the final report of the engineer and viewers, and the railroad company shall have the right to file objections to the report and to appeal from the findings of the board of commissioners in the same manner as any landowner. But such an appeal shall not delay or defeat the construction of the improvement. (1909, c. 442, s. 27; C.S., s. 5347.)

Vision Books Order Form

Fax Orders:	1-980-299-5965
Phone Orders:	1-704-898-0770
E-mail Orders:	www.visionbooks.org
Mail Orders:	Vision Books, LLC P.O. Box 42406 Charlotte, NC 28215

Shipp To:
Name_____
Address_____
City_____State_____Zip_____
Phone_____Fax_____
Email_____@_____

Bill To: We can bill a third party on your behalf.
Name_____
Address_____
City_____State_____Zip_____
Phone____(_____)_____Fax_____
Email_____@_____

Pamphlet Number ($15.00 Each)	Qty	Total Cost
_____	_____	_____
_____	_____	_____
_____	_____	_____
_____	_____	_____
_____	_____	_____
_____	_____	_____
_____	_____	_____
Full Volume Set 1-92	92 Pamphlets	1,380.00

Free Shipping & Handling on Full Volume Orders
Add $1.00 Shipping & Handling Per Pamphlet $_____

Total Cost $_____

Thank you for your support. Management!

DID YOU ENJOY THIS BOOK?

Vision Books, LLC would like to hear from you! If you or someone you know has been fasely imprisoned, we would like to hear your story. If the 'North Carolina Criminal Law and Procedure' has had an effect in your life or if you have suggestions, we would like to hear from you. Send your letters to:

Vision Books, LLC
Attn: Staff Writers
P.O. Box 42406
Charlotte, NC 28215
Email: staff@visionbooks.org

Order Additional Copies:

Fax Orders: 1-980-299-5965

Phone Orders: 1-704-898-0770

E-mail Orders: www.visionbooks.org

Mail Orders: Vision Books, LLC
                       P.O. Box 42406
                       Charlotte, NC 28215

www.ingramcontent.com/pod-product-compliance
Lightning Source LLC
Chambersburg PA
CBHW051630170526
45167CB00001B/131